Women in
Religion

THEMES IN RELIGIOUS STUDIES SERIES

Series Editors: Jean Holm, with John Bowker

Other titles:

Worship
Making Moral Decisions
Myth and History
Attitudes to Nature
Human Nature and Destiny
Sacred Writings
Picturing God
Rites of Passage
Sacred Place

Women in Religion

Edited by

Jean Holm

with John Bowker

PINTER
PUBLISHERS
LONDON, NEW YORK

Distributed exclusively in the United States and Canada by St. Martin's Press

Pinter Publishers Ltd.
25 Floral Street, London WC2E 9DS, United Kingdom

First published in 1994

Distributed exclusively in the USA and Canada by St. Martin's Press, Inc. Room 400, 175 Fifth Avenue, New York, NY 10010, USA

British Library Cataloguing in Publication Data

A CIP catalogue record for this book is available from the British Library

ISBN 1 85567 108 5 (hb)
ISBN 1 85567 109 3 (pb)

Library of Congress Cataloging in Publication Data

Women in religion / edited by Jean Holm, with John Bowker.
    p.   cm. – (Themes in religious studies series)
    Includes bibliographical references and index.
    ISBN 1-85567-108-5 (hb). – ISBN 1-85567-109-3 (pb)
    1. Women in religion.   2. Religions.   I. Holm, Jean, 1922– .
II. Bowker, John Westerdale.   III. Series.
BL458.W564   1994
200'.82–dc20   94–13748
                                                                      CIP

Typeset by Mayhew Typesetting, Rhayader, Powys
Printed and bound in Great Britain by Biddles Ltd., Guildford and King's Lynn

Contents

Series Preface

The person who knows only one religion does not know any religion. This rather startling claim was made in 1873, by Friedrich Max Müller, in his book, *Introduction to the Science of Religion*. He was applying to religion a saying of the poet Goethe: 'He who knows one language, knows none.'

In many ways this series illustrates Max Müller's claim. The diversity among the religious traditions represented in each of the volumes shows how mistaken are those people who assume that the pattern of belief and practice in their own religion is reflected equally in other religions. It is, of course, possible to do a cross-cultural study of the ways in which religions tackle particular issues, such as those which form the titles of the ten books in this series, but it soon becomes obvious that something which is central in one religion may be much less important in another. To take just three examples: the contrast between Islam's and Sikhism's attitudes to pilgrimage, in *Sacred Place*; the whole spectrum of positions on the authority of scriptures illustrated in *Sacred Writings*; and the problem which the titles, *Picturing God* and *Worship*, created for the contributor on Buddhism.

The series offers an introduction to the ways in which the themes are approached within eight religious traditions. Some of the themes relate particularly to the faith and practice of individuals and religious communities (*Picturing God, Worship, Rites of Passage, Sacred Writings, Myth and History, Sacred Place*); others have much wider implications, for society in general as well as for the religious communities themselves (*Attitudes to Nature, Making Moral Decisions, Human Nature and Destiny, Women in Religion*). This distinction, however, is not clear-cut. For instance, the 'sacred places' of Ayodhya and Jerusalem have figured in situations of national and international conflict, and some countries have passed laws regulating, or even banning, religious worship.

Stereotypes of the beliefs and practices of religions are so widespread that a real effort, of both study and imagination, is needed in order to discover what a religion looks – and feels – like to its adherents. We have to bracket out, temporarily, our own beliefs and presuppositions, and 'listen in' to a religion's account of what *it* regards as significant. This is not a straightforward task, and readers of the books in this series will encounter a number of the issues that characterise the study of religions, and that have to be taken into account in any serious attempt to get behind a factual description of a religion to an understanding of the real meaning of the words and actions for its adherents.

First, the problem of language. Islam's insistence that the Arabic of the Qur'ān cannot be 'translated' reflects the impossibility of finding in another language an exact equivalent of many of the most important terms in a religion. The very word, Islam, means something much more positive to a Muslim than is suggested in English by 'submission'. Similarly, it can be misleading to use 'incarnation' for *avatāra* in Hinduism, or 'suffering' for *dukkha* in Buddhism, or 'law' for Torah in Judaism, or 'gods' for *kami* in Shinto, or 'heaven' for *T'ien* in Taoism, or 'name' for *Nām* in Sikhism.

Next, the problem of defining – drawing a line round – a religion. Religions don't exist in a vacuum; they are influenced by the social and cultural context in which they are set. This can affect what they strenuously reject as well as what they may absorb into their pattern of belief and practice. And such influence is continuous, from a religion's origins (even though we may have no records from that period), through significant historical developments (which sometimes lead to the rise of new movements or sects), to its contemporary situation, especially when a religion is transplanted into a different region. For example, anyone who has studied Hinduism in India will be quite unprepared for the form of Hinduism they will meet in the island of Bali.

Even speaking of a 'religion' may be problematic. The term, 'Hinduism', for example, was invented by western scholars, and would not be recognised or understood by most 'Hindus'. A different example is provided by the religious situation in Japan, and the consequent debate among scholars as to whether they should speak of Japanese 'religion' or Japanese 'religions'.

Finally, it can be misleading to encounter only one aspect of a religion's teaching. The themes in this series are part of a whole interrelated network of beliefs and practices within each religious tradition, and need to be seen in this wider context. The reading lists at the end of each chapter point readers to general studies of the religions as well as to books which are helpful for further reading on the themes themselves.

Jean Holm
November 1993

List of Contributors

Jean Holm (EDITOR) was formerly Principal Lecturer in Religious Studies at Homerton College, Cambridge, teaching mainly Judaism and Hinduism. Her interests include relationships between religions; the relationship of culture to religion; and the way in which children are nurtured within a different cultural context. Her publications include *Teaching Religion in School* (Oxford University Press, 1975), *The Study of Religions* (Sheldon, 1977), *Growing up in Judaism* (Longman, 1990), *Growing up in Christianity*, with Romie Ridley (Longman, 1990) and *A Keyguide to Sources of Information on World Religions* (Mansell, 1991). She has edited three previous series: *Issues in Religious Studies*, with Peter Baelz (Sheldon), *Anselm Books*, with Peter Baelz (Lutterworth) and *Growing Up in a Religion* (Longman).

John Bowker (EDITOR) was Professor of Religious Studies in Lancaster University, before returning to Cambridge to become Dean and Fellow of Trinity College. He is at present Professor of Divinity at Gresham College in London, and Adjunct Professor at the University of Pennsylvania and at the State University of North Carolina. He is particularly interested in anthropological and socio-logical approaches to the study of religions. He has done a number of programmes for the BBC, including the *Worlds of Faith* series, and series on Islam and Hinduism for the World Service. He is the author of many books in the field of Religious Studies, including *The Meanings of Death* (Cambridge University Press, 1991), which was awarded the biennial Harper Collins religious book prize in 1993, in the academic section.

Rita M. Gross has been a leader in feminist studies in religion for twenty years. She is a founder of the Women and Religion section of the American Academy of Religion, and has worked and written on a wide variety of topics pertaining to women and religion. Her book, *Unspoken Worlds: Women's Religious Lives* (edited with Nancy Auer Falk), is widely used in courses on women and world religions. *Buddhism After Patriarchy: A Feminist History, Analysis and Reconstruction of Buddhism* was published by SUNY Press in 1992. She is currently writing a textbook on religious studies for basic women's studies courses, *Feminism and Religious Studies: Transformations of a Discipline*. Professor Gross has also played a leading role in Buddhist–Christian dialogue in North America.

Clare Drury has been a Lecturer in Theology at St Hugh's College, Oxford since 1992. Previously, she was Fellow, Tutor and Director of Studies in Theology at Newnham College, Cambridge. She teaches the New Testament and reviews for a number of journals.

Sharada Sugirtharajah lectures on Hinduism at Westhill College in Birmingham. She has led sessions on topics ranging from Hindu spirituality to women's issues for clergy, nurses, social workers, counsellors and multi-faith groups. She has co-authored the text for a photo learning pack on Hinduism (a resource for primary and secondary religious education) and has also contributed articles to journals.

Leila Badawi is a freelance journalist and broadcaster based in London. She has published several articles in the national press and has broadcast on the BBC World Service and national radio and television on Islam and women and on the Middle East. She has also spoken at a number of conferences. She was educated in Britain and has a special interest in Islam in South Africa and Nigeria, and women in Muslim societies.

Alexandra Wright is rabbi of Radlett and Bushey Reform Synagogue in Hertfordshire, and Lecturer in Classical Hebrew at Leo Baeck College, London. She has written several articles on women and Judaism. Her area of research interest is the sixteenth-century Bohemian Rabbi Judah Loew ben Bezalel.

Kanwaljit Kaur-Singh is a local authority inspector for primary education. Her research interests concern the contribution of women to Sikh society. She has spoken extensively on issues relating to Sikhism and primary education, and has written articles on education and racial equality, Sikh women and the Sikh religion. Dr Kaur-Singh is currently Chair of the British Sikh Education Council.

Stewart McFarlane is a Lecturer in Religious Studies at the University of Lancaster, specialising in Chinese Religion and Philosophy; he is also Visiting Professor at the Chung-Hwa Institute of Buddhist Studies in Taiwan. He has published numerous articles and chapters on Buddhist ethics and society. He is a member of the editorial board of the *Journal of Asian Philosophy*. He is currently writing a book on 'Culture, Identity and Power in Chinese Martial Arts'.

D.P. Martinez is Lecturer in Anthropology with reference to Japan at the School of Oriental and African Studies (SOAS), University of London. Previously, she studied at the University of Chicago before going on to do a DPhil in anthropology on Japanese diving women at Oxford University. Among her recent publications are 'The dead: Shinto aspects of Buddhist ritual' in *JASO* vol. 21 (2), 1990; and 'Women as bosses: perceptions of the *ama*' in *Japanese Women Working*, edited by Janet Hunter (Routledge, 1993).

Introduction: Raising the Issues

Jean Holm

Two striking facts about the status and role of women in religion emerge from the contributions to this volume. First, in several religious traditions the position of women was higher at an earlier period in their history than it later became. For example, Japanese women had a higher status in all spheres of life before the feudal period (twelfth century CE), and Hindu women enjoyed equal status with men in many ways in the vedic period (from about 1500 BCE), when *upanayana*, the rite of initiation, was open to them, husband and wife jointly performed ritual acts, and widows were allowed to remarry.

The founders or significant figures in four religions were amazingly radical when seen against the background of their times. The Buddha acceded to the request of his disciple, Ananda, and allowed the creation of a nuns' as well as a monks' order, and so provided women for the first time with an alternative to domesticity. Jesus included women among his followers, and is recorded as having welcomed contact with women who were regarded as 'beyond the pale' in the society of his day, while Paul, who has suffered from the reputation of being a misogynist, declared that there was 'neither male nor female; for you are all one in Christ Jesus'. Muhammad greatly enhanced the status of women in Arabia, ensuring that they were entitled to a share of inheritance, taking steps to provide for widows who were left destitute, and banning infanticide (which usually affected girl babies), and he is even recorded as having appointed a woman to lead the prayers in a household of men and women. Guru Nanak proclaimed the equality of men and women, and both he and the Gurūs who succeeded him allowed women to take a full part in all the activities of Sikh worship and practice.

The second striking factor to emerge from the contributions to this volume is the contrast between the classical teachings of religions about the equality of men and women and the actual lived experience of women. Expressions that occur frequently include 'inferior', 'polluting', 'male-dominated', 'patriarchal', 'androcentric'. Throughout history men have formulated the beliefs of religions, composed and transmitted the sacred writings and been their sole interpreters, created the religious – and secular – institutions of their societies, and controlled worship and other important rituals. History has been written by men, and by and large there is a resounding silence about the activities and the achievements of women. There are now moves to match 'history' by 'herstory', and research in recent decades has uncovered a great deal of information about the part that women have played in their communities, including holding positions of leadership. Kanwaljit Kaur-Singh gives one example: although a very able woman ran the Sikh community in the Panjab for a period, records gave the credit only to her male adviser.

Women do, of course, have a part to play in many religions, but it is almost always subordinate to the role of men, and it is likely to be in the private rather than in the public sphere. D.P. Martinez comments that in Japanese folk religion it is the women who hold the knowledge of the rituals, and who organise everything for them, but it is only men who take part in the actual public performance. Stewart McFarlane refers to female shamans in Chinese popular religion dealing with *yin* forces and lower order spirits associated with women's illnesses, childbirth and infancy problems, while male shamans or Taoist priests deal with higher forces such as *yang* spirits and gods, and are seen as ritually more powerful.

The major world religions have been if anything even more male-dominated. In Buddhism, the most senior nun must defer to the most junior monk. In Judaism, the discussion of *halakhah* has been a male preserve, and public worship in Orthodox Judaism has involved the full participation only of men. In Christianity, many of the most influential ideas were worked out by (celibate) men in the first five centuries of the Church's history, and the significant developments of the medieval Church and the Reformation were also shaped by men. In Islam, all legal rulings have been made by men, and in some regions of the world women are not even allowed to be present in the mosque for worship. In Hinduism, the Brahmanic priesthood has been confined to men. Even in Sikhism, in which all offices are open equally to men and women, there is only a very small minority of women holding official positions on gurdwara committees or as leaders of worship.

Many men would dispute the assertion that religions treat women as second-class citizens. Frequently used expressions are 'equal but different' and 'equal but complementary'. However, women are increasingly feeling able to articulate their experience, in which such expressions work out in practice as 'unequal and different'. If women were able to share in making decisions in even those matters which affect women themselves, they might be happier with 'equal but different'!

The way in which women are treated within their religious traditions has to be seen in the wider context of the almost universal phenomenon of men being regarded as superior to women. There are many cultural factors which are independent of specific religious teachings but which have been absorbed into religions. For example, the birth of a boy has traditionally been welcomed with much greater enthusiasm than the birth of a girl. Men's activities are regarded as more important than women's activities – even though in another society those same activities might be undertaken by women. Men's greater physical strength and their ability to protect their families from physical danger has provided the (no doubt unconscious) excuse to claim that the restrictions placed on women's dress, behaviour and freedom of association are for their 'protection'. It is interesting to note that in some cultures western dress is regarded as a sign of corruption in women, but not in men.

Sexuality

Female sexuality is probably the most deep-seated cause of men's negative attitudes to women. This relates on the one hand to menstruation and childbirth, and on the other hand to myths about women's sexual nature. Menstruation and childbirth are almost universally regarded as polluting.[1] In many traditions women are forbidden to enter sacred places or touch sacred objects during their menstrual period. In Hinduism, for example, women should not approach the family shrine during menstruation or pregnancy, and they should keep away from the kitchen area and have nothing to do with the preparation of food – a much more difficult rule to observe in a nuclear family than in the traditional large joined family. Muslim women may not touch the Qur'ān during menstruation, nor may they pray, or enter a mosque. In some religions the ban applies to women altogether, for instance, the exclusion until recent times of women from the sanctuary of a Christian church. In others it applies to the period between puberty and the menopause. One example of this is that women are not allowed to make the pilgrimage to Sabari, in Kerala, South India, unless they are post-menopausal. In some African religions women can actually become ritual priests after the menopause.

In almost every society childbirth has been assumed to render a woman ritually unclean, and each religion has specified the period of isolation and the rituals for removing the pollution and bringing the woman back into the community. Christianity has traditionally had 'churching of women' after childbirth, though this came to be modified into a thanksgiving service for the safe delivery of the baby. Alexandra Wright points out that the biblical laws surrounding childbirth (which ruled that the period during which a woman was ritually unclean was twice as long after the birth of a daughter as after the birth of a son) are nowadays observed by only a minority of Jewish women, in the Orthodox traditions. Leila Badawi states that in Islam giving birth is a witness and not a regrettable pollution, but even so, *ghusl*, the greater ablution, is needed after it.

The tantric tradition, within Buddhism and Hinduism, provides a stark contrast to the attitudes just described. In one form of Tantrism a woman's menstrual blood has been regarded as so powerful that ritual sexual intercourse ideally should take place during menstruation. Those things which were taboo because of pollution in the mainstream religion were ritualised in Tantrism.

When we come to the question of the essential nature of women, we find a surprising diversity, not only among the religions, but also within them. Rita Gross comments, 'In every period of Buddhist history there are at least two views about women', and she describes the differing opinions about whether women could achieve enlightenment only in male form. The writers of the popular *Jataka* tales, aware of the temptations facing monks who embrace the ascetic life, most often portray women as beautiful but fickle, and with voracious sexual appetites. On the other hand, in the light of the Buddhist belief in *śunyatā* (emptiness), femaleness – like maleness – is recognised as an illusion. Hinduism, characteristically, contains a number of differing views. For example, Advaita Vedānta has placed emphasis on the ascetic life, and on the concept of *ātman* as the sexless 'self'. In theistic Hinduism *śakti*, the feminine principle, is the divine creative energy, without which the masculine principle is powerless. However, as Sharada Sugirtharajah points out, in contrast to the role of *śakti* in the myths, in society a woman's power or *śakti* is largely confined to the domestic sphere. She also describes the reversal of gender roles in the *bhakti* tradition, and especially in Tantrism.

In Chinese thought the two categories, *yin* and *yang*, represent the pairs: female and male, earth and heaven, dark and light, cool and hot, moist and dry, passive and active. Stewart McFarlane explains that it was believed that in sexual intercourse each partner absorbed the other's essences, but the fact that women's *yin* essences were regarded as inexhaustible while men's *yang* essences as easily depleted was one of the reasons for men's fear of women's sexuality. He also refers to Taoism's elevation of the feminine principle, which, however, did not affect the general devaluation of women in Chinese history.

Clare Drury discusses Christianity's ambivalence in its attitude to women, symbolised most clearly in the persons of Eve and the Virgin Mary. Although the Genesis story speaks only of the sin of disobedience, it came to be accepted that Eve introduced Adam to sexuality, and thus there developed the characterisation of woman as temptress.[2] Woman's image was not helped by the Church's adoption of Aristotle's belief that a woman was a malformed male, or by the teachings of some of the early theologians, for example Augustine, that only man was made in the image of God, woman being made in the image of man. In the birth stories in the gospels Mary was said to be a virgin, and the cult of the Virgin Mary certainly exalted a woman in a male-dominated Church. However, Mary's motherhood was linked to her virginity, and there was therefore no contradiction of the negative attitude to woman's sexuality.

Signs of hope

Generalisations are dangerous and can be misleading. There are positive as well as negative features in all religions in relation to the role and status of women. Rita Gross comments that in the wide sweep of Buddhist history the bias against women is becoming less acceptable, and she looks forward to 'post-patriarchal Buddhism' which could result from the religion's move into the West, where many of the most dedicated Buddhists are laywomen who expect to take leadership roles in their religious communities. Leila Badawi points out that the relationship between Muslim society and Muslim law, and therefore the status of women, is complex and subtle, and that Muslim religious law is not the same as social conservatism. Examples of Muslim law favouring women include the wife keeping her family name and choosing which school of law she will give her allegiance to, and the compassionate legal fiction of the 'sleeping foetus'.

Alexandra Wright chronicles developments in Judaism, especially in the Progressive movements, which give women much greater equality with men. Reform Judaism, for example, has allowed women to be ordained as rabbis since 1972. Similarly, many Christian churches are giving women a greater role in both decision-making and worship, with women ministers and priests, and even (at this date) three Anglican women bishops. Perhaps more surprising is what Pope John Paul II wrote in his 1988 Apostolic Letter, *Mulieris Dignitatem*:

> The Scriptures confirm the equality between men and women. . . . Men and women are equally images of God. That is why Scripture ascribes to God masculine and feminine characteristics. God is Father and Mother.

Against the stream

It is not only in recent times that women have, either by their words or their lives, stood out from the mass of their contemporaries. Every religion can tell of able, and often courageous, women of earlier centuries. Alexandra Wright points to outstanding women leaders in biblical times, such as Deborah and Miriam, and to more recent women such as those of the famous seventeenth-century Modena family in Italy. Rita Gross mentions the biographies of an influential group of Chinese Buddhist nuns who lived in the fourth to sixth centuries CE. In addition, the important eighth-century Tibetan Buddhist *siddha*, Yeshe Tsogyel, and Buddhist nuns in the early period of Indian Buddhism both left significant writings, including passages that reveal the difficulties which faced the women of their day. Sharada Sugirthirajah describes not only outstanding historical figures, such as Mirabai and Sarada Devi, but women in Hindu mythology – Kālī, Durgā and Draupadī – whose actions challenge the conventional Indian view of women as gentle and submissive.

Leila Badawi says, 'Strong women are the keystones in the foundation of Islam', referring especially to Khadijah and A'isha, Muhammad's first and last wives, and to Fatima, his daughter. The responsibilities they carried within the religion are an encouragement to Muslim women today, who find themselves with a much less significant role to play. Kanwaljit Kaur-Singh lists a number of women who have been important in the history of Sikhism, including some who fought alongside men on the battlefield.

There are records of many outstanding women in Christian history. Clare Drury mentions a number of them, particularly in the medieval period (for example, the remarkable mystic, Julian of Norwich) and in the seventeenth century (for example, Margaret Fell, the Quaker who exercised an extensive and intensive preaching ministry). The seventeenth century produced some amazing Christian women, many of whom practised their ministry under great difficulties in the Puritan communities of New England. However, it was not only Dissenters who challenged male authority. A contemporary English woman, with a number of publications to her name, had no hesitation in arguing for women's rights and standing up to the men of her day. In *The Christian Religion as Profess'd by a Daughter of the Church of England* (1705), Mary Astell wrote:

> If God had not intended that Women shou'd use their Reason, He wou'd not have given them any, for He does nothing in vain. If they are to use their Reason, certainly it ought to be employ'd about the noblest Objects, and in business of the greatest Consequences, therefore in Religion.[3]

Women's movements

In one sense religious orders could be described as the most widespread of all women's movements; they are certainly the earliest. To observers, a nun's life might appear incredibly constrained, but although nuns lived lives of great self-discipline, and often under rules decided by men, the advantages were great. In *Therigatha* ('Song of the Sisters'), the Indian Buddhist nuns sing of their joy at being free from the restrictions of being a woman in the society of their day. Christian ascetics also rejoiced in the freedom which being a nun gave them, allowing them time and opportunity to study, and certainly freeing them from the drudgery and oppression of domestic life.

Women mystics followed a different path, but nevertheless one which gave them great freedom. Whether they were individual mystics, or lived as members of a group, they by-passed the authority of male leadership, and neither their religious experience nor its interpretation was dependent on the male-dominated religion. This was particularly important in the early days of the Hindu *bhakti* tradition in South India, with devotional worship open to both men and women of all castes, in stark contrast to the male-dominated Brahmanical religion.

The nineteenth and twentieth centuries have seen the creation of a large number of new religious movements, particularly in Africa and Japan. Many of their founders have been women. A very high proportion of their members are women. However, many of the new religions have experienced the phenomenon which is typical of new religious movements worldwide. As they grow and become established as institutions, control tends to move into the hands of men. A new movement within Buddhism has so far managed not to succumb to such a fate. Won Buddhism gives women an equal place with men, including ordination, and it has women in the top administration. It has attracted a large number of able and well-educated young women, and by 1993 it had 850 nuns and 150 monks. It is now spreading from Korea, and has about ninety branches in Taiwan and eight in the United States of America.

During the past hundred and fifty years feminist movements have been most numerous in the United States and Europe, and within religions they have been largely confined to Christianity and Judaism. However, this has now changed, though women's movements in the Middle East and Asia are developing their own characteristics. Many of them started from women working alongside men in struggles for independence, or to build a stable community, rather than from women confronting men and demanding their 'rights'. Out of the early shared struggle came moves to improve the lot of women. These movements are seldom

heard of in the West. For example, in January 1957, soon after
Tunisia, a Muslim nation, gained its independence it introduced a
Code of Personal Status, which gave women a great deal of freedom,
because of the need to modernise the country and improve the
economy. Another movement that raised the status of women was
the Arya Samaj, founded in India in the nineteenth century in
reaction against western criticism of Hinduism; it went back behind
the 'accretions' of more than two millennia, and included in its
reforms practices from the vedic period, allowing women to recite
the Vedas and perform vedic rituals.

Western women's movements have been criticised by women from
Asia and the Middle East, on the grounds that the western emphasis
on individualism is in conflict with their cultural values. This
rejection is expressed forcibly in Hussain (1984):

> Doctrines of emancipation and feminism have sought to transform
> Muslim women into Westernized women – alienating them from their
> own cultures to the extent that they become strangers in it and cannot
> relate to their past or present heritage. . . . Western women themselves
> have struggled to gain freedom in their societies not by following alien
> ideologies but through the evolution of their own cultures. . . . Muslim
> women have to liberate themselves from the yoke of feudalism in their
> societies and place themselves under God.[4]

A similar need to develop their own distinctive character has been
expressed by Asian Christian women theologians. In 1983 they
formed the Women's Commission in Asia of the Ecumenical
Association of Third World Theologians, and in 1988 they
established in Hong Kong the Asian Women's Resource Centre for
Culture and Theology. Their experience is expressed in the
introduction to *We Dare to Dream: Doing Theology as Asian
Women*:

> Since the 1970s, women theologians in Asia have felt the need of a
> theology that is more cognizant of their context and inclusive of the
> women's viewpoint. However, with few exceptions . . . [it reflected
> either] the thinking of Third World male liberation theologians or First
> World feminists. More recently, Christian women have become aware
> that without their distinctive voices as Asians and as women, the

emerging theologies in Asia cannot be liberating or relevant, not for themselves or for the Church or society at large.[5]

Women's movements within religions, like secular feminist movements, have been divided over the approach they ought to take. Some feel that it is right to take a confrontational line, rejecting sexist culture and institutions. Others want to reappropriate and value the traditions of their culture. This is particularly significant in relation to symbolism. Religious symbols operate at a deep level, shaping our culture and defining our values. Religious symbol systems that are almost exclusively male make a powerful statement about their societies. Can religious images be reclaimed, or must they be rejected? Won Buddhists felt strongly enough about the power of images to adopt the symbol of a circle in place of the image of the (male) Buddha.

A feature of some women's movements has been a recovery of the distant past, and an appropriation of what had been rejected or repressed by the mainstream religion. This may mean a new interest in the worship of the Mother Goddess, or in female shamans, or in folklore or pagan mythology and practices. Jewish feminists have reclaimed Lilith, the legendary first wife of Adam (made, like Adam, from the dust of the ground). She was a powerful, even a demonic, figure, who demanded equality with Adam, and when he would not agree, she left him. A Jewish women's magazine is called *Lilith*. Two Indian women significantly called their publishing venture Kālī, after the powerful and terrifying Hindu goddess, rather than choosing one of the less aggressive deities. (The same motif seems to lie behind the choice of 'Virago' for the British women's publishing house.)

Some women's movements are anti-religious. In China one movement has been anti-Confucian because of the rigid hierarchical structure that Confucianism advocates for society. In Asia and the Middle East some women have turned to secular feminism or Marxism, and in Europe and the United States of America a number of women have despaired of religions being able to reform themselves – or believed that the reformation of institutions so profoundly steeped in patriarchal imagery, doctrines and structures was impossible. However, as the contrast between the classical teachings of the religious traditions represented in this book and the experienced reality of women shows, it is possible to condemn a religion for its oppression of women and yet to recognise that it is from that religion that we gain the criteria which we use for our appraisal.

> Religion is both a problem . . . where its structures of dominance have oppressed women, as well as the solution where its vision of liberation has generated powerful movements for social change.[6]

NOTES

1. The classic anthropological study of pollution and purity is *Purity and Danger*, by Mary Douglas, London, Routledge and Kegan Paul, 1966.
2. In neither Judaism nor Islam is Eve assumed to carry the responsibility for the disobedience in the Garden of Eden.
3. *Mary Astell, 1668–1731, The First English Feminist* (1986) Edited by B. Hill, Gower/Temple Smith, p. 197.
4. Hussain, F. (ed.) (1984) *Muslim Women*, London, Croom Helm, pp. 58 and 60.
5. Fabella, Virginia and Park, Sun Ai Lee (eds) (1989) *We Dare to Dream: Doing Theology as Asian Women*, Asia Women's Resource Centre for Culture and Theology and the EATWOT Women's Commission in Asia, p. vii.
6. Eck, Diana and Jain, Devaki (eds) (1986) *Speaking of Faith: Cross-cultural Perspectives on Women, Religion and Social Change*, London, The Women's Press.

1. Buddhism

Rita M. Gross

Modern commentators on the participation of women in Buddhism are likely to focus on two broad generalisations. The first observation is that the core teachings of this 2,500 year-old tradition are gender-free and gender-neutral, perhaps to a greater extent than is the case with any other major religious tradition. Contemporary Buddhist teachers themselves often respond to questions about the role of women in Buddhism by stating that the Buddha's teachings apply, without exception, to all sentient beings and that no relevant distinctions can be made between women and men regarding their ability to become enlightened and realise Buddhism's deepest insights into reality. But, this has not meant that women and men have been accorded the same status or expected to accomplish the same things throughout most of Buddhist history. Buddhism emerged in a culture that was quite male-dominated and in which there were strong gender roles. Throughout its history Buddhism has accommodated itself more to these patriarchal norms than it has stood against them, though in every period of Buddhist history there are records of highly accomplished women and of great teachers who argued against cultural perceptions of female inferiority. When asked to comment on this historical and institutional slighting of women throughout Buddhist history, many contemporary Buddhist teachers attribute it to 'cultural factors', thus agreeing with the conclusion that such disempowerment of women does not accord well with basic Buddhist teachings. However, to date, little has been done within Buddhism to correct these 'cultural factors' that have been so detrimental to women.

In this chapter, I shall focus on those aspects of Buddhism, both institutional and doctrinal, that most easily enable us to discern

1

women's participation in Buddhism and Buddhist attitudes towards women. After a brief outline of Buddhist teachings, I shall discuss issues pertaining to women in each of the three major phases of Buddhist intellectual-spiritual development: early Indian Buddhism, Mahāyāna Buddhism, and Tantric or Vajrayāna Buddhism. Then I shall rapidly survey the development of Buddhism outside India, with reference to women's roles in those developments. In conclusion, I shall discuss the situation of women in the contemporary Buddhist world, surveying new developments, both theoretical and practical, that redefine women's presence in Buddhism.

Survey of major Buddhist teachings

Buddhism is a non-theistic religion. Its central teachings point out to its adherents the cause of and the cure for human suffering, locating both within human attitudes towards life. Buddhism is not concerned about the existence of a supreme being, because a supreme being would be unable to relieve human suffering, as it is defined by Buddhists. A supreme being cannot cause humans to give up the attitudes that produce human misery. Only human beings are capable of that feat.

According to Buddhism, the cause of misery is located in negative habitual patterns common to all unenlightened beings. Succinctly put, human beings suffer because, while still unenlightened, all beings strive with all their energy for unattainable goals. Disliking boredom and discontent, they strive for perfect complete bliss; disliking uncertainty, they strive for complete security; and disliking death and finitude, they strive for perfect complete permanence in personal immortality. According to Buddhism, these desires are completely impossible to attain under any conditions; therefore, striving to attain them is counterproductive, and serves only to deepen the pain of inevitable failure. That is the bad news, traditionally communicated by Buddhism's first and second noble truths – the truth that conventional existence is pervaded with suffering, and the truth that the cause of such suffering is desire rooted in ignorance.

The good news, according to Buddhism, is that human beings do not have to remain in such useless and counterproductive, desire-ridden states of being; they can lay down the burden and experience the calm and tranquillity of enlightenment. This is the third truth, the truth of the cessation of suffering. The best news of all is that there is a simple and workable path that can be used to good effect by everyone who wants to diminish the burden of excessive desire and compulsion. Called the eight-fold noble path, it is commonly summarised as consisting of three main disciplines: wisdom, morality, and meditation.

Buddhism can seem like an extremely complex religion, especially when one first begins to study it. But all the doctrinal developments found in its many schools and denominations, and all the manifold philosophical texts and meditation manuals it has produced, could well be considered commentary on the four noble truths, discovered by Siddartha Gautama, the Buddha of our historical epoch, during his enlightenment experience, and outlined above.

Buddhism can also seem to be an excessively difficult religion to comprehend at the beginning of one's studies. This difficulty may well be due to Buddhism's extreme simplicity. The four noble truths are extremely simple and basic, but psychological and spiritual truths that are simple in their profundity are often glossed over, resisted, or made unduly complex in conventional thinking. Initially, most people do not want to hear that the solution to human misery lies in giving up unattainable desires, rather than in attaining what one desires, whether by one's own efforts or as the gift of a supreme being.

Women and early Indian Buddhism

Two stories, both extremely well known in Buddhist literature, set the tone for discerning attitudes towards women during Buddhism's first several hundred years. The first story recounts how the future Buddha, having resolved that he would abandon the householder life to become a world renouncer in order to seek enlightenment, silently and secretly gazed upon his sleeping wife and new-born baby, but did not awaken them to bid them farewell. The second story occurs about five years after the Buddha's enlightenment experience, when women loyal to the new religion first gained formal permission to adopt the world renouncer's life-style favoured by the Buddha. His aunt and foster-mother, who had raised him from early infancy, came with five hundred women followers to ask

3

the Buddha for admission to the monastic order, already well-established for men. They were refused the first time they asked, but they persisted and asked again at a later date. At that time, the Buddha's personal attendant, Ananda, took up their cause. He asked the Buddha if women could achieve the same spiritual states as could men. The Buddha replied that they could, whereupon Ananda suggested that, since women could benefit spiritually from living the homeless life, they should be allowed to renounce the world. The Buddha agreed, contingent upon the condition that the women world renouncers accept eight special rules, the effect of which was to make the nuns' order dependent upon and subservient to the monks' order. The eight special rules were accepted and the nuns' order began.

Both these stories are set in the context of the belief that world renunciation is essential to the successful pursuit of the religious life. That is why the future Buddha felt compelled to abandon his wife and child, and why it was so essential for women to found a nuns' order parallel to the monks' order. If the nuns' order had not been established, early Buddhism would have been an extremely disadvantageous religion for women, since they would not have been able to participate in its fundamental institution and, consequently, would have been greatly hampered in their ability to attain its highest goals. Though Buddhism has also devised various methods for lay or householder participation in the religious life throughout its history, reliance on a monastic core has been both the strength and the weakness of Buddhism in its various cultural manifestations. Therefore, it is important to understand what this life-style involved and why it was valued so highly.

Siddartha Gautama, the Buddha, did not originate the world renouncer life-style; he was merely adopting a value widespread in the India of his day. The life-style involved renouncing the securities of conventional life along with its major tasks of economic production and biological reproduction. Without significant possessions, without consort, without significant ties to parents or children, and often without a permanent dwelling, the world renouncer's life was dedicated full-time to the pursuit of spiritual insight, meditative calm and awareness, and detachment. Such achievements brought freedom from the curse of rebirth into the endless rounds of cyclic existence that was believed to be the lot of those who remained fettered to their desires and compulsions. The householder's life, by contrast, was burdened with cares and responsibilities; deep insight into reality, calm awareness, and detachment were thought to be almost impossible to attain while involved in economic or reproductive pursuits.

These assessments of the relative value of householder or monastic life-styles did not turn on a body–spirit dichotomy and did not regard sexuality or the body as evil and degraded, as did similar western forms of monasticism. Rather, the problem that had to be overcome was attachment, clinging, or desire. One life-style bred those enslaving attitudes; the other fostered freedom from them. Thus, when Siddartha Gautama abandoned his wife, it was not because of her evil or sexual nature, but because of his own attachment to her. Other monks, whose attitudes are recorded in early Buddhist texts, could not so readily locate their problems in their own attachments, but blamed women for their sexual desires. Because of these stories and statements, some scholars have regarded early Buddhism as misogynist in its views of women, but I believe that such views do not represent the norm in early Indian Buddhism. Attachment itself, rather than that to which one is attached, was recognised as the fundamental obstacle by the tradition as a whole.

The other major story raises much more serious questions about the treatment of women in early Indian Buddhism. Why did the Buddha resist the women who wished to renounce the world, as men had already done? Why didn't the Buddha himself encourage women, as well as men, to leave the householder life-style behind? Why did he hedge the nuns' order in with the eight special rules? And why did he predict that the Buddhist religion would last only five hundred years, instead of one thousand years, as a consequence of the women's ordination? None of these questions is easy to answer and probably cannot be answered with certainty. That these events were included as part of the Buddhist record demonstrates that, from its beginnings, Buddhism was male-dominated or patriarchal, even though it was not misogynistic.

Though various explanations for these attitudes and practices have been put forward, I believe the simplest and most adequate explanation recognises that the Buddha, though enlightened regarding certain deep spiritual truths, was not entirely free of the social conditioning of his times. I do not believe that enlightenment entails a timelessly perfect social conscience or universal scientific and historical knowledge. Therefore, it did not occur to the Buddha to encourage women to be equal to men in their unconventionality and counter-cultural activities. Nor did he immediately welcome the idea of a parallel women's order. Good guesses as to why he did not welcome the women renunciants include the fear of hostility from householders if their wives and daughters suddenly had an option to renounce their domestic roles, and fear of gossip regarding the interactions of nuns and monks. And it is very clear from another story that, even after he had accepted the idea of a women's order, he could not fathom any other principle than a male-dominant gender hierarchy by which to regulate the inter-actions of the two orders. The first of the eight special rules decreed that even the most senior nun must defer to the most recently ordained monk. The founder of the nuns' order is said once to have asked the Buddha for a special boon – that monks and nuns greet each other by seniority, without regard for gender. The Buddha is said to have replied that even in poorly run sects, the men never deferred to the women and that such behaviour would be unthinkable for his order.

Women in early Indian Buddhism were, however, far more able to participate fully in their tradition as nuns who had to observe the eight special rules than they could have if the nuns' order had not been founded at all. Thus, though the modern tendency may be to criticise the Buddha for his unequal treatment of women, it is probably far more accurate, in the historical context, to recognise how radical it was to provide women with an alternative to domesticity. Furthermore, the eight special rules in no way inhibit women's spiritual development, since women practise a religious life identical with that practised by men.

According to the records of early Indian Buddhism, women used their option well. Many women, in varying domestic situations – married, widowed, abandoned, suffering from the death of children, leaving their children behind, with grown children – renounced their domestic lives. Many attained the tradition's goal of freedom, peace, and release from cyclic existence. Many are celebrated as having become highly accomplished at various achievements valued by the tradition. Their stories and poems are recorded in the *Therigatha*, one of the most remarkable and under-recognised texts in world religious literature. In these poems, women sing of their joy in liberation, of their former sorrow and attachment, and their freedom from the constraints of gender stereotypes. Though not nearly so frequently mentioned by historians of Buddhism as is the story of the Buddha's reluctance to initiate the nuns' order, these stories of the great female exemplars of the early tradition deserve to become a prominent part of the record regarding women and Buddhism. If they were better known, scholars and students of Buddhism could form a more balanced and complete picture of the role of women in early Indian Buddhism.

In the long run, however, the nuns' order did not fare as well as did the monks' order, in India or elsewhere in the Buddhist world. The nuns' order may have existed in India for about fifteen hundred years, until the final days of Buddhism there, but its fortunes eventually declined from the glory of its earlier years. There were fewer nuns; they appear to have been poorly supported by the laity and they were poorly educated. There is no indication that they were involved in the great monastic universities, such as Nalanda University, that were so famous in the late period of Indian Buddhism.

It is difficult to isolate a single cause for this decline, but several interrelated factors probably explain why the order declined in India and was not carried with other aspects of Buddhism to some Asian Buddhist countries. Probably the single biggest difficulty faced by the nuns was the patriarchal definition of women's place as the domestic and reproductive sphere. This cultural norm at first limited even the Buddha's vision regarding the nuns' order. Throughout Asian patriarchal cultures, people simply could more easily envision men taking up the homeless life than they could imagine women taking up the same life-style. In such cultures, they could also more easily give men the prestige and the economic support accorded to those who do renounce the conventional life-style in favour of spiritual development. The eight special rules also seem to have played a part in this decline (Falk 1989: 159). Because nuns were forbidden by the eight special rules to instruct monks, nun scholar-teachers could not build the basis of prestige that their male counterparts could, even if they were well-educated, which became more difficult for them over the centuries. Lay donors preferred to contribute to famous rather than obscure monastics, which meant that the nuns were last on the list and became poorer and less well-educated. Furthermore, such a community was unattractive to more capable recruits. And so a downward spiral developed, which, once in place, was difficult to reverse.

7

Women in Mahāyāna Buddhism

By five hundred years after the beginnings of Buddhism, another school of Buddhism, the Mahāyāna, had developed and was being practised along with the older schools. Mahāyāna Buddhism is famous for its philosophical teachings concerning emptiness, which can be briefly defined as the claim that lack of a permanent essence or lack of independent existence is the central trait of all phenomena. Mahāyāna Buddhism is equally famous for its elaboration of the *bodhisattva* ideal. The *bodhisattva* vows to achieve 'complete perfect enlightenment' for the sake of all beings, over the course of many lifetimes, rather than to rest content, achieving only her own freedom from cyclic existence. Though monasticism continued to be popular, at least theoretically, Mahāyāna Buddhism also elevated the lay, householder life-style to a much higher status. No longer was it assumed that only monks and nuns stood any chance of achieving enlightenment, and Mahāyāna texts are full of tales of householders, both women and men, who are highly advanced.

In principle, these Mahāyāna innovations have great implications for women's participation in Buddhism. Unfortunately, in terms of historical records, little is available and there is little indication that women's roles in Buddhist life and institutions were different in any significant way from what they had been in older forms of Buddhism. But the literature of Mahāyāna Buddhism includes a wide variety of opinions about women and their potential for spiritual achievement. From this literature, it is evident that, even if there was not a women's movement in Mahāyāna Buddhism, the intellectual foundations for such a movement were being laid.

Some famous and important Mahāyāna scriptures reinforce the view, already articulated in early Indian Buddhism, that female rebirth is an unfortunate condition. This view is easily misunderstood in a cultural context, such as that of the West, in which belief in rebirth is not assumed and in which many religious symbols encode a view that women are evil and inferior. On the contrary, the emphasis of the Mahāyāna texts that do speak of the misfortune of female rebirth is that, since women (under patriarchal conditions) suffer many liabilities that men do not suffer, their greater suffering must be a result of their more negative *karma*, or inherited moral balance sheet from previous lives. In the future, however, this misfortune can and will be overcome. Therefore, for example, the all-compassionate Buddha Amitābha graciously arranges that in his Pure Land there will be no unfortunate rebirths, including no female rebirths, and that women, in their current lives, can assure themselves of rebirth into the Pure Land as easily as can men. To a modern western feminist, the evaluation that female rebirth is unfortunate sounds very negative, but it is important to realise that the Buddhist who holds this belief and the feminist agree on an important issue. They agree that women's lives in patriarchal societies are painful and filled with suffering. What they disagree about is that the feminist would eliminate patriarchy, rather than female rebirth. But that option probably seemed impossible to most people in the societies in which such texts were written.

Other Mahāyāna texts concern themselves with the question of how much spiritual depth a person might develop while manifesting in a female rebirth. Most of them consciously refute the claim that only in a future male rebirth could a female really attain deep insight. Instead, they demonstrate that *presently*, in her female body, a person has attained the highest levels of wisdom and insight. Many texts include narratives in which the highest truths and most complex philosophical arguments of Mahāyāna thought are articulated, with complete ease and competence, by a woman, often a young girl, to an astounded audience of male elders, who cannot believe what they are hearing. Thus the Mahayanist demonstrates that religious attainment is not restricted to a monastic élite, that even those most disadvantaged under the prevailing system can experience and express the indwelling enlightenment common to all beings, according to Mahāyāna analysis.

In these Mahāyāna texts, a range of levels of acceptance of such accomplished and competent women is found. In many texts, the conservative male elders remained adamantly unconvinced until the woman or girl performs an instantaneous sex change into a male. In one famous story the woman, instead, briefly changes her adversary into a woman. In some widely used and important texts, the teacher is a mature woman who expounds Buddhist teachings with great clarity and skill to an audience which accepts her without challenge to her womanhood as incongruent with her accomplishments.

In the first motif to be analysed, the girl or woman accomplishes a sexual transformation to confirm her demonstration of her advanced understanding of the Buddhist teachings and her status as an advanced *bodhisattva*. Stories of this genre occur in many Mahāyāna texts, indicating that the ideas behind it were widespread among Mahayanists. In the story, the female uses both logic and magic to demonstrate her advanced understanding. It is important to see the place of each clearly; otherwise it would be easy to draw the conclusion that, in the long run, all highly competent and advanced beings must be or become males.

We may use the famous story of the Nāga Princess in the *Lotus Sūtra* as a good example of this genre. The eight-year old Nāga Princess is praised by Mañjuśrī, the *bodhisattva* of wisdom, as 'superior in knowledge and understanding'. Another *bodhisattva* objects to his judgement, stating that because of the amount of time it takes to attain the *bodhisattva* way, such a young girl would not have been able to acquire so much wisdom. Suddenly the Nāga Princess appears and proclaims that she will teach the *dharma* (Buddhist teachings) which liberates from suffering. Sariputra, exemplar of older, more conservative forms of Buddhism, objects that she cannot accomplish that goal because a female cannot attain the 'five stations'. (These are five positions attained by a future *buddha* on the path towards buddhahood that women were not allowed to fill in Indian society.) To demonstrate to him that she will attain buddhahood anyway, she gives a jewel to the Buddha, which he accepts. She asks Sariputra to confirm that the Buddha accepted the jewel quickly, not slowly. Then she declares that she will attain 'the unexcelled perfect way and achieve supreme enlightenment even more quickly than that'. In that instant, her 'female organ disappeared and the male organ became visible'. She appeared instantly as a *bodhisattva* and then immediately thereafter as a *buddha* with the thirty-two marks of an enlightened being teaching the *dharma* (Paul 1979: 187–90).

The point of her becoming male, by means of her magical powers, is not that males are more worthy, but that only such a demonstration would convince the thick-headed (and male chauvinist) Sariputra. The knowledge possessed by a *bodhisattva* or a *buddha* was hers already; they were not added on with the penis she grew when she changed her empty form from female to male. But her knowledge and logic had been overlooked by those who fixated on her empty female form as if it had intrinsic essential traits that defined her. She must demonstrate more concretely an important implication of the Mahāyāna teachings about emptiness – gender, like every other phenomenon, has no fixed essence and so does not limit those who bear its illusory outward signs.

Another famous Mahāyāna story again involves Sariputra. In the *Vimalakīrtinirdeśa Sūtra*, he is discussing Buddhist philosophy with a mature female called simply 'the goddess', who has been meditating and studying for twelve years. He is extremely impressed with her understanding and asks her (apparently not remembering the act of the Nāga princess) why she doesn't change her female sex. Her reply is classic: 'I have been here twelve years and have looked for the innate characteristics of the female sex and haven't been able to find them. How can I change them?' She compares her femaleness to the femaleness of a magically created illusion of a woman, which Sariputra agrees could not be changed since it possesses no innate determinative characteristics of its own. Her femaleness, she says, no more has innate characteristics than does the femaleness of the illusion. Then she changes Sariputra into a likeness of herself and herself into a likeness of Sariputra and asks Sariputra, who has been changed into a female form, 'Why don't you change your female sex?' Sariputra is quite confused and the goddess lectures to him that if he could be changed into a female form, then all women could also change, which is why the Buddha said, 'all are not really men or women'. After changing him back into his original male form, she asks him where the innate female traits were now. His reply demonstrates that he has acquired a much deeper understanding of emptiness. 'The female form and innate characteristics neither exist nor do not exist' (Paul 1979: 230).

The final Mahāyāna text to be discussed presents an example of a great female Buddhist teacher who simply, and with great authority, teaches advanced Buddhist doctrine. She is the heroine of the *Srīmālādevī Sūtra*, a laywoman and queen of her people. Her parents perceived her extraordinary abilities as a child and brought a teacher to her. She immediately received a prediction that she would attain buddhahood. But, unlike many other stories involving the prediction that a woman would eventually attain buddhahood, no sex change is predicted or hinted at in her story. She does not, for example, receive as part of her prediction a male name that she will bear when she becomes a *buddha*. After completing her studies, she preaches 'eloquently with the "lion's roar" of a Buddha' (Paul 1979: 292–301). No one challenges her in any way, nor is her female gender even discussed. At the end of the *sūtra*, everyone in her realm

11

converts to Mahāyāna Buddhism, beginning with the women, who are followed by her husband, and then, finally, by the rest of the men.

In her study of this *sūtra*, Diana Paul has argued that implicitly Queen Srīmālādevī is a *buddha* in female form, since she receives a prediction that she will achieve full and complete buddhahood in the future, and in her present incarnation she preaches with the eloquence and effect of a *buddha*. That is the meaning of her epithet, 'one who has the lion's roar'. Thus her story takes us far beyond the most conservative Mahāyāna viewpoint in which the compassionate Amitābha creates a Pure Land where the misfortune of female rebirth will not be known.

Women in Vajrayāna Buddhism

The third major phase of Buddhist spiritual-intellectual development is called the Vajrayāna, or Tantric Buddhism. Building upon early Indian Buddhism and the Mahāyāna as essential foundations which must first be mastered, Vajrayāna Buddhism mainly involves elaborate and esoteric meditation practices that are believed to speed up enormously the progress of a *bodhisattva* towards complete perfect enlightenment. The emergence of this form of Buddhism is difficult to date with certainty, but by the sixth century CE, it was well established in parts of India. Somewhat later, it was well known at the great monastic universities of late Indian Buddhism. Eventually this form of Buddhism was carried to Tibet, where it became the dominant form of Buddhism and has flourished until the present. Today, it is mainly represented in Tibetan refugee communities and by great Tibetan *lamas*, who are teaching around the world.

Though the situation of the majority of ordinary Buddhist women probably did not change significantly under Vajrayāna influence, theoretical concepts about femininity and women did change significantly. These changes correlated with changes in views about sexuality and the emotions. Rather than being dangerous territory that was best avoided, sexuality and the emotions are regarded as an extremely provocative working basis for enlightenment, *provided that they are experienced with mindfulness and detachment rather than with absent-minded lust*. Thus, a whole new symbolic, meditative, and ritual universe was developed to train Buddhists in a mindful, detached, and liberating approach to sexuality and the emotions, whether they were experienced in actual rituals or internally through visualisations.

Vajrayāna Buddhism is concerned with the vivid, but relative, phenomena that arise out of emptiness, with 'suchness' (*tathatā*), as it is technically known in Buddhist thought. Relative phenomena, seen with clear or purified perceptions, are methods of experiencing ultimate reality, which is to say that phenomena are symbols of ultimate reality. Among phenomenal symbols, none more clearly express the Vajrayāna view of reality than sexuality, than the dynamic and dyadic unity of a couple in sexual embrace. In the Vajrayāna view, unity and harmony are the underlying reality not always evident in ordinary experience. This unity, however, is not static or monolithic; it is colourful, playful, and multiform. The varied elements in phenomenal reality retain their distinctiveness within their unity. No symbol better expresses this complex, subtle insight, which is almost inexpressible in words, than the symbol of a couple, multiple yet unified, consisting of distinctive elements, yet one entity. Therefore, this symbol became perhaps the central image in Vajrayāna Buddhism, painted, sculpted, visualised, sometimes physically acted out, not as an endorsement of lust but as a method of experiencing reality and enlightenment.

In this symbolism, masculine and feminine principles each clearly and consistently stand for basic elements in the dyadic unity. Most of the important aspects of the phenomenal and spiritual universes are seen as aspects of either masculine or feminine principles and are paired with each other. Thus, the feminine principle is seen in the openness of vowels, the vividness of red, the constancy and brilliance of the sun, the all-pervasive basicness of space or emptiness, the sharp clarity of wisdom, and the left side of the body, among others. The masculine principle, in unifying contrast, is seen as the specificity of consonants, the foundational quality of white, the reflective illuminating power of the moon, the definiteness and specificity of forms that arise in space, the accommodating, out-reaching quality of compassion, and the right side of the body. The two principles are also symbolised by the ritual implements that the meditator holds in the left and the right hands – the bell in the left, feminine, hand, and the *vajra*, or ritual weapon and sceptre, in the right, masculine hand. When the left and right hands, holding the

13

bell and the *vajra*, are crossed in the ritual gesture (*mudrā*) of embracing, the feminine and masculine principles are united. When the hands form independent gestures, in correlation with each other, the masculine and feminine principles co-operate in constructing the world and seeking enlightenment.

These symbolic associations are also personified in the mythological universe of Vajrayāna Buddhism. A vast pantheon of *yidam*s, perhaps best translated as 'non-theistic' deities, and understood as 'myth-mirrors' or as 'personifications of enlightenment', is known and available to the Vajrayāna meditator, who, when properly initiated, meditates on herself as one of the *yidam*s or as the dyadic unity of a male with a female *yidam*. Because enlightenment is personified and because the initiated meditator can identify with these personifications, the body, whether female or male, is spiritually acknowledged and valorised. This valorisation extends to specifically female or male biology, a phenomenon rare in the great world religions.

Among human beings, however, the enlightened meditator is not bound by or limited to the traits that correspond to his or her physiological sex. Women do not exemplify only the feminine principle, nor men the masculine. In so far as they might be so limited in earlier stages of spiritual development, this is seen as a problem rather than a requirement or an ideal. Therefore, male and female initiates are given identical meditational exercises, in which both identify themselves with both masculine and feminine principles in order to develop their inherent enlightenment.

This high evaluation of the feminine principle, combined with the practice of training women and men in the same spiritual disciplines, might lead one to expect the status of women to be high under Vajrayāna Buddhism. One might expect that options previously closed to women would be opened and that women would take a more equal role in the religious community. But the social situation for women under Vajrayāna Buddhism does not correspond completely with the symbolisms outlined above. In some ways, social norms did change to reflect the increased appreciation of women and femininity, but in other ways, longstanding patriarchal social realities were too deeply entrenched for such changes to occur.

The importance and high regard given to feminine symbolism does seem to have had a direct impact on certain standards and norms central to Vajrayāna Buddhism. In addition to the vows of refuge in

14

the Three Jewels (Buddha, *Dharma* and *Saṅgha*), taken to affirm basic Buddhist affiliation, and vows of aspiration to be a *bodhisattva*, taken to affirm one's Mahāyāna affiliation, Tantric practitioners have additional obligations to uphold and downfalls to avoid. Among these obligations, which become downfalls if they are not fulfilled, is the fourteenth:

> If one disparages women, who are of the nature of wisdom, that is the fourteenth root downfall. That is to say, women are the symbol of wisdom and *śūnyatā*, showing both. It is therefore a root downfall to dispraise women in every possible way, saying that women are without spiritual merit and made of unclean things, not considering their good qualities.

> (Willis, 1973: 103)

This obligation, which is the normative social and religious view regarding women, nevertheless contrasts sharply with many popular attitudes. Widely held popular belief still regards female rebirth as 'low' and unfortunate, compared with male rebirth. This attitude is so pervasive that the Tibetan word for woman literally translates as 'born low', a connotation that is fully known to all users of the language (Aziz 1989: 79). These attitudes result in a socially created sense of inferiority that begins with reactions to the birth of a girl and lasts throughout a woman's life. Even women who take up a life-style involving serious spiritual discipline often retain such attitudes about being female (Tsomo 1989: 123).

Given these various attitudes towards women and femininity, it is not surprising that the institutions of Vajrayāna Buddhism do not either completely support or suppress women's spiritual inclinations. Women who wished to become nuns did not fare well under Vajrayāna Buddhism, despite the fact that their male counterparts were honoured, both in India and Tibet. By the time Vajrayāna Buddhism emerged in India, the nuns' order was already in serious decline. Apparently, full ordination for nuns was never transmitted to Tibet along with the rest of Vajrayāna Buddhism, though the novice ordination was. Throughout the history of Tibetan Vajrayāna Buddhism, many women have taken vows and lived all their lives as novice nuns. Though in some ways, such as dress and behaviour, they are very much like fully ordained nuns, they were never as well supported or educated as their male counterparts, nor did their

15

renunciation bring them the prestige and value that it brought to the monks.

Vajrayāna Buddhism did, however, bring a new role to women. Many of the most famous and highly regarded practitioners of Vajrayāna Buddhism did not observe monastic vows, though they were completely dedicated to a life of spiritual discipline, but did not live as conventional householders either. Known either as *siddha*s (accomplished ones) or as *yogis* and *yoginīs*, these seekers often lived highly unconventional lives on the fringes of society and achieved deep levels of realisation. Frequently, part of their *sādhana*, or the spiritual exercises assigned to them by their religious teachers, included actions contrary to older Buddhist requirements for spiritual discipline. For many of them, spiritual discipline included living with a consort who was a partner on the path toward enlightenment.

Women did become *siddha*s. Because the literature focuses more on the male practitioners, we often read about the nameless consort of a male *siddha*. This lack could give us the impression that the consorts were mere enablers or ritual implements used by the male *siddha* in his spiritual practice. But that impression is probably incorrect, because the literature about the *siddha*s often includes the comment that both partners attained high states of realisation. In a much smaller sample of the stories, the main character is a female *siddha*, and the focus is on her struggles and her accomplishments. Though such women are much rarer and even more unusual than their male counterparts, those who did manage to break away from conventional life and to achieve deep levels of spiritual insight, are valued equally with the male *siddha*s. Every *siddha* struggles greatly against conventional expectations, since they keep the norms of neither monastics nor householders, but the women seem to have faced even greater obstacles than did the men in being able to pursue their unusual spiritual vocation. Negotiating their way out of conventional marriage was much more difficult for them than it was for male *siddha*s, just as men could more easily abandon their wives to become monks during the period of early Indian Buddhism than women could abandon their husbands to become nuns. Once on the path of a *siddha*, however, the women experienced no greater difficulties than did the men, thus bearing out the conclusion, already reached by Mahāyāna Buddhists, that 'the *dharma* is neither male nor female'.

The most famous of these female *siddha*s, perhaps the single most famous woman in Buddhist history, was Yeshe Tsogyel, an eighth-century Tibetan woman so important to the transmission of Buddhism to Tibet that she is still included by some schools of Tibetan Buddhism among the revered lineage holders of the *dharma*, standing between the historical Buddha and the present lineage holders. Her story, part of the biographical literature that functions to inspire present-day meditators to great effort in their spiritual discipline, recounts how, despite many obstacles, she attained buddhahood in a single lifetime, thus refuting frequent claims in older Buddhist literature that such a feat was impossible for a woman. Though her story is filled with exemplary incidents, we can learn a lot about the situation of women overall in Buddhism by quoting in full her own assessment of how women are treated and her teacher's assessment of their potential – two passages found almost back to back in her biography. She describes what happens to her:

> I am a woman – I have little power to resist danger.
> Because of my inferior birth, everyone attacks me.
> If I go as a beggar, dogs attack me.
> If I have wealth and food, bandits attack me.
> If I do a great deal, the locals attack me.
> If I do nothing, the gossips attack me.
> If anything goes wrong, they all attack me.
> Whatever I do, I have no chance for happiness.
> Because I am a woman, it is hard to follow the *Dharma*.
> It is hard even to stay alive.
>
> (Tarthang Tulku 1983: 105)

From her own perspective, she sees all the additional obstacles put upon her by a culture hostile to accomplished women. But her teacher, who as a male is less aware of how debilitating such obstacles can be, focuses on her outstanding qualities, which he claims as the potential of all women:

> Wonderful *yoginī*, practitioner of the secret teachings!
> The basis for realizing great enlightenment is a human body.
> Male or female – there is no great difference.
> But if she develops the mind bent on enlightenment,
> The woman's body is better.
>
> (Tarthang Tulku 1983: 102)

17

A summary of traditional Buddhist attitudes towards women

Vajrayāna Buddhism represents the last major new intellectual development in Indian Buddhism. As Buddhism spread beyond India into the rest of Asia, new developments occurred, but none of them constitutes a whole new phase of Buddhist thought, as does the passage from early Indian Buddhism to Mahāyāna Buddhism and then to Vajrayāna Buddhism. Furthermore, no great elaborations or additions to the attitudes towards women or institutional innovations regarding their participation in Buddhism occurred in these non-Indian movements. Therefore, before surveying what happened to Buddhism outside India and what is happening currently regarding women's issues in Buddhism, it is useful to summarise briefly the history surveyed above.

Three generalisations, also important to understanding the role of women in Buddhism altogether, provide such an overview. First, in every period of Buddhist history, there are at least two views about women, neither of which ever fully wins out. Some texts record fairly negative views of women, even some outright misogyny, though it is important to remember that misogyny is different from patriarchy or male dominance. The negative views of women often see them as more materialistic, emotional and sexual than men, less able to renounce desire, and generally less capable of making significant progress on the Buddhist path. Not uncommonly, their best hope was thought to be rebirth as a male, whether offered out of pity and compassion, given the difficulties of women's lives, or recommended out of scorn for women's limited abilities. But, in every period, others stated and argued that women were not inherently deficient or inferior to men in their ability to achieve the calm and insight required to attain Buddhism's highest goals. This opinion is attributed even to the historical Buddha, despite his reluctance to found the nuns' order, and some rather nasty comments about women also attributed to him.

The second major generalisation is that in the broad sweep of Buddhist history, from early Indian Buddhism to Mahāyāna to Vajrayāna, the bias against women becomes less acceptable. The more important texts, stories, and teachers argue that 'the *dharma* is neither male nor female', and that to denigrate women 'who are the symbol of wisdom and Śūnyatā, showing both' is a serious root downfall.

18

Thirdly, on the whole, Buddhist attitudes towards women throughout history are not overwhelmingly misogynistic, if misogyny is narrowly defined, and not confused with male dominance. This judgement is especially clear when Buddhism is compared with other major world religions. However, androcentrism and male dominance are almost unrelieved throughout Buddhist history. Most of the inadequacies regarding Buddhist treatment of women that would be pointed out by many contemporary Buddhists sympathetic to feminism stem from Buddhism's traditional androcentrism and male dominance.

Women in Buddhism outside India

Buddhism is among the minority of major religions that have spread successfully beyond their homeland into cultures very different from the one that gave them birth. Such religions always focus on a message that is relatively culture-free and universal in its implications; furthermore, they do not emphasise a detailed, and therefore culture-bound, code for daily living. Thus the same factors that make Buddhism relatively gender-free, at least in its abstract teachings, also worked in favour of Buddhism's success as a portable religion. However, the cultures into which Buddhism spread were just as male-dominated as the Indian culture from which Buddhism came. Therefore, its institutionalised practices favouring monks and men in general were not challenged or modified during its wanderings throughout Asia. However, as Buddhism, in fulfilling ancient but enigmatic prophecies it has retained for centuries, comes to the West, it is encountering, for the first time, the challenge to mesh its gender-free vision with more egalitarian-feminist praxis.

In India, Buddhism was always largely carried and maintained by its monastic core, and the monastic life-style was usually regarded as the ideal method for practising Buddhism, even among Mahayanists. This monastic core, usually consisting of monks rather than nuns, was also critical in the spread of Buddhism to other Asian countries. For the most part, Buddhism did not spread primarily in conjunction with colonialism or military conquest. Instead, wandering monks, often travelling with trading caravans, spread the religion, which was adopted slowly by an élite and then from the top down in the receiving society. In addition, once Buddhism became established to any degree in a society, inhabitants of that country frequently went on arduous pilgrimages to the lands from which Buddhism had come, in an attempt to gain deeper understanding of their newly adopted religion. Monks were also well suited to these reverse missions. All these factors together meant that monasticism also dominated Buddhism in its non-Indian developments. In fact, monasticism was so highly valued that some would claim that Buddhism is not genuinely established in a country until it can boast a flourishing monastic community. Because of the continued emphasis on monasticism, a survey of women's involvement in Buddhism outside India yields little information on Buddhist laywomen throughout the centuries in the Asian Buddhist countries.

Unfortunately, even more than had been the case in India, the monastic community, with a few notable and important exceptions, favoured monks over nuns. For a variety of reasons, many Asian Buddhist countries do not have a nuns' order. To be fully ordained, according to the ancient and nearly universal Buddhist regulations for monastics, a nun must be ordained by a group of ten monks and ten nuns. Without the initial group of ten nuns, a broken lineage could never be restored nor proper ordination procedures begun. Due to the greater difficulties and diminished support often experienced by the nuns, that initial group of nuns required to begin an ordination lineage was often difficult to assemble. Sometimes, not enough nuns could travel to a newly established outpost of Buddhism. Sometimes, after the lineage was destroyed, its re-establishment was opposed. Under such circumstances, women who wish to live as renunciants must resort to makeshift approximations of ordination, often without much support from their culture. They may live and dress as nuns, but they are regarded as novices or laywomen by the Buddhist establishment. As such, they do not receive the economic support, education, or respect that would be due to them as nuns. Nevertheless, in all Buddhist countries where monks are found, some form of nuns' community is also found, with the exception of Mongolia (Tsomo 1988: 103). Under such conditions, it is noteworthy that some version of nunship does exist in all Asian Buddhist countries.

Theravadin Buddhism, directly descended from the ancient Indian Buddhism characteristic of the first period of Buddhist intellectual and spiritual development, has become the dominant form of Buddhism in Southeast Asia. Most of the values of ancient Indian

Buddhism, including its very strong emphasis on monastics as the ideal Buddhist practitioners, and its views about women, have been faithfully transmitted to Southeast Asia. Though the nuns' ordination lineage was transferred to some Theravadin Buddhist countries, it has since been lost in all of them. Under current conditions, it would be relatively easy to re-introduce the ordination lineage from China, but many Theravadin authorities are quite unsympathetic to this development.

Sri Lanka was the first country outside India to become Buddhist. Usually the initial conversion is credited to the son and the daughter of the Indian Emperor Asoka, who founded, respectively, the Sri Lankan monks' and the nuns' orders in the third century BCE. The nuns' order existed until at least the ninth century CE and is usually credited as the source of the ordination lineages still preserved by Chinese nuns. In the eleventh century, the monastic institutions were severely damaged, if not destroyed, by South Indian invaders. When efforts were made, successfully, to re-introduce monks' ordination lineages from other Theravadin Buddhist countries, there were, apparently, no attempts to re-introduce the nuns' ordination lineages as well. Until the twentieth century, it does not seem that Sri Lankan women had any formally organised and recognised renunciant community. During this century, women have begun to take up the nuns' life-style but, without the formality of full ordination, they lack prestige and support from their Sri Lankan compatriots.

The current situation of nuns in Myanmar (Burma) and Thailand, the other major Theravadin countries, is similar. Women live the nuns' life-style and dress distinctively, but they do not receive formal vows and are not legally or religiously treated as nuns by either their governments or the religious establishments in their countries. Often, though their discipline is strict, they are poorly supported and poorly educated. A woman who takes up the life of such a nun does not receive the praise and respect that her male counterpart would receive. There is evidence that the nuns existed in Myanmar as late as the eleventh to the thirteenth centuries CE, but most commentators conclude that the nuns' ordination never reached Thailand (Tsomo 1988: 105).

In Mahāyāna Buddhist countries, the situation varies considerably. The East Asian culture area received Buddhism through China and all the East Asian forms of Buddhism retain some Chinese imprint.

The nuns' order has been rather strong in China for many centuries and ordination lineages have been preserved there, which has affected other East Asian forms of Buddhism to some extent. Between 429 and 433 CE, when Buddhism was becoming a dominant influence in China, nuns from Sri Lanka travelled to China to provide the quorum of ten nuns required for ordination as a full-fledged nun (Tsomo 1988: 106). Since then, these lineages have been preserved in China and in many overseas Chinese communities, as well as in Korea and Vietnam. Today, in many non-mainland Chinese Buddhist communities and in some Korean communities, nuns out-number monks, are almost completely independent to run their own affairs, and include many young, well-educated women, a situation not found elsewhere in the Buddhist world.

Historically, there are also a number of strong and noteworthy figures. A Chinese text, the *Bi-qui-ni-chuan* (*Lives of Eminent Nuns*), contains biographies of sixty-five Chinese nuns who lived between 317 and 516 CE. They were a 'highly literate, active, influential group of women' (Schuster 1985: 98). At least one Chinese Ch'an (Zen) Buddhist nun is recorded in Ch'an records as an important teacher and a highly realised being (Levering 1982). Buddhist laywomen of the Imperial court also gained considerable power at some points in Chinese history. Probably the most successful and important was Empress Wu (625–705 CE), who, though maligned by later Chinese historians, ruled China successfully and well, using Buddhist ideas to justify her rule and her policies (Paul 1989).

In Japan, the prestige of the monastic community has broken down more than anywhere else in the Buddhist world, so that today, though Buddhism is thoroughly intertwined into Japanese culture, celibate monks or nuns ordained according to ancient Indian norms used elsewhere in the Buddhist world are almost non-existent. At one time, monks were ordained according to the Indian texts and rules, but the full quorum of ten nuns required to confer the nuns' ordination was never successfully assembled in Japan. However, early in the ninth century, under the influence of one of Japan's greatest Buddhist teachers, the idea that receiving the *bodhisattva* precepts was equivalent to receiving the monastic precepts was introduced. Over the centuries, particularly as Japan began to allow and affirm a married Buddhist priesthood, this form of ordination took precedence over the form of monastic ordination used elsewhere in the Buddhist world. All nuns are ordained in this 'non-monastic' fashion, though they live a life-style much closer to the ancient Indian norms for monks and nuns than do their male counterparts. Unlike most male 'monks', they do not marry or drink alcohol. Sometimes they serve as temple priests, though, unlike their male counterparts, they would not marry if they are to be considered nuns. Currently, there is also a growing number of married female priests or priests' wives who have taken on many of the duties and privileges of priesthood. However, becoming a nun is not currently a popular option in Japan.

Vajrayāna Buddhism came to Tibet directly from India, beginning in the seventh century. By the mid-eighth century, monastic ordination had begun, but again, the quorum of ten nuns required to initiate the nuns' ordination lineage was never assembled in Tibet. From the beginning, however, many Tibetan women have taken novice ordination, worn monastic robes, and lived a monastic life-style. Though they are not as well supported economically, and generally not as well educated as their male counterparts, and do not have the same level of prestige as do monks, they are regarded as monastics, not laywomen, by their culture. Some of them come to be very highly regarded for their discipline and spiritual attainments. Because Vajrayāna Buddhism is the major form of Buddhism in Tibet, the *siddha* or *yoginī* ideal prevails beside the monastic ideal. Throughout the centuries, many dedicated and determined Tibetan women have not taken vows as novice nuns, but have lived as wandering *yoginī*s or as strict retreatants instead. If anything, the women who have chosen this path are even more respected and renowned than are the nuns. The most famous and important of them are Yeshe Tsogyel (Gross 1989) (see p. 17) and Machig Labdron, but many others are known (Allione 1984). Today, Tibetan Buddhism survives mainly in exile communities in India and among a rapidly growing number of western converts. The exile communities are often poor; even when they are not, support for women religious seekers is not high on the list of favoured projects, despite the honour accorded theoretically to women and to the feminine principle.

The latest development in the long history of Buddhism is its transmission to the West, begun early in this century but growing exponentially during and after the 1960s. At present, all major forms of Buddhism are represented in western countries, especially in

23

North America and Europe. Buddhism is coming to the West, not only with Asian immigrants who maintain Buddhism as part of their ethnic tradition, but also as the religion of choice of an articulate, dedicated, and idealistic minority of Europeans and Americans of European descent. These European Buddhists are well-educated, both in western and in Buddhist learning and often are extremely dedicated to their new religion. Some of them become monks and nuns, but thus far, the majority of them remain laypeople. Because of their dedication to Buddhist learning and meditation practice, they may well be in the forefront of a new style of Buddhism, which would not be so characterised by the dichotomy between monks and laypeople.

Of utmost importance for the future of Buddhism is the fact that many of the most dedicated and able European Buddhists are women who are not content with the role traditionally allotted to women in Asian male-dominated forms of Buddhism. They study Buddhist doctrine and practise Buddhist meditation equally with their male counterparts and expect to take leadership roles in emerging Western Buddhism. In the endless debates and comments about similarities and differences between Asian and western forms of Buddhism, it has been noted, cogently, that the single biggest difference is the presence of numerous women in meditation halls and classrooms, studying and practising with men. As these women gain greater understanding of Buddhism and greater self-confidence, major new developments in Buddhism are likely, as Sandy Boucher has indicated by the title of her book, *Turning the Wheel: American Women Creating the New Buddhism* (Boucher 1988).

Current issues involving women and Buddhism

The major contemporary issues concerning women and Buddhism are also important issues for the future of Buddhism as a whole. They turn on the age-old problem in Buddhism of the relationship between the monastic and the lay communities, and on the need for both of them to be renewed and modernised.

The issues and the needs regarding women and the monastic community are relatively simple and straightforward, which does not mean that they will be easily resolved within the Buddhist world. Many voices call for the re-introduction of the nuns' ordination into those forms of Buddhism in which it has been lost. Given modern means of transportation and the existence of fully ordained nuns in some parts of the Buddhist world, the solution would seem to be straightforward. A quorum of ten nuns could ordain a group of women (at least ten, preferably more) who meet the criteria for ordination and wish to be ordained, but cannot in their own form of Buddhism because the lineage has died out there. Once a quorum of nuns exists in Theravadin or Tibetan communities, it could again become self-maintaining. Unfortunately, some powerful Buddhist monks are quite opposed to this possibility, especially in Theravadin countries. They claim that ordination of Theravadin Buddhists by representatives from lineages currently existing only in Mahāyāna Buddhism, would be unacceptable from a Theravadin point of view. It can easily be countered that the differences between Theravadin and Mahāyāna Buddhism are doctrinal, not behavioural, and that, in fact, there are no significant differences between Theravadins and Mahayanists regarding monastic discipline. Others worry that perhaps at some point in history, the Chinese nuns' ordination lineages were improperly maintained, which would invalidate the ordinations they confer. However, similar fears about the validity of male ordination lineages are seldom, if ever, voiced. In the Tibetan monastic community, there are some fears and hesitations regarding these Chinese ordination lineages, but important authorities, such as the Dalai Lama, have voiced their general support of the movement to institute full ordination for nuns in Tibetan Buddhism (Tsomo 1988: 268–9).

Deeper problems concerning attitudes towards women would still remain, however. Throughout Buddhist history, and in most parts of the contemporary Buddhist world, nuns simply are not as well supported or as well respected as are monks. As a result, they are often poor, which inhibits their efforts to develop themselves through study and practice. They often have only minimal opportunities for Buddhist education and often experience great difficulty in taking on the more advanced meditations that are so important in many schools of Buddhism. Because their attainments are low, a vicious downward spiral is maintained. They are less attractive recipients of support than their more accomplished male counterparts, and so the cycle continues, as it seems to have spun itself out time after time in Buddhist history.

Receiving full nuns' ordination would probably alleviate some of

25

these problems, since Chinese and Korean nuns do seem to be better educated and better supported than Tibetan or Theravadin women who practise either as novices or as 'lay nuns' (Tsomo 1988: 103–6). However, even fully ordained nuns must deal with certain liabilities *vis-à-vis* the monks, especially their inability to develop fully as teachers, given the confines of the eight special rules. The eight special rules are themselves rooted in and reflective of the androcentric consciousness and male-dominant world-view that were characteristic of ancient India. Really solving, in any definitive way, the problems facing Buddhist women is unlikely so long as Buddhism remains androcentric in its outlook and male-dominant in its praxis.

To reform the androcentrism and male dominance of classical Buddhism is an immense task. If it can be accomplished at all, many of the reforms are likely to come from lay Buddhists, and from Western Buddhists, especially from the women who simply would not adopt Buddhism if they were required to conform to conventional male-dominant Buddhist practices in order to be Buddhists.

A potentially extremely significant development in Buddhism is the emergence of groups of Buddhist laypeople who, nevertheless, define themselves as serious Buddhist practitioners striving for the same goals that are often thought of as goals attainable only by monastics – some deep level of personal transformation through the realisation of insight and tranquillity. The means pursued to attain these goals are also the classic monastic methods – study of Buddhist teachings and the practice of meditation. In their life-style, these lay meditators usually combine elements of the householder life-style with elements of the monastic life-style. Meditation centres, for the first time in Buddhist history, can include childcare facilities. People with families periodically withdraw from economic and domestic responsibilities for intensive study and practice. When they return to their economic and domestic responsibilities, they seek to infuse their ordinary activities with meditative awareness cultivated during their retreats. In short, the dichotomy between serious, detached monastic Buddhists and hopelessly attached, desire-driven Buddhist householders is being broken down. This development is even more significant for women than it is for men, because precisely those 'lay' activities that traditionally are women's sphere – sexuality, family, and reproduction – are the most destructive aspects of worldly life, according to traditional Buddhism.

Lay Buddhism is significant for women also because it is much easier and more attractive for most women to become involved in serious lay Buddhism than in monastic Buddhism. And many, many women are becoming so involved in all forms of Buddhism, especially among Westerners. Most of them are still undergoing traditional Buddhist training, but eventually, whether authorised by their communities or by their own inner transformation, they will begin, indeed already have begun, to lead their communities and to teach. The emergence of a large and strong core of women teachers who are well-educated, well-practised, articulate, and not male-identified, will be one of the most significant events ever in the intellectual and spiritual development of Buddhism. Because of androcentrism, male dominance, and the eight special rules, it has never before happened. Previously, those women who did excel at Buddhist practice and understanding rarely taught; those few who did teach did not seek to overcome the traditional androcentrism and male dominance of Buddhism, probably because the historical causes and conditions favouring such a transformation were not yet in place.

It is possible to envision Buddhism after patriarchy (Gross 1991b), a Buddhism no longer driven by subtle or obvious preference for men and their interests. As is the case with most major world religions, post-patriarchal transformation in Buddhism is likely to include two basic developments. In the first development, the resources of Buddhism will be utilised to call for a prophetic reform of Buddhist institutions that brings Buddhist praxis in line with Buddhist vision. It can easily be argued (Gross 1991a) that the normative teachings of Buddhism are remarkably free of gender bias favouring either women or men, that the fundamental teachings of Buddhism apply, without exception, to all human beings, without reference to gender, race or class. It can be shown with equal ease that Buddhism, in its institutional forms, both monastic and lay, has never lived up to its own vision, or even come close to living up to its own vision. But, it would be argued, given the intolerable contradiction between view and practice, the practice of male dominance, rather than the view of gender neutrality, should be given up. To begin that task, Buddhists would need to introduce nuns' ordination everywhere in the Buddhist world, upgrade the status and well-being of nuns, and take laywomen seriously as Buddhist practitioners. These steps are already occurring, at least to some extent, and are being discussed by all Buddhists.

27

Post-patriarchal Buddhism, however, also involves a deeper question, the same question brought up in most major religions by the post-patriarchal revolution. Once the male-dominant institutions are reformed, will everything else stay as it has always been? Or will some of the rules of the game change with the input of women's culture? Women's spirituality and feminist psychology are now well-developed resources that can hardly be ignored by anyone seeking to understand and experience personal and social transformation. Those resources suggest that post-patriarchal Buddhism will need to emphasise connection, community and communication in ways that will go beyond what has previously been the norm for Buddhism, though they will not contradict those norms. In this subtle, but profound revalorisation of Buddhism, alienation between people and between humans and our environment may well come to be viewed as problematic for spiritual well-being, in the same way that attachment has always been viewed as a major obstacle for spiritual well-being by Buddhists. Balancing out the fear of attachment with an equal fear of alienation may well bring Buddhists to a deeper understanding of a Middle Way that is equally relevant to women and men.

FURTHER READING

Allione, T. (1984) *Women of Wisdom*, London, Routledge and Kegan Paul.

Aziz, B. (1989) 'Moving toward a sociology of Tibet', in J. Willis (ed.) *Feminine Ground: Essays on Women and Tibet*, Ithaca, NY, Snow Lion.

Boucher, S. (1988) *Turning the Wheel: American Women Creating the New Buddhism*, San Francisco, Harper & Row.

Falk, N. (1989) 'The case of the vanishing nuns: the fruits of ambivalence in ancient Indian Buddhism', in N. Falk and R. Gross (eds) *Unspoken Worlds: Women's Religious Lives*, Belmont, CA, Wadsworth.

Gross, R. (1989) 'Yeshe Tsogyel: enlightened consort, great teacher, female role model', in J. Willis (ed.) *Feminine Ground: Essays on Women and Tibet*, Ithaca, NY, Snow Lion.

—— (1991a) 'The Dharma is neither male nor female: Buddhism on gender and liberation', in H. Grob, H. Gordon and R. Hassan (eds) *Women's and Men's Liberation: Testimonies of Spirit*, New York, Greenwood Press.

—— (1991b) 'Buddhism after patriarchy', in P. Cooey, W. Eakin and J. McDaniel (eds) *After Patriarchy: Feminist Reconstructions of the World's Religions*, Maryknoll, NY, Orbis.

Horner, I.B. (1930) *Women Under Primitive Buddhism: Laywomen and Almswomen*, New York, E.P. Dutton.

Levering, M. (1982) 'The Dragon Girl and the Abbess of Mo-Shan: gender and status in Ch'an Buddhist tradition', *Journal of the International Association of Buddhist Studies*, 5(1): 19–35.

Paul, D. (1979) *Women in Buddhism: Images of the Feminine in Mahayana Tradition*, Berkeley, Asian Humanities Press.

—— (1989) 'Empress Wu and the historians: a tyrant and saint of classical China', in N. Falk and R. Gross (eds) *Unspoken Worlds: Women's Religious Lives*, Belmont, CA, Wadsworth.

Schuster, N. (1985) 'Striking a balance: women and images of women in early Chinese Buddhism', in Y. Haddad and E. Findly (eds) *Women, Religion and Social Change*, Albany, NY, State University of New York Press.

—— (1987) 'Buddhism', in A. Sharma (ed.) *Women in World Religions*, Albany, NY, State University of New York Press.

Tsomo, K.L. (1988) *Sakyadhita: Daughters of the Buddha*, Ithaca, NY, Snow Lion.

—— (1989) 'Tibetan nuns and nunneries', in J. Willis (ed.) *Feminine Ground: Essays on Women and Tibet*, Ithaca, NY, Snow Lion.

Tulku, Tarthang (trans) (1983) *Mother of Knowledge: The Enlightenment of Yeshe Tsogyel*, Berkeley, Dharma Publishing Co.

Willis, J. (1973) *The Diamond Light: An Introduction to Tibetan Buddhist Meditations*, New York, Simon & Schuster.

29

2. Christianity

Clare Drury

The primary source of authority for Christians has always been the Bible. It is on biblical texts that Christian attitudes to women are based, but this does not mean that there is any straightforward biblical teaching about women which everyone accepts. For the Bible is made up of many different books written and altered over many centuries and not designed to be bound together as one volume. Furthermore, the interpretation of the Bible changes as society changes, so that what seems to fit the scientific and cultural ideas of one century may look quite different in the next.

For some Christians, however, even now, the Bible is felt to have an authority which transcends time and place, so that words written centuries ago in an entirely different culture can be read and believed without reference to the social, cultural or religious conditions in which they were written. But modern scholarship has brought an awareness of the importance of a society's historical and cultural background when interpreting its documents, so that Christian scholars read Paul's teaching on marriage in 1 Corinthians 7, for example, with the knowledge that he expected the world to end in a very short time.[1] When Paul discourages his readers from marrying, it is because 'the appointed time has grown very short', and they should be concentrating on their new faith and not on the worldly cares of the newly married. Jesus, too, had called people to prepare for the coming Kingdom of God, proclaiming its imminence and its radical demands. In the centuries following, some Christians have taken these demands seriously even without the urgent eschatological motivation of the earliest teachers, while others have tried to accommodate the teaching to existing social conditions. In the present century, feminists have been able to point out how radical

30

some of the New Testament teaching about women really was when understood against its contemporary background. They claim that this radicalism was lost during centuries of patriarchal domination of the Church.

Attitudes to the position of women in Christianity, therefore, depend first on which biblical texts one chooses, then on how one reads the Bible and how much weight is given to the contexts in which it was written. The women's movement has begun to interpret the Bible in its own, feminist, way, recognising the almost totally male dominance of both writers and interpreters of the Old and New Testaments, drawing out teaching more positive towards women which has often been overlooked before. Following the extreme change in attitudes towards sexuality and gender issues in modern western society, Christian women have begun to assert their right to equality inside the Church as well as in secular life. Recently, as women have gained unprecedented freedom in the West, the Churches have begun to mirror these changes. But in societies which have given women a more restricted role and function, the Church has continued to reflect this state of affairs. Some modern scholars[2] have recognised that many of the most influential ideas about women in the Church have come from celibate male writers whose fears about their own sexuality were projected on to women. They chose to emphasise teaching that was negative towards women so that women could be kept at a safe distance and in a secondary position within the Church.

A less radical, but still inegalitarian, view of women, found today among some conservative Protestant groups, is that they have a role different from, but complementary or subordinate to, men. Some Churches, such as the Quakers, the Methodists, the Baptists and some provinces of the Anglican Communion, treat women as men's equals at all levels and some appoint them as ministers, priests or even bishops, while others, such as the Roman Catholics, still demand celibacy of their all-male priesthood. Some allow women control over their bodies in, for instance, contraception and even abortion, while others regard both as sinful. Since the Bible is the primary authority for these contradictory positions, it is necessary first to look at what it has to say about gender, sexuality and marriage and then at how the Church has interpreted these texts. Much of the seminal work of interpretation was done in the first four centuries of Christianity and those interpretations have formed the basis of most Christian attitudes towards women until the twentieth century.

Women as part of the created order

Christians adopted as their own the Jewish Scriptures because they believed that Jesus was the Christ, or Messiah, to whom the Scriptures referred. They soon began to write their own books some of which, in time, also achieved the status and authority of Scripture. The two groups of writings together came to be called the Old and New Testaments. Both are thought by Christians to record the activities of the same God who is responsible for creating the world and sustaining it, and for providing salvation for his people. So Christians, like Jews, believed that the world had been created by God, that God was beneficent, that he approved his creation and wished it well, 'And God saw everything that he had made, and behold, it was very good' (Gen. 1:31). On the other hand, the world was obviously not a perfect place where God's work was undeniably present; suffering and pain could not be explained as the creation of a good God. Genesis 3 places the responsibility for the sufferings of the human race on the shoulders of Adam and Eve for their act of disobedience to God. Christians accepted the stories of creation they found in the Jewish Scriptures and adapted them only to the extent of introducing the pre-existent Christ into the scheme of creation, so that the redeemer of the world was also seen to take part in its creation (John 1:1–18; Col. 1:12–20; Heb. 1:1–2:13). They felt that through the death and resurrection of Christ, God had provided a way of reversing the sin of Adam and Eve. 'For as in Adam all die, so also in Christ shall all be made alive.' (1 Cor. 15:22, cf. Rom. 5:12ff). Because Christians believed that Jesus was the Jewish Messiah and that Jewish history had been building up to and working towards the coming of the Messiah, they felt entirely justified in interpreting the Jewish Scriptures in ways which suited their own purposes, but which were foreign both to the probable original intentions of the writers and to their Jewish interpreters.

The story of the Creation and Fall in Genesis 1–3 was perhaps the most influential Old Testament text affecting woman's place in society, her relationship with her husband and with God. The first thing that must be said is that Genesis 1–3 clearly incorporates two distinct accounts of the Creation myth; Genesis 1:1–2:3 dates from about 400 BCE and is more sophisticated than the Genesis 2:4–3:24 account, which includes the story of the Fall and which was written about five hundred years earlier. From the woman's point of view the separation of the two stories is vital. In the later account, God creates the world in six days ending with the creation of human beings. In this account man and woman are created at the same time, they are the high point of creation and are given dominion over all the other creatures, 'So God created man in his own image, in the image of God he created him; male and female he created them' (Gen. 1:27). There is no distinction in status, there is no subjugation of one sex to the other implied. Both are created in the image of God, and the significance of the gender difference is made clear immediately with the injunction, 'Be fruitful and multiply'. Male and female are differentiated primarily for procreation – the commandment to procreate was understood in a positive way by the Jews as long as sexual intercourse took place within marriage. The image of God is not tied to the male, the whole human race is in the image of God. There was a tendency among Christians to conflate the two accounts so that the one in Genesis 1:1–2:3 is seen to describe the perfect state of human beings in Paradise before the fall, the state which, through Christ, it was possible to regain. This may be the basis of a passage in Galatians where Paul seems to be describing Christianity as a faith in which distinctions of race, social status and gender do not apply. 'There is neither Jew nor Greek, there is neither slave nor free, there is neither male nor female; for you are all one in Christ Jesus' (Gal. 3:28).[3] The equality of the status of the sexes before God is therefore recognised among redeemed – that is Christian – men and women, at any rate by Paul. But as far as most Christian women are concerned, the equality of status has had little effect in their everyday lives until this century, especially since elsewhere in Paul's letters and in those written by his followers, this egalitarian ideal seems to be contradicted (e.g., 1 Cor. 11:7–9, 14:34–36, 1 Tim. 2:9–15).

The older account of the Creation (Gen. 2:4–3:24) is more primitive in style. God uses the dust of the ground to create Adam, the first man, and breathes into his nostrils the breath of life, 'and man became a living being'. God went on to create a garden for man to live in with trees bearing fruit for him to eat. He only commanded Adam not to eat fruit from the tree of the knowledge of good and

33

evil. God then created all the birds and animals with the aim of finding a helper fit for man, but he could not. So God sent Adam into a deep sleep and created the woman, out of Adam's rib. She is created to provide a companion suitable for him, and their original belonging together as one creature is the explanation for 'the two becoming one flesh' in marriage (Gen. 2:24, cf. Mark 10:8). It is she who persuades Adam to disobey God's commandment not to eat of the tree of the knowledge of good and evil.

Christian writers from Paul onwards used this story in two ways. First, it showed that women are subordinate to men because they are created after men and from men and for men. It is the origin of the idea which many feminist Christians find abhorrent, that humankind is to be understood in terms of the male. There is a natural hierarchy; to be male is the norm, the female half of the human race is other and subordinate. Paul uses the story to justify his system of authority, explaining it as a kind of divine order given in nature: 'For man was not made from woman, but woman from man. Neither was man created for woman, but woman for man' (1 Cor. 11:8–9).

The second way in which Christian writers came to use this version of the Creation myth was to emphasise the fundamental wickedness of women. They are responsible for leading men astray; if the woman had not tempted the man, he would not have sinned. 'For Adam was formed first then Eve; and Adam was not deceived, but the woman was deceived and became a transgressor' (1 Tim. 2:13–14). The punishment meted out to Adam and Eve after their disobedience is in line with this sort of interpretation. Adam will find it difficult to provide a livelihood because the earth has been cursed and growing food will be arduous and painful. But the woman's punishment is more integral to her very existence and her purpose in life. She will have pain in child-bearing and yet she will desire her husband and he will have authority over her (Gen. 3:16–19). This emphasis on Eve's primary guilt is exacerbated by the idea which became prevalent among many Christians that the knowledge which Adam and Eve gained from eating the fruit of the tree of knowledge was carnal knowledge. In other words, Eve was responsible for introducing Adam to sexuality. Women are temptresses in what came to be seen in the Church as the greatest of all temptations, sex.

According to the gospels of Matthew and Mark, Jesus joined the two stories together to support his radical opposition to divorce.

34

But from the beginning of creation, 'God made them male and female.' 'For this reason a man shall leave his father and mother and be joined to his wife, and the two shall become one flesh.' So they are no longer two but one. What therefore God has joined together, let no one put asunder.

(Mark 10:6–9, cf. Matt. 19:5–6)

The two accounts have been conflated in Christian tradition ever since. So, it has been necessary to reconcile the idea that women, like men, were made in the image of God, with the idea that men were made in the image of God and women, created later, were secondary and inferior.

This latter view became prevalent in the Church partly because it meshed so well with most secular views in the late antique world in which Christianity grew up. Aristotle (fourth century BCE) had introduced the idea that the male seed provides the 'form' of the human body. The woman's part is passively to receive the formative power of the male seed and so conceive a child. If all goes well, the baby will be male, but if some accident occurs the male form is subverted and produces an inferior or malformed, that is female, baby (Aristotle, *Generation of Animals*, 2.3). He believed that there was a natural hierarchy with free men, who were naturally more rational than women, ruling over wives, slaves and children (e.g., *Politics*, 12.1). Men were seen as fiery, hot and active; women as cold, clammy and wet and passive. Aristotle's writings continued to be very influential in the Church for many centuries, partly because they seemed to reflect the actual state of affairs. It was not until 1827, for instance, when K.E. von Baer discovered the ovum, that it was recognised that women have an equal share in the reproductive process. In the early centuries of this era, every girl baby was deemed a failure, less than the ideal, useful only for her ability to bear children, 'Yet woman will be saved through bearing children, if she continues in faith and love and holiness, with modesty' (1 Tim. 2:15).

Although the Church chose to emphasise the sin of Eve by concentrating on the older creation story, yet Genesis 1:27 could not be entirely ignored: 'In the image of God he created him; male and female he created them'. Augustine (354–430 CE), Bishop of Hippo in North Africa, was possibly the most influential Christian writer of all outside the New Testament. He combined the texts of Genesis

35

1:27 with 1 Corinthians 11:7–16 to argue that woman was not made in the image of God in the same sense that man was.

> But we must see how the words spoken by the Apostle, that not the woman but the man is the image of God are not contrary to that which is written in Genesis: . . . For he says that human nature itself, which is complete in both sexes, has been made to the image of God. For after he had said that God made man to the image of God, he went on to say: 'he made them male and female'. In what sense then are we to understand the Apostle, that the man is the image of God, and consequently is forbidden to cover his head, but the woman is not, and on this account is commanded to do so? The solution lies . . . in that the woman together with her husband is the image of God, so that the whole substance is one image. But when she is assigned as a help-meet, a function that pertains to her alone, then she is not the image of God; but as far as the man is concerned, he is by himself alone the image of God, just as fully and completely as when he and the woman are joined together in one.
>
> (Augustine, *de Trinitate*, 12.7.10)

He believed that the serpent had approached Eve first, because she represented 'the frailer part of human society', the more gullible partner. Later theologians such as Thomas Aquinas (*d.* 1274) revived Aristotle's definition of a woman as a malformed male, but claimed that the innate inferiority had been exacerbated by sin. He followed closely Aristotle's view of the relations of men and women. Woman was only created for her role in procreation; children were encouraged to follow their fathers rather than their mothers: 'The father is more to be loved than the mother because he is the active generative element, whereas the mother is the passive' (*Summa Theologica* II/II q. 26, a. 10). Women were more sexually incontinent than men (ibid. q. 156, a. 1). Aquinas believed that for companionship at any rate, another male was infinitely superior because of his greater rationality and self-control.

These are only two examples of male writers in the late antique and middle ages, but they are typical of the prevalent attitude among educated men of the whole period. Their ideas are responses to their own life situations and their social contexts where women were perceived as a threat to men's ability to avoid sin. But the very persistence of such statements from many different writers reveals that in reality women's lives did not always conform to this pattern. There were noble and notable exceptions to the rule; for example, two powerful and erudite abbesses in the twelfth century – Hildegard of Bingen and Heloise, whose tutor, Abelard, had become her lover, thus giving substance to some of the male fears about women – were admired and praised by even the most misogynist celibates. Many other aristocratic women were educated to an advanced level, often as well as their brothers,[4] to enable them to take on responsibilities when their husbands were away from home. Some were taught the arts of medicine and herbs so that they could heal the sick and wounded. But this was a two-edged sword; learned women and particularly those skilled in medicine were in danger of being feared as much as revered. A combination of men's fear of women's sexuality and of their skill and erudition could lead to accusations of witchcraft which in turn resulted in inquisitions and terrible persecutions.[5]

It was, however, usually perfectly acceptable for a woman to be well-educated, fluent in languages, well-read in the Scriptures and the Christian Fathers, as long as she did not try to teach men or produce theology of her own, for they claimed that Paul had taught the same. 'Let a woman learn in silence with all submissiveness. I permit no woman to teach or to have authority over men; she is to keep silent' (1 Tim. 2:11–12). Mysticism was sometimes an exception to this rule, and mysticism was an area of Christianity particularly attractive to women in the middle ages for the revelations given to mystics came directly from God or from Christ, they by-passed the authority of the leaders and teachers of the Church. One such woman was Julian of Norwich, a fourteenth-century anchoress or recluse whose *Revelations of Divine Love* were written down by a scribe. She, like others before her, understood Christ's role partly in terms of motherhood.

> Thus in Jesus, our true Mother, has our life been grounded, through his own uncreated foresight, and the Father's almighty power, and the exalted and sovereign goodness of the Holy Spirit. In taking our nature he restored us to life; in his blessed death upon the cross he bore us to eternal life; and now, since then, and until the Day of Judgement, he feeds and helps us on – just as one would expect the supreme and royal nature of motherhood to act, and the natural needs of childhood to require.

> (*Revelations*, 63)

Her understanding of the motherhood of God is revealed in Christ, both as nurturing carer, and as creator and saviour of the whole person, body and soul.

As well as these lofty and inspiring exceptions, there are indications that the realities of everyday life for ordinary women in the middle ages did not always conform to the theories of celibate male writers. The Wife of Bath's Prologue in Chaucer's *Canterbury Tales*, published in the fourteenth century, deals at length with contemporary attitudes towards sexuality and the scriptural texts on which they were based. Here she summarises the misogyny of the priests:

> For take my word for it, there is no libel
> On women that the clergy will not paint,
> Except when writing of a woman-saint, . . .
> By God, if women had but written stories
> Like those the clergy keep in oratories,
> More had been written of man's wickedness
> Than all the sons of Adam could redress.

Margery Kempe, a fifteenth-century married woman from Norfolk, who had borne fourteen children, decided to take a vow of chastity and to travel on pilgrimages throughout Europe and as far as the Holy Land. She was guided in her actions by revelations of Christ, who encouraged her at one point to bargain with her husband that if she ate with him on Friday instead of fasting, he would make no sexual demands on her. Her outlandish behaviour and outspoken teaching led to accusations of heresy and of disobeying Paul's injunction that women should not preach. She defended herself bravely before the Archbishop of York and the Mayor of Leicester, arguing her case as an equal.

The attitude of Protestant theologians in the sixteenth century was a little more positive towards women than that of the celibate priests of the Catholic Church, for although they also emphasised the sin of Eve and her innate inferiority to Adam, they thought that she also was created in the image of God and was destined to 'inherit the glory of the future life' (Martin Luther, *Lectures on Genesis*, 1:27).

> For the punishment that she is now subjected to the man was imposed on her after sin and because of sin, just as the other hardships and

dangers were: travail, pain and countless other vexations. Therefore Eve was not like the woman of today: her state was far better and more excellent, and she was in no respect inferior to Adam, whether you count the qualities of the body or those of the mind.

(*Lectures on Genesis*, 2:18)

This means that Eve's sorrows, which she would not have if she had not fallen into sin, are to be great, numerous and also of various kinds. The threat is directed particularly at birth and conception. . . . Now there is also added to those sorrows of gestation and birth that Eve has been placed under the power of her husband, she who previously was very free and, as the sharer of all the gifts of God, was in no respect inferior to her husband. This punishment too springs from original sin; and the woman bears it just as unwillingly as she bears those pains and the inconveniences which have been placed upon her flesh. The rule remains with the husband, and the wife is compelled to obey him by God's command. He rules the home and the state, wages war, defends his own possessions, tills the soil, builds, plants, etc. The woman, on the other hand, is like a nail driven into the wall. She sits at home . . . the wife should stay at home and look after the affairs of the household as one who has been deprived of the ability of administering those affairs that are outside and concern the state. . . . In this way Eve is punished.

(*Lectures on Genesis*, 3:16)

Martin Luther, himself a married man who had started his career as a celibate, could value women in a positive way even if still very much from a male point of view; 'wives are adorned with the blessing and glory of motherhood, namely that we are all conceived, born, and nurtured by them' (*Lectures on Genesis*, 3.16). He claims that it is the fault of 'ungodly celibacy that aspersions are cast against the female sex' (*Lectures on Genesis*, 2.18), yet he accepts that God has assigned to them the care of children and kitchen: to Kinder, Küche, Kirche under the authority of their husbands.

In the religious turmoil of mid-seventeenth-century England, a group of Dissenters, led by George Fox, held radical views about the equality of women and men which proved in the long term to be very influential. The sect which became known as the Quakers flourished in England in spite of persecution, and soon spread to America. Fox and an early convert, Margaret Fell, who later became his wife, believed that women and men were both created in the image of God; inequality was a result of the sin of Adam and Eve, and that equality had been restored by Christ for those who followed him. So that in a Quaker marriage husband and wife are theoretically equal. The woman does not promise to obey her husband, both husband and wife promise to obey God. The Quakers have no priests, no set forms of worship or sacraments. At meetings the Spirit descends on men and women alike, there is no need for priestly authority, the emphasis is on the individual's sense of the divine and responsibility for others. The Quakers set up their own educational system, since, as Dissenters, the universities were closed to them, and boys and girls were educated in schools together as early as the eighteenth century. Women quickly developed a sense of responsibility against this background; in 1666 separate women's meetings were established to supervise marriages, women's and children's affairs and the welfare of the poor.

The Shakers, a sect which originated in an eighteenth-century Quaker revival, flourished in North America. They went further in egalitarian behaviour than the Quakers. The Shakers live a celibate life (though marriage is not absolutely forbidden), but one in which brothers and sisters are equal; separated from the world, they live in 'family' communities. There is no natural hierarchy of gender, so there is no difference in status between men and women in their communities.

Such groups represent a trend which ran against the tide of mainstream Christian thought until the nineteenth and twentieth centuries, when the increase in biological knowledge and a belief in some sort of evolutionary process rather than divine creation in seven days made the Churches rethink their most fundamental beliefs. A different attitude to biblical texts, for example, reading Genesis 1–3 as mythological rather than as historical truth, has allowed more Christians to accept the principle of sexual equality and to remove guilt from women just for being women . This is still not universally true, however, and the Church's negative attitude to sexuality and to women as the dangerous 'other' who might lead men astray, still persists in many places.

The ideal of celibacy

In the world of the Roman Empire in which Christianity took shape, the need to produce children to replace the lives of those lost in war or from disease was very great. People were expected to get married young – many girls would marry at fourteen – and to produce several children. Life expectancy was short, few people reached the age of fifty, so marriage and procreation were strongly encouraged. Christianity was remarkable for its idealisation of celibacy and virginity: 'Their contempt for death is patent to us every day, and likewise their restraint from intercourse. For they include not only men but also women who refrain from intercourse all through their lives' (attributed to Galen).

Although virginity was not unknown in pagan religions, it was often not undertaken for life; it was frequently not chosen by the individual herself, but by her father or other authorities, and the need for virgins or celibates was usually related to the need for purity at the altar. So although Christianity's sexual restraint was unusual, the traditionally accepted view that the Church provided a haven of respectability in a pagan world of debauched sexuality is far from the truth. Apart from a recognition that adolescent boys would experience strong sexual urges, Graeco-Roman society expected its citizens to be reasonably chaste and monogamous after marriage. This was partly for biological reasons: 'Frequent sexual activity was frowned upon. It decreased the fertility of the male seed and hence the father's chance of children.'[6] Sexual intercourse, if conducted with proper decorum, would have a positive effect on the character of the child. But the values of the state were to be reflected in the life of the family and household; loyalty and self-control were highly valued in the Roman Empire of the first few centuries CE.

The Christian ideal of celibacy which flourished against this background had different roots as well. For women especially, virginity was seen as a way of becoming closer to the lost ideal of being in the image of God, closer to what Eve was before she sinned and was cursed. It also has roots in the Jewish idea of single-minded devotion to God, the idea that the whole person owes him allegiance. Whereas in the Graeco-Roman world the soul was thought to rule the rebellious body – the body could be held in check by the restraint of the soul – for the Jew, both body and soul were part of God's creation, and both would be liable to judgement.

The Essenes, a Jewish sect contemporary with Jesus, shunned pleasure and disdained marriage (Josephus, *War*, ii: 119f). The Qumran sect – possibly to be identified with the Essenes – also encouraged celibacy, openness and wholehearted obedience to God: 'That they should seek God with a whole heart and soul . . . and no longer follow a sinful heart' (*Community Rule* 1). These Palestinian Jewish ideas about wholeness and single-heartedness helped form the Christian attitudes towards sexuality, even when the religion had left Palestine and was predominantly a religion of the Graeco-Roman cities.

Celibacy as an ideal is found in the New Testament both in the teaching of Jesus and in that of Paul. According to Matthew 19:10–12, Jesus encouraged celibacy in his followers: 'Not all can receive this precept, but only those to whom it is given. For there are eunuchs who have been so from birth, and there are eunuchs who have been made eunuchs by men, and there are eunuchs who have made themselves eunuchs for the sake of the Kingdom of Heaven.' In third-century Alexandria, Origen took the saying quite literally and castrated himself for the sake of the Kingdom of Heaven. But much of the Church's teaching on celibacy, as on marriage and divorce, derives from Paul's first letter to the Corinthians:

> I wish that all were as I myself am [i.e., able to exercise sexual self-control]. But each has his own special gift from God, one of one kind and one of another. To the unmarried and the widows I say that it is well for them to remain single as I do. But if they cannot exercise self-control, they should marry. For it is better to marry than to be aflame with passion.
>
> (1 Cor. 7:7–9)

Paul seems to be advocating celibacy as the best way, and allowing marriage as a concession to those whose sexual feelings are so strong that otherwise they would commit the sin of fornication. For Paul, brought up as a strict Jew, sexual intercourse was intended for the purpose of procreation and should therefore only take place between married couples.

This passage, along with Matthew 19:10–12, has been used by the Church over the centuries to argue for the ideal of celibacy. Until recently the teaching was taken out of its context and accepted as authoritative just as it stood, without reference to its time or place of composition and ignoring the clear evidence elsewhere in the letter and in the Gospels that the earliest apostles were married (1 Cor. 9:5, Mark 1:30 and parallels). In the West, in 1139, it became illegal for priests to marry, or for married men to become priests. The legitimacy of married priests had been a subject for discussion in the Church since the fourth century, and it was one important element in the split between Eastern and Western Churches. For the Eastern Churches continued to allow their priests to marry, though their bishops had to be celibate. The effect of this on women has again been to see them as second-class citizens; not only could women not be priests, but in the Roman Catholic Church at any rate, they were not even allowed to marry priests.

However, looking at the historical and sociological background of 1 Corinthians will produce a different picture of what Paul was trying to say. Since Paul expected the world to end very soon, his somewhat negative attitude to marriage arises as much from a recognition that a married man is bound up in worldly cares because of his wife, as from a disdain for sexual passion: 'Yet those who marry will have worldly troubles, and I would spare you that. I mean, brethren, the appointed time has grown very short' (1 Cor. 7:28–29). In fact, Paul's attitude to sexual intercourse within marriage is surprisingly egalitarian:

> The husband should give his wife her conjugal rights, and likewise the wife to her husband. For the wife does not rule over her own body, but the husband does; likewise the husband does not rule over his own body, but the wife does.
>
> (1 Cor. 7:3–4)

He even goes on to teach against complete celibacy within marriage:

> Do not therefore refuse one another except perhaps by agreement for a season, that you may devote yourselves to prayer; but then come together again, lest Satan tempt you through lack of self-control.
>
> (1 Cor. 7:5)

The eschatological dimension forms the background to all Paul's teaching. If one really sees no future ahead in worldly terms, then undertaking marriage, which is a commitment to a particular

43

worldly future, becomes nonsensical. So marriage is permitted as a concession to prevent fornication because the other more positive reasons for getting married, such as having children, are no longer relevant.

Sociological studies of first-century Corinth also provide a picture which is different from the traditional one.[7] There seems to have been an enthusiastic, spirit-filled group in Corinth who were taking ideas about sexual equality too literally and their behaviour was threatening the stability of the Corinthian Church, which depended for its continuing success on its acceptance by the well-to-do heads of households. So Paul's teaching on marriage and divorce is a holding action, designed to permit such families to continue to live normally in their pagan societies while accepting his teaching in their Christian lives. Paul was not afraid to compromise for the sake of the spread of the Church. He was 'all things to all men'.

Paul's teaching on divorce arises out of the same social and eschatological background. There is no time to waste on the business of getting divorced; attention should rather be focused on the individual's faith and the coming transformation of the world: 'Are you bound to a wife? Do not seek to be free. Are you free from a wife? Do not seek marriage' (1 Cor. 7:27). Paul argues that no one should try to change the state in which they were called to be a Christian – they should not seek freedom from slavery or a change in marital status; such changes involve time and attention which would be diverted from the important matter in hand.

In the centuries which followed, when eschatological fervour had died down, the ideals of celibacy and virginity gained popularity as ways of demonstrating one's wholehearted acceptance of the Gospel message. For women especially, retaining one's virginity was a sign of freedom and equality in Christ. At a time when women were regarded as inferior to men in every way, and were under the authority of a man, whether father or husband, a refusal to become married was tantamount to rebellion. It was a denial of the principles on which the Graeco-Roman world was founded. Women had to choose between obedience to their earthly father and obedience to God. One of the earliest accounts of a case like this is the fictional account of Thecla, found in the second-century *Acts of Paul and Thecla*. Thecla was engaged to a man named Thamyris, but was converted to Christianity on the eve of her marriage by Paul's preaching. She took a vow of celibacy and refused to marry

Thamyris. Her family and fiancé were so incensed that Thecla was persecuted and condemned to death. Saved by a miracle, she accompanied Paul to Antioch. Condemned to fight with wild beasts in the arena, she baptised herself and the beasts did her no harm. Many people, particularly women, were converted by her activities and her preaching. Like Paul she travelled the Mediterranean proclaiming the Christian message, and converting many to the faith. Thecla's story is the first of many accounts of women all over the Christian world, many of whom came to be revered as saints, who refused marriage on the grounds of wholehearted devotion to the Gospel message. But, at the same time, they were exercising their independence and freedom to be individuals in their own right, quite separate from fathers and husbands.

There were other models of celibacy growing up alongside these rather spectacular ones. Women of well-to-do families would renounce marriage because they felt that virginity left them closer to the ideals of the Kingdom as proclaimed by Christ (Matt. 19:12, Luke 20:35) and by Paul (1 Cor. 7:6). Others, like the wealthy Melania, in the fourth century, submitted to her family's demands that she marry, and to her husband's demand that she produce two children, but she then became celibate and with her husband, Pinian, renounced the world and lived a life of penitent obedience to Christ. Jerome, an older contemporary of Augustine, and an ascetic of great erudition, set himself up as a spiritual mentor to a group of rich, aristocratic women, first in Rome, then outside Bethlehem. Jerome claimed that virginity and chastity were infinitely superior to marriage and would bring with them rewards of eternal life better than those awaiting married people. He warned his female followers repeatedly against the dangers of mixing in worldly company:

Do not court the company of married ladies . . . women of the world, you know, plume themselves because their husbands are on the bench or in other high positions. . . . Learn in this respect a holy pride; Know that you are better than they.

(Jerome, *Epistle to Eustochium*, 22.16)

This teaching had tragic consequences for the family of one of Jerome's most faithful supporters in Rome, the wealthy widow, Paula. The superiority of asceticism and chastity was impressed so strongly on two of her daughters, Blaesilla and Eustochium, that when Blaesilla's husband died, she acceded to Jerome's suggestion that she should adopt a radically austere regime which, within three months, led to her death. Jerome was fiercely criticised and blamed by many of his contemporaries for her death. In fact, his negative attitude towards sexuality was by no means universally popular. Jovinian, a celibate Christian monk, criticised the growing popularity of Jerome's views, arguing that God himself had commanded Adam and Eve to procreate, 'Be fruitful and multiply and fill the earth', and that this command, first found in Genesis 1:28, was repeated by Jesus himself. Concentrating on deutero-Pauline texts, he was also able to draw out teaching positive to marriage from the epistles. 'I desire, therefore, that younger widows marry and bear children', and 'marriage is honorable to all, and the marriage bed undefiled' (1 Tim. 5:14 and Heb. 13:4, quoted in *Jerome Against Jovinian*, 1.5). However, the opposition was too great, and the idealisation of virginity and celibacy as the most desirable way of following Christ continued to grow in strength. This controversy illustrates the difficulty of basing the Church's teaching on scriptural proof. The texts are chosen selectively, and there are always other texts which can be used to disprove the case.

Not long after Jerome's departure from Rome, Paula and Eustochium also travelled to Bethlehem and set up a community of celibate women there near Jerome's small monastic community, supporting both him and themselves with their great wealth. These women found the advantages of their celibate state lay not only in the renunciation of the social and marital obligations of high-born Roman women, but also that they were able to read, study and absorb the scriptures in their original tongues and the Christian writers who had interpreted them under the guidance of learned men such as Jerome. Although it was the norm for aristocratic women to be highly educated, for they often had to take responsibility for their husbands' estates and businesses when they were away from home, Christian women who adopted the celibate life had greater freedom in the disposal of their money and their time than their married sisters. The women who followed Jerome into a life of intellectual asceticism were not encouraged to write themselves, but their minds and intellects were as highly trained and learned as many of their male contemporaries.[8]

Throughout the middle ages, the tendency continued, among

aristocratic women at any rate, to renounce the life of marriage and follow the more meritorious route of celibacy. Virginity was recognised as a powerful and compelling religious ideal. The woman who was intact and whole, who had devoted herself mind and body to Christ, was felt to have extraordinary power and was open to the inspiration of the spirit in a unique way. During the twelfth century the number of women choosing to follow the only religious role available to them grew rapidly, but the rules defining how they could renounce the world were still firmly in the grasp of men. When, in the thirteenth century, St Clare tried to follow Francis of Assisi as a mendicant, she was refused and forced to retire to a convent, to keep some of her wealth and her servants. Such a dangerous and wandering life was not suitable for a woman. Within convents, in the tenth to the twelfth centuries, women had even had some authority to exercise clerical roles such as hearing confessions from the nuns under them, preaching and sometimes even celebrating mass. But in the later middle ages this was stopped; the powerful abbesses of the earlier period are no longer found.

At the same time women were finding new ways of living their religious lives. The established orders demanded such high dowries from women wanting to enter their convents that only the very rich could afford it. Among the new bourgeoisie and the lesser nobility of the towns in northern Europe, many women chose to become beguines. Beguines were women who set themselves apart from the world and devoted their lives in celibacy to prayer, manual work and charity. They took no vows, had no rules or hierarchy, but lived in loosely organised groups or at home. In southern Europe, the movement of tertiaries developed at the same time; these were women who were affiliated with mendicant orders but who devoted themselves to prayer, asceticism and charitable works. The rapid rise in the number of women religious in this period has been explained by social historians as resulting from their desire to avoid the dangers of childbirth and the possible brutalities of marriage, or on the difficulty and expense of finding a husband and a dowry. But the religious life of renunciation and the women's wish to express their faith through their whole lives must still have been the main impetus.

So there was a variety of ways for women to express their religious ideals in the middle ages, generally involving the vow of chastity. The decision to give one's whole life to God was the most powerful decision a girl or a woman could make. It expressed total devotion to God but at the same time enabled her to exercise control over the only area of her life where she had control – her body. She also gained, thereby, a measure of autonomy not otherwise to be found in the world of men. It is no accident that this autonomy – through renunciation – fitted so neatly with the idea prevalent at the time that women were dangerous tempters of men.

The Virgin Mary

The theory of learned, celibate men, based on their readings of Scripture, that women were second-class human beings and a threat to men, was supported by the growth of the popularity of the cult of the Virgin Mary. Reverence for the Virgin bridged the gap between popular feelings and intellectual theories. The New Testament basis for the growth of the cult is extremely sparse. Paul, the first New Testament writer, mentions Jesus' birth only once, in Galatians 4:4: 'But when the time had fully come, God sent forth his Son, born of a woman, born under the Law'. This amounts only to a claim that Jesus was a Jewish male baby; it says nothing about who his mother and father were. Similarly, in Mark's gospel, which is commonly thought to be the earliest of the four gospels, apart from a reference to Mary, his mother and his brothers and sisters, to point out how incredible is the authority with which Jesus teaches (Mark 6:1–6), Jesus' mother appears only once, again in the company of his brothers, and is treated by Jesus with some disrespect:

> And his mother and his brothers came; and standing outside they sent to him and called him. And a crowd was sitting about him; and they said to him, 'Your mother and your brothers are outside, asking for you.' And he replied, 'Who are my mother and my brothers?' And looking around on those who sat about him, he said, 'Here are my mother and my brothers! Whoever does the will of God is my brother, and sister, and mother.'
>
> (Mark 3:31–35)

Certainly Mark does not seem to be aware that Mary was a virgin, and she is not shown the deference which was later to become her due. John's gospel also gives Jesus' mother no name, and although she appears at his first miraculous sign (John 2:1–11) and at the crucifixion (John 19:25–27), she is never said to be a virgin and there is little in these stories to give rise to her adoration.

It is on the birth narratives in Matthew and Luke that the cult of the Virgin Mary is based. Whether or not Jesus' mother conceived him as a virgin, gave birth to him as a virgin or continued to be a virgin for the rest of her life, as the Roman Catholic Church claims, is not at issue here and has been very fully discussed elsewhere.[9] What is significant, is that both Matthew and Luke believed that Jesus' birth had been special, possibly unique, and that in some sense it originated with God. The title 'Son of God', understood elsewhere in the New Testament in a metaphorical way as referring to God's special messianic envoy, was apparently understood by Matthew and Luke in a physical sense. At a time when the biological under-standing of how conception took place was dominated by Aristotle's active and passive, giving and receiving imagery, the possibility of a girl conceiving by the Holy Spirit was universally believable and not unparalleled in pagan mythology.

The story of the conception and birth of Jesus is told in quite different ways by Matthew and Luke. Matthew portrays Mary as a passive character. The story is told from the point of view of Joseph, the putative father, who is instructed by an angel not to divorce his betrothed, as she has not been unfaithful, 'for that which is conceived in her is of the Holy Spirit' (Matt. 1:20). In typical Matthean fashion, the conception is said to have come about to fulfil the Scriptures. The rest of Matthew's story – the visit of the magi, the massacre of the children, the flight into Egypt (none of which appear in Luke's account) – also fulfils scriptural prophecy or has scriptural resonances. Like Matthew, Luke names Mary and Joseph, and, like Matthew, places the birth in Bethlehem, but, whereas in Matthew's account Mary and Joseph seem to live in Bethlehem, according to Luke, they come from Nazareth in Galilee and travel to Bethlehem because of a census. It is shepherds, not the more glamorous magi, who visit Jesus, but most important of all, it is Mary to whom the announcement of the birth is made by the angel Gabriel, and Mary who responds first with incomprehension and then with faithful acceptance: 'Behold, I am the handmaid of the Lord; let it be to me according to your word' (Luke 1:38). Each evangelist told the story of Jesus' birth in a way which suited his own purpose in writing and the needs of the people for whom he was writing.

49

However, as with the creation narratives in Genesis, the two gospel stories were soon conflated by the Church in worship and doctrine so that a much more elaborate picture of Mary developed, fleshed out by material in other writings such as the Protevangelium of James,[10] where her 'immaculate conception' is described. Not only did she conceive her son without a human father, she herself was conceived without sexual intercourse when her parents embraced after a period of separation and penitential prayer. Her young life was dedicated to God from the start (Protevangelium of James 7.1–8.1). The idea gained popularity because only if Mary herself was free from sin could her body provide a womb fit for the Son of God. So either she must have been preserved from actual sin, or, by conception without sexual intercourse, she was preserved from original sin which has tainted the rest of the human race from Adam onwards. Some medieval theologians found it impossible to accept the idea that Mary, uniquely among human beings, was free from the contagion of sin and therefore not in need of the redemption brought by Christ. They got round this by believing that the redemptive gifts had been awarded to her in advance by God so that she was fit to bear his Son. In 1854 Pope Pius IX declared the immaculate conception of Mary to be a dogma of the Roman Catholic Church. The Church had also decided officially, though the idea had been current since the second century, at the First Lateran Council in 649 CE that Mary was a virgin not only before Jesus' birth, but during it and ever afterwards as well.[11] The brothers of Jesus mentioned in the New Testament were considered to be either sons of Joseph by a previous marriage, or merely cousins.

In parallel with the separation of Mary from ordinary human sexual experience, she began to assume her own soteriological significance. The second-century writers, Justin and Irenaeus, portrayed her as the new Eve, who by her obedient acceptance of the angel's message showed herself to be the disobedient Eve's opposite. Just as Jesus had undone the sin of Adam (Rom. 5:12–21, 1 Cor. 15:20–22, 45–50), so Mary had reversed the condemnation of Eve. Just as a man and a woman had been involved in introducing sin into the world, so Mary with Jesus came to play a part in the redemption of the world.

Alongside this antisexual imagery, there grew up the veneration of Mary's motherhood. This is the image so familiar in Christian art from earliest times throughout the middle ages, of a mother holding an infant in her arms, in various poses, with expressions from that of the happy mother proudly presenting her infant son, to the mother whose look shows that she knows what fate awaits him. These artistic representations of Mary as mother are reflections of the popular interest in her motherhood. In 451 CE at the Council of Chalcedon, the title 'Mother of God' was accepted by the Church after decades of bitter dispute. But the result of the decision was to open the way for her veneration almost as a goddess. For Christianity, like Judaism and later Islam, is notable for having only one God and he is decidedly male. Although there are occasional references to God in a female role in the Old Testament (e.g., Isa. 49:1, 15, 66:13), and Jesus refers to himself as being like a mother hen protecting her chicks (Matt. 23:37), and uses the image of a woman searching for lost coins to represent God seeking sinners (Luke 15:8–10), nevertheless the overriding biblical picture of God is of a male deity with stereotypical male characteristics – he is strong, war-like, vengeful, a judge; the husband of unfaithful Israel, or the father of his people. For Christians the masculinity is emphasised by teaching about God's fatherhood. Jesus, the Son of God, became human so that human beings can become sons of God (e.g., Rom. 8:3 and 14). The paradigmatic prayer taught to his disciples by Jesus begins, 'Our Father . . .'. God is male and so is his Son. The third member of the Christian Trinity, the Holy Spirit is of indeterminate gender – the Greek word for spirit is *pneuma*, a neuter word, and the Latin, *spiritus*, is masculine. But female the Holy Spirit is certainly not. So the gradual rise of the cult of Mary, first as virgin, then also as mother, and later still as Queen of Heaven, filled a need in Christianity, especially among the less well-educated.

Because there was no mention of her death in the gospels, popular stories grew up about the end of her life. Some believed that she had not actually died, but this view was never officially sanctioned because it would deny her full humanity. So, in the Eastern Church the tradition of the Dormition grew up. Mary's body is laid to rest and Jesus receives her soul into heaven. In the West, she is taken to heaven body and soul. Although this element of the story did not become dogma as the Assumption until the papal decree of 1950, it had been the basis for believing in Mary as Queen of Heaven since the early middle ages. During the middle ages, she was worshipped as the Queen of Heaven and became an object of prayer and devotion. She was seen as a mediator, someone who, because of her feminity and motherhood, could sympathise with and plead the case of Christian sinners. As the *mater dolorosa*, the bereaved mother, sharing the universal human experience of grief and loss, she became the great focus as comforter and consoler.

In the courtly life and literature of the twelfth and thirteenth centuries, the idealisation of the Virgin which was reaching its zenith in the Church, was reflected in the idealisation of the chaste and untouchable female figure familiar to us from the Arthurian legends and other traditions of courtly love.[12] It was during the same period that the Church began the long process of sacralising marriage, introducing rules of degrees of blood relationship, the enforcement of monogamy and indissolubility, and most important of all for women, consent. Although in theory the woman's situation had improved, she could be revered as a chaste and obedient wife, or the object of devotion of a faithful knight, yet she was still her husband's inferior and subject to his control. Idealised in a role designed by men, she had little freedom and certainly no sense of equality. In northern Europe in Protestant Churches, this idealisation diminished as reverence for the Virgin gradually disappeared, but the role assigned to women by Luther continued to be generally accepted for centuries.

The other woman and other women

The cult of the Virgin Mary and the corresponding idealisation of chastity caught the imagination of people and scholars alike, presenting fascinating intellectual problems as well as spiritual and emotional solace. But the ideal she presents of perfect mother as well as spotless virgin has always had its negative aspects for women as well. It is an impossible ideal for a human mother to live up to. Feminists argue that that is partly why celibate male priests have encouraged it for so long: women can never attain the ideal of redeemed womanhood as presented by the virgin mother and feel confident in their femininity. The ideal is unattainable. The best a woman can do is remain celibate and deny herself her biological destiny as a mother.

There are plenty of other women in the New Testament and in the tradition of the Church who provide different sorts of role models from the virgin mother, but whose part in the origins of Christianity has usually been played down. In the gospels, many women appear as part of Jesus's following whose lives are by no means blameless but who are praised by Jesus for their faith and insight. The most well-known story is that of the 'woman of the city who was a sinner' who anointed Jesus for burial before his death. The story is told in all four gospels (Matt. 26:6–13, Mark 14:3–9, Luke 7:36–50, John 12:1–8).

And while he was in Bethany in the house of Simon the leper, as he sat at table, a woman came with an alabaster jar of ointment of pure nard, very costly, and she broke the jar and poured it over his head. But there were some who said to themselves indignantly, 'Why was the ointment thus wasted? For this ointment might have been sold for more than three hundred denarii, and given to the poor.' And they reproached her. But Jesus said, 'Let her alone; why do you trouble her? She has done a beautiful thing to me. For you always have the poor with you and whenever you will, you can do good to them; but you will not always have me. She has done what she could; she has anointed my body beforehand for burying. And truly, I say to you, wherever the gospel is preached in the whole world, what she has done will be told in memory of her.'

(Mark 14:3–9)

All except Luke place the story at the beginning of the Passion Narrative so that the anointing is seen to have direct relevance to Jesus' death. Luke is the only evangelist actually to state that the woman was a sinner, but the story in all the gospels is an illustration of one of the main complaints by the authorities against Jesus and his followers, that he mixed with and sat at table with tax-collectors, sinners and prostitutes (Mark 2:16). For a first-century Jew this was extremely radical behaviour. Tax-collectors and criminals were social outcasts, and women, let alone prostitutes, would not be acceptable table companions. The details of the story are different in each gospel; Luke, for example, places it in the house of Simon the Pharisee to highlight more clearly the contrast between the sinner whose act of goodness is praised and the official 'good' man, the Pharisee. But the point is made in all of them, that forgiveness or approval by Jesus is given to a woman of dubious character. She 'belongs' in a way that some of his friends and close followers do not: 'Truly, I say to you, the tax-collectors and harlots will go into the kingdom of God before you' (Matt. 21:31). This woman came to be identified with Mary Magdalene by the Church, though there is no link in the gospels between the woman who washed Jesus' feet with her tears and the woman who in all the gospel accounts was one of the first witnesses to the resurrection.

In John's gospel there is another story where a 'sinful' woman is contrasted with 'good' scribes and Pharisees. The woman had been caught in adultery which was a capital offence for a woman; the authorities brought her to Jesus to test his attitude. He responded by saying, 'Let him who is without sin among you be the first to throw a stone at her'. Obviously she survived, and was sent on her way by Jesus with the words, 'Neither do I condemn you; go, and do not sin again' (John 8:1–11). Although the authenticity of this passage is very doubtful, it reflects an image of Jesus as the protector of the female 'sinner'. He gets into conversation with a Samaritan woman in John 4, a woman who had had five 'husbands', and reveals his messiahship to her. He heals a woman who was ritually unclean because of her constant haemorrhage (Mark 5:24–34), and a gentile woman's daughter (Mark 7:24–30). All these women would have been outcasts in contemporary Jewish society, but the evangelists seem to be making a point of their inclusion among those who are to enter the kingdom of God. Other well-known women from Old Testament stories whose sexual life was the cause of disapproval are mentioned in Matthew's genealogy of Christ. Along with the famous patriarchs and kings, Tamar, who slept with Judah, her father-in-law, Rahab the harlot and Ruth, who slept with Boaz before she married him, are also part of his ancestry. Perhaps Matthew wanted to provide the unmarried mother, Mary, with some suitable prototypes, who were Jewish heroines in spite of their tarnished reputations. Rahab is also mentioned in the Epistle to the Hebrews as one of the people who showed great faith during Israel's past (Heb. 11:31), and in James 2:25 she is praised as an example of faith demonstrated by works. The 'good harlot' became a stereotype in Christianity as an alternative to that of the virgin.

In 1666, while in prison for her Quaker beliefs, Margaret Fell wrote *Women's Speaking Justified by Scripture*, a pamphlet which defended women's right to speak in public religious contexts. Basing her arguments on examples from Scripture, she demonstrated that women were capable of receiving divine inspiration and that they had been of central importance throughout biblical history. She pays special attention to the women in the gospels:

> Thus we see that Jesus owned the love and grace that appeared in women, and did not despise it, and by what is recorded in the Scriptures, he received as much love, kindness, compassion and tender dealing towards him from women, as he did from any others, both in his life time, and also after they had exercised their cruelty upon him, for Mary Magdalene, and Mary the mother of Joses, beheld where he was laid. . . . Mark this, ye despisers of the weakness of women, and look upon yourselves to be so wise: but Christ Jesus does not so, for he makes use of the weak: for when he met the women after he was risen, he said to them, 'All hail', and they came and held him by the feet, and worshipped him, and then said Jesus unto them, 'Be not afraid, go tell my brethren that they go into Galilee and there they shall see me.' . . . What had become of the redemption of the whole body of mankind, if they had not believed the message that the Lord Jesus sent by these women . . .

It is not surprising that the authorities found this kind of argument hard to take. Both Margaret Fell and George Fox, who supported her arguments to the full, found themselves repeatedly persecuted and imprisoned for publishing such statements.

Although in the narrative parts of the New Testament – the gospels and Acts – women do seem to have played an important part in earliest Christianity in all sorts of roles, it is from the teaching within the epistles, especially those that come from second- or third-generation Christians, such as Ephesians, and the Pastoral epistles to Timothy and Titus, and the epistles of Peter, that much of the material comes which has kept women in a secondary role in Christianity, subordinate and obedient to men: 'Wives be subject to your husbands as to the Lord. For the husband is the head of the wife as Christ is the head of the church' (Eph. 5:22–23, cf. also Col. 3:18); 'And so train the young women to love their husbands and children, to be sensible, chaste, domestic, kind and submissive to their husbands, that the word of God may not be discredited' (Titus 2:4–5). They had to be quiet and submissive in public, and were denied the authority to teach or preach to men: '. . .the women should keep silence in the churches. For they are not permitted to speak, but should be subordinate even as the law says' (1 Cor. 14:34, cf. also 1 Tim. 2:11–12). The difference can be explained by a recognition that the gospel accounts reflect the radical nature of the renewal movement of first generation Palestinian Christianity, while the deutero-Pauline epistles reflect the later, more settled, urban situation of the Church in Hellenistic society.

Women as priests and ministers

It is to this primitive, radical form of Christianity that Christian women have always turned when seeking to be treated as men's equals in the Church. The mention of women playing significant roles in the Church in the lists of greetings in the epistles, in Acts and in apocryphal works like the *Acts of Paul and Thecla*, led Margaret Fell in the seventeenth century, as it does women today, to argue for equal status within the Church. Paul names several women in Romans 16 who are active in the Church, for instance, Phoebe the deacon (Rom. 16:1) and Prisca, a fellow worker with Paul (Rom. 16:3), who also appears in Acts 18 as Priscilla. The arguments have prevailed in some Churches; the Lutherans, the Methodists, the United Reformed Church all have women clergy. Among the Churches of the Anglican Communion, opinion is still divided, but most now have women priests, and in the United States and New Zealand there are women bishops as well as priests and deacons. The Roman Catholic and Eastern Orthodox Churches, however, still find authority in their traditional teaching about women and resist the idea. There is little that is new in any of the arguments; they have all been rehearsed before, but changes that have taken place in society in the West during the twentieth century have made it much easier for women's voices to be heard. Women are seen publicly in roles of importance and authority in secular life, so that some of the old arguments based on women's innate inferiority to men have disappeared in the Church as well.

But the influence has not been only in one direction; it was the firmly held belief among Quakers that women and men were equal in the sight of God, which enabled Quaker women to fight for the emancipation of slaves in the nineteenth century and the liberation of women in the nineteenth and twentieth centuries. It was not just their beliefs which enabled them to contribute so much to changes in attitude, but because from the beginning they were used to running their own meetings, and to concerning themselves with the poor and under-privileged, they had the resources to organise and equip themselves to help.[13]

The movement towards equality for women within the Church has picked up speed enormously in the twentieth century, and their status as men's equals is now accepted by many Christians. The question remains: how far-reaching will be the effect of having women as priests, ministers and bishops on the religious language and doctrines of the Church, dominated by men for so many centuries? (see Loades 1990).

NOTES

1. Albert Schweitzer (1931) *The Mysticism of Paul the Apostle*, London, A. & C. Black, was a key exponent of this view, as is E.P. Sanders in, for example, *Paul*.
2. See Marina Warner, *Alone of All Her Sex*, e.g., pp. 76ff., Caroline Walker Bynum (1987) *Holy Feast and Holy Fast*, Berkeley, University of California Press (pp. 15ff.) who refers to and draws psychological inferences from R.W. Southern (1970) *Western Society and the Church in the Middle Ages*, Harmondsworth, Penguin.
3. This text has been an important one for Christian women from the earliest Quakers to modern feminist Christians such as Elisabeth Schussler Fiorenza, *In Memory of Her*, Chapter 6.
4. Patricia Labalme (1980) *Beyond Their Sex*, New York, New York University Press.
5. The origins of the widespread accusations of witchcraft in western Europe in the later middle ages and up to the seventeenth century are described in Norman Cohn (1975) *Europe's Inner Demons*, Sussex University Press (1976 edn, London, Paladin).
6. Peter Brown, *The Body and Society*, p. 18.
7. Wayne Meeks, *The First Urban Christians*, especially pp. 76–77 and 106.
8. Peter Brown, *The Body and Society*, pp. 369f. For women as well as men celibates, intellectual creativity could be understood as fertility.
9. Marina Warner, *Alone of All Her Sex*, summarises the developments in the myths surrounding Mary.
10. The second-century Protevangelium, or Book, of James can be found in *The Apocryphal New Testament* (trans. and ed.) (1924) M.R. James, Oxford, Oxford University Press. It was revered by the Church and, with other apocryphal works, provided much of the material which became inseparably associated with the cult of Mary, but which never attained the canonical status of Matthew, Mark, Luke and John.

11. See Marina Warner, *Alone of All Her Sex*, pp. 22ff.
12. See Marina Warner, *Alone of All Her Sex*, Chapter 9 and references.
13. See Margaret Hope Bacon (1980) *Valiant Friend. The Life of Lucretia Mott*. New York, Walker and Co.

FURTHER READING

Social history of the New Testament period:
Meeks, Wayne (1983) *The First Urban Christians*, New Haven, Yale University Press.

Introductions to the thought of Paul:
Sanders, E.P. (1990) *Paul*, Oxford, Oxford University Press.
Ziesler, John (1983) *Pauline Christianity*, Oxford, Oxford University Press.

Feminist approaches to Christianity:
Schussler Fiorenza, Elisabeth (1983) *In Memory of Her*, London, SCM Press.
Loades, Ann (ed.) (1990) *Feminist Theology. A Reader*, London, Society for Promoting Christian Knowledge.

Historical and critical studies:
Brown, Peter (1988) *The Body and Society. Men, Women and Sexual Renunciation in Early Christianity*, New York, Columbia University Press (1989 edn, Faber & Faber).
Pagels, Elaine (1988) *Adam, Eve and the Serpent*, London, Weidenfeld & Nicolson.
Trevett, Christine (ed.) (1989) *Women's Speaking Justified: and Other Seventeenth Century Quaker Writings About Women*, London, Quaker Home Service.
Warner, Marina (1976) *Alone of All Her Sex, the Myth and Cult of the Virgin Mary*, London, Weidenfeld & Nicolson.

3. Hinduism

Sharada Sugirtharajah

Hindu women come from diverse cultural, linguistic, geographical and social backgrounds, and their roles have been varied in history, literary tradition and society. This chapter looks at the varied scriptural, mythological, sociological and philosophical perspectives on women.

Women in *śruti* literature (1500–500 BCE) (The Vedas, *Brāhmaṇa*s, *Āraṇyaka*s and *Upaniṣad*s)

The Aryan pastoralists who came to India from the northwest around 1500 BCE were part of the Indo-European patriarchal tradition. The religion they brought with them involved elaborate rituals, including the sacrificial use of fire. It was patriarchal, family-based and life-affirming. The vedic pantheon is dominated by male deities whereas the pre-Aryan and post-vedic traditions are replete with feminine images of the Divine.

THE VEDAS

The earliest scripture of the Aryans, the *Ṛg-veda*, throws some light on the position of the upper-class women in ancient India. Despite the family being patriarchal and patrilineal, women were accorded a significant place within the family and society. Although the roles of wife and mother were of supreme importance, women's intellectual and spiritual quests were recognised. The rite of initiation (*upanayana*), which marked the beginning of vedic studies, was open to both men and women. In contrast to later periods, education was not an obstacle to marriage. On the contrary, it was essential as some knowledge of rituals was required in order to be able to participate in religious activities, which were jointly performed by the husband and wife.

Despite male dominance, women seers, poets and philosophers were held in high esteem in the vedic period. A few of the hymns in the *Ṛg-veda* are attributed to women seers such as Ghoṣā, Apālā, Viśvavārā and Lopāmudrā.

Even though the *Ṛg-veda* shows a marked preference for sons, daughters were not devalued as in the *Atharva-veda* and later scriptural texts. The vedic deity, Usha, goddess of Dawn, is described as a beautiful maiden who never grows old. There is reference to young maidens and women participating in a recreational festival called *Samana*, and mixing freely with men and women. It appears that both the sexes had some freedom in the choice of marriage partners although parental guidance and protection played an important part. References suggest that marriage was not compulsory for women and that very early marriages were not prevalent during the vedic period. Ghoṣā figures as an unmarried woman living in her father's house (RV 1.117.7).[1] The few references to the life of a widow suggest that widowhood did not pose any serious problems as it did in subsequent periods. The vedic texts indicate that the widow could marry her brother-in-law (RV 10.40.2).[2] The rite of *satī* (self-immolation of widows) was merely symbolic during the vedic period (see pp. 77–8).

Despite patriarchal orientation, the Ṛg-vedic hymn (8.31.5–9)[3] emphasises the equality of wife and husband. This is also indicated by the use of the term *dampati*, meaning the married pair (although in some contexts it may signify the 'Lord of the house'). Even to this day the term is used when blessing a newly married couple. The new bride is called *sumaṅgalī* (fortunate). Her presence is considered auspicious and she is associated with prosperity, well-being and happiness. She is warmly welcomed and accorded an honourable position in the family. The Ṛg-vedic marriage hymn welcomes her arrival to take charge of the entire household and to take care of the physical and spiritual welfare of all its members. Her varied roles are indicated by terms such as *Jāyā*, *Janī* and *Patnī*: 'Jāyā has the special sense of a sharer of the husband's affections; Janī, the mother of children; and Patnī, the partner in the performance of sacrifices' (Shastri 1954: 17–18).[4]

60

Marriage being the ideal upheld in the vedic religion, and home being the centre of religious practice, the woman was indispensable both from the domestic and religious point of view. She was important for bearing children, especially male children, and her presence and participation in religious activities were essential. In the Ṛg-vedic marriage hymn, the couple are described as jointly performing ritual acts. They both wash and press the *soma* juice, and pluck the sacred grass for sacrifice (RV 8.31.5 & 6).[5]

THE *BRĀHMAṆAS*

Women's ritual and educational roles came gradually to be marginalised in the *Brāhmaṇa* texts, which were primarily concerned with the ritualistic side of sacrifice. With ritual specialists becoming teachers, the gap between men and women widened. Sons came to be valued more highly and rituals were performed to prevent the birth of a daughter. The birth of a son came to be seen as a blessing as it was thought that he alone could ensure the future well-being of the family. Although vedic education was open to women, few were able to undertake it as it became extensive and complicated and the period of study was extended to take up twelve to sixteen years. Without a proper vedic education participation in sacrifices was not possible.

Women came to be trained in domestic activities and a minimal ritual knowledge was imparted to qualify them for their participation in the sacrifices. They also came to be seen as being impure during menstruation and pregnancy. This no doubt affected the ritual status of women as in other traditions.

THE *ĀRAṆYAKAS* AND *UPANIṢADS*

In the *Āraṇyakas* and the *Upaniṣads* there is a shift from ritual to 'knowledge', or wisdom, which came to be seen as the means to salvation. While the Ṛg-vedic texts exalt marriage and family, the *Upaniṣads* extol the ascetic life. The emphasis on meditation, knowledge and asceticism affected the later position of women in Hindu society. With the emergence of Buddhism in the sixth century BCE, challenging Brahman ritualism and priesthood, an uneasy tension arose between vedic orthodoxy and the ascetic ideal (upheld by both the *Upaniṣad*s and the Buddha). Unlike Buddhism, in which nuns have a place, Hinduism was not favourably disposed towards women embracing the monastic ideal. Although learned women figure in the *Upaniṣad*s, women ascetics were less common. In the later vedic period there were two classes of educated women: *brahmavādinī*s and *sadyodvāhā*s. For the former, education remained a life-long pursuit and they were initiated into vedic learning. The latter studied only until they got married. Although the rite of initiation (*upanayana*) was open to both, it was nominally performed for those who desired to get married.

In the *Brāhmaṇa* texts women were already marginalised. Their eligibility to take up the monastic ideal was almost a closed issue except in the case of the few women who remained single and pursued religious studies. The two well-known women in the *Upaniṣad*s, Gārgī and Maitreyī, display their critical skills in philosophical discourses, but there is little evidence to suggest that they desired to become ascetics.

In the *Bṛhadāraṇyaka Upaniṣad* (2.4.1–5),[6] Maitreyī and her husband Yājñavalkya discuss how to attain immortality. Yājñavalkya, who is about to take up the life of an ascetic, desires to settle his property between his two wives, Maitreyī and Kātyāyanī. Maitreyī asks her husband whether she would become immortal if she owned the whole earth and all its riches. Yājñavalkya tells her that there is no hope of immortality in wealth. She then asks her husband to enlighten her with his knowledge. Then Yājñavalkya goes on to expound the nature of the true Self which alone could lead to immortality.

In the same *Upaniṣad* (3.6)[7] Gārgī Vācaknavī emerges as the leading figure in the philosophical debate that takes place in the court of King Janaka of Videha. She challenges the learned sage Yājñavalkya on abstruse and esoteric topics.

Although there were a few female ascetics, the monastic ideal was primarily associated with men. The life of a man came to be divided into four stages: student (*brahmacārin*), householder (*gṛhastha*), forest dweller (*vānaprastha*) and renunciant (*sannyāsin*). Marriage was important in the stage of a householder, when a man shared his domestic and religious duties with his wife. The desire for the ascetic way of life and *mokṣa* (salvation) diverted his attention from family to other-worldly concerns. In the legal texts women could accompany their husbands into the forest only if the husbands so wished. Even in the forest women's ascetic way of life was devoted to serving their husbands selflessly and observing chastity. While men were entitled to seek *mokṣa* or salvation, women's goals were seen in terms of marriage and rebirth.

Women in myths

The two Hindu epics, the *Mahābhārata* and the *Rāmāyaṇa* (probably compiled around 400 BCE–200 CE), offer a variety of images of ideal womanhood. The epics focus on the fidelity of women and the ordeals they are prepared to undergo for the sake of their husbands. Even though the *Mahābhārata* has contrasting feminine images, the image of Sītā in the *Rāmāyaṇa* has had a greater impact on Hindu society. The epic figures such as Sītā, Savītrī and Draupadī are known for their wifely devotion and marital fidelity.

SĪTĀ

Sītā figures in the *Rāmāyaṇa* as a devoted wife to Rāma. She chooses to follow her husband into the forest and live in exile with him for fourteen years. When Rāma dissuades her she tells him that a woman's place is with her husband. While in the forest she is abducted by the demon King Rāvaṇa and is held captive in his palace. He desires to marry her but she does not succumb. Her devotion to Rāma remains steadfast and finally he rescues her from Rāvaṇa, with the help of Hanumān (the monkey-god) and his tribe.

The story reaches an unexpected climax when Rāma renounces her. Although he knows that Sītā is chaste and devoted to him, there is no means of proving it to his subjects. Against his personal wishes he is forced to renounce her. Society will not consider her acceptable because she has lived in another man's house. In the classical version of the *Rāmāyaṇa* Rāma's rejection of Sītā is linked with the notion of the ideal king whose duty (*rājadharma*) it is to respect the sentiments and wishes of his subjects at the cost of personal suffering. Sītā is shocked at Rāma's behaviour towards her but that does not make her less devoted, though wifely devotion does not prevent her from questioning Rāma's attitude to her abduction by Rāvaṇa:

> If some are faithless, wilt thou find
> No love and truth in woman-kind?
> Doubt others if thou wilt, but own
> The truth which all my life has shown.

(*Rāmāyaṇa* 118.8)[8]

Her honour is at stake. She decides to prove that she is pure and blameless by asking Rāma's brother Lakṣmaṇa to prepare a funeral pyre for her. When she emerges unharmed from the fire her chastity is affirmed and Rāma and Sītā are reunited.

The story does not end there. Rāma is again forced to renounce her though he knows she is pregnant, as society, despite the fire ordeal, seems reluctant to accept Sītā fully. While in the forest, in the cottage of the sage Vālmīki, Sītā is blessed with twins, Lava and Kuśa. When Rāma comes to know that they are his children, he calls for Sītā. Sītā makes her appearance but decides to follow her own course of action. She prays to the Mother Earth to swallow her up and disappears into it – an appropriate ending as she was found in a 'furrow' by her father and named Sītā, meaning furrow.

In the oral tradition Sītā shows her anger and disapproval of Rāma's treatment of her, and her sons are given a matrilineal heritage. While Sītā's earlier decision to follow Rāma into the forest fulfils traditional expectations of an ideal woman, her role towards the end of the story can be seen as a departure from traditional norms. She emerges as a woman who is capable of shaping her destiny and affirming her deeper self.

Sītā is not worshipped in her own right, as Lakṣmī, Sarasvatī and Pārvatī are. She is always seen with Rāma and his brother Lakṣmaṇa. Although she has popular appeal, she plays an intermediary role – devotees approach her to seek Rāma's grace.

SĀVITRĪ

In another legend in the *Mahābhārata*, Princess Sāvitrī, like Sītā and Draupadī, emerges as a devoted wife and a woman of great spiritual strength. She shows remarkable fortitude and firmness in accomplishing her ideal. She chooses her own husband, Satyavan, although she knows that he has only a year to live. When Yama, the Lord of Death, takes him away, she pleads with him to restore Satyavan to life. Yama commends her wifely devotion and is prepared to offer her any boon other than bringing Satyavan back to life. Sāvitrī requests Yama to grant her the boon of offspring and cleverly argues that her duties as a wife do not end with the death of her husband. Finally, Yama is persuaded to grant her boon and she is reunited with Satyavan and gives birth to many sons. By her wifely devotion she conquers death and brings Satyavan back to life.

Although the main emphasis is on Sāvitrī's fidelity and devotion to her husband, the legend also illustrates the powerlessness of the male without his female counterpart. In other words, *Sakti*, the feminine consciousness and energy, is seen as necessary for man to achieve immortality. Sri Aurobindo (a twentieth-century mystic and philosopher) has transformed the legend of Sāvitrī into a spiritual symbol in his monumental epic *Sāvitrī*. The birth of Sāvitrī indicates 'the arrival of the New Dawn, the descent of a new consciousness' into humanity.

DRAUPADĪ

Draupadī is strikingly different from other epic figures in some respects. In the *Mahābhārata* she is married to the five Pāndava brothers. Although monogamy was seen as the ideal norm, polygamous and polyandrous marriages were not unknown in certain parts of India.

Draupadī's polyandrous marriage, which is explained and justified in a variety of ways (both figuratively and literally), is not the central theme of the story. Arjuna, one of the five Pāndava brothers, wins the hand of Draupadī, the Princess of Pañcāla, at a contest held by her father King Draupada. The Pāndava brothers return to their home in the forest (where they were living in disguise as begging Brahmans and sharing alms) and tell their mother of the 'alms' they had obtained. Kuntī, without looking up to see what Arjuna had won, asks them to share it. The five sons fulfil their mother's wish.

Draupadī is visible in both the domestic and public spheres. She is both ideal wife and queen. She emerges as a dynamic and devoted wife. She follows her husbands into the forest after all their wealth is lost in gambling with their cousins. She not only offers them comfort and solace, but also rouses them to action when their spirits are low. But she does not hesitate to show her rightful anger when one of them, Yudhiṣṭhira, pawns her after having forfeited his brothers and himself. Her refusal to yield to the command of Duryodhana (the cousin of the Pāṇḍavas) that she should serve as a servant in his household, shows her as a woman of courage and determination. She sends off the charioteer who has come to fetch her, saying:

> O charioteer, return. Ask of him who played the game whether in it he first lost himself, or his wife. Ask this question in the open assembly; bring me his answer and then you can take me.

> (*Mahābhārata* XXV)[9]

Draupadī is forcibly dragged by her hair to an assembly of elders. On regaining her composure she points out to the assembly that Yudhiṣṭhira was tricked into this game and that, after having lost all his wealth and freedom, he had no right to pawn his wife and moreover she belonged to all five Pāṇḍava brothers. She questions the integrity and justice of the Kauravas who resorted to unfair means to achieve their goals.

Draupadī suffers the worst form of humiliation in the court of Duryodhana. His brother insults her by stripping off her sari but she is miraculously saved by Lord Kṛṣṇa who restores it. Seeking to avenge herself, Draupadī does so in the battlefield where she smears Duryodhana's blood on her hair. She emerges as a powerful person who will not allow others to dictate to her.

Conformity to tradition

In a predominantly patriarchal culture women's roles are defined and interpreted by men. Although the idealised images of women in the epics belong to the aristocratic class, their experiences have some relevance to all women in Hindu society.

While these images of women have been a source of great comfort to some Hindu women, others find them less liberating. Like the epic heroines, some women see themselves in terms of giving rather than receiving. Their happiness and well-being are seen in terms of encouraging their husbands to achieve success.

It is a common belief among devout Hindu women that their fasts and vows will protect their husbands and children. Even young unmarried women fast so that they may be married to suitable partners. While in worship, devotion is directed to God, in marriage it is directed to one's husband.

Feminists in the Hindu tradition look to Draupadī who challenges her husband's right to pawn her, or to the goddess Kālī who inspires terror and awe.

Women in the *bhakti* tradition

With the emergence of *bhakti*, devotional movements centred on Śiva and Viṣṇu in South India (sixth and seventh centuries CE) and later in North India, the religious status of women improved considerably. The impact of these movements was not significant at the social level but women were allowed greater participation in the religious realm. Being non-Brahman in origin, the *bhakti* cults challenged the hierarchical caste structures, Brahman orthodoxy and ritualism. They were open to all regardless of caste or sex. *Bhakti* required only an intense personal relationship with one's chosen deity. Most of the devotional literature has non-Brahman authors, including women. The songs of the Vaiṣṇava saint Āṇḍāl are sung in Vaiṣṇava shrines and homes even today.

Bhakti allows different kinds of relationships with one's deity. The exact form it takes is less important. One could conceive of God as lord, master, father, mother, friend, child, and even as one's beloved, but here God is the male and the worshipper is the female. In the *madhura bhava* relationship (God as beloved and the devotee as lover), God is the only male and both male and female devotees are spiritually female.

Strangely enough, in the *bhakti* tradition a reversal of gender-related roles is called for. A male who seeks union with Kṛṣṇa will have to transform himself psychologically into a woman and identify with her love and longing for Kṛṣṇa. In devotional literature one finds poets identifying themselves with *gopīs*, cowherd girls who yearn for Kṛṣṇa. Anyone who desired an intimate relationship with Kṛṣṇa had to become one of his *gopīs*. History provides examples of male devotees such as Jayadeva (twelfth century) and Caitanya (fifteenth century) who suspended their masculinity in order to relate to Kṛṣṇa as their beloved. Even Sri Ramakrishna, the nineteenth-century saint, dressed like a woman and identified with Rādhā. Another significant aspect that emerges in the relationship with Kṛṣṇa is the illicit love-affair of the *gopīs* who are already married but flock to him when they hear the sound of his flute. To identify with Kṛṣṇa's *gopīs* verges on adultery. This also means transcending social norms and becoming natural and spontaneous as the *gopīs* did in their relation to Kṛṣṇa.

Among women devotees of Kṛṣṇa two saints stand out. Andal, a saint well-known in South India (sixth century CE), is the only female saint among the twelve male devotees of Viṣṇu called Ālvārs. Even from her early years she began to look upon herself as the bride of Kṛṣṇa. She imagined herself to be Kṛṣṇa's *gopī*, pining for his love and suffering from pangs of separation. Her *Song Divine* (*Tiruppāvai*) speaks of her devotional love for Kṛṣṇa. Her spiritual yearning finds expression in her *Sacred Utterance* (*Tirumozhi*). In the South Indian classical dance, *Bharatanatyam*, Andal's love and yearning for Kṛṣṇa are given a unique place.

Mirabai (sixteenth century CE), a Rajput saint, was devoted to Kṛṣṇa even as a young child. Although married at a young age to a Rajput prince, she continued to look upon Kṛṣṇa as her husband and spent most of her time in the company of saints singing the praises of Kṛṣṇa. Her fervent devotion to Kṛṣṇa enraged her in-laws, who tried unsuccessfully to poison her. While her early poems express her agony over separation from Kṛṣṇa, her later poems speak of her spiritual identity with him. Her devotional songs have captured the hearts of musicians, dancers and ordinary householders.

The traditional ideal of womanhood did not mean much to Mirabai. On becoming a widow she did not, like most Rajput princesses of her time, opt for self-immolation on the funeral pyre of her husband, but proclaimed that she was wedded to Kṛṣṇa.

Women saints in the Śaivite tradition

In the long list of canonised saints in the Śaivite tradition in South India, women are held in high esteem. Of the three women saints, Karaikkal Ammaiyar is the best known.

Even as a young child she was devoted to Lord Śiva. She was a devoted and dutiful wife to her husband but at the same time her devotion to Lord Śiva never diminished. According to legend, Karaikkal Ammaiyar prayed to Lord Śiva to transform her beautiful body into a ghostly one (symbolic of her severance from the world), afterwards continuing to sing his praises in her new form. She composed verses in praise of Śiva, known in Tamil as *Arpuda Tiruvantādi* and *Tiru Iraṭṭai Maṇimālai*, which are included in the scriptures of Śaivism.

Modern women saints

Modern Hinduism also has examples of such saintly figures. One of them is Sarada Devi, who was married at an early age to Sri Ramakrishna, a well-known saint of nineteenth-century Bengal. He recognised the spiritual eminence of his wife and looked upon her as an equal partner in his spiritual mission or journey. She became his disciple, helpmate and spiritual partner, and combined the roles of wife, ascetic, mother and *guru*. Sri Ramakrishna taught her not only the sacred *mantra*s for the worship of the Divine Mother, but also how to initiate people into them. After the death of Ramakrishna she became the spiritual guide to all disciples – monks as well as laypeople – of the Ramakrishna Order.

There are a few well-known contemporary female *guru*s such as Mother Jnanananda and Sati Godavari Mataji. The final stage of *sannyās* (renunciation), normally not open to women, was taken up by Mother Jnanananda. She is perhaps the only woman to be initiated into *sannyās* by the present Śaṁkarācāraya (follower of the advaitic or non-dualistic philosophy of Śaṁkara) of Kanchipuram in South India. Now Mother Jnanananda herself initiates both men and women into *sannyās*. Sati Godavari Mataji trained young girls, women and widows to read the Vedas in Sanskrit, perform religious rites and follow the path of selfless service.

Women in the law books

The *Dharmaśāstra*s, the legal texts, were composed some time during the first two centuries of the Common (or Christian) Era by

Brahman men. The contradictory views on women in the law books are attributed to the sage, Manu, the legendary author of the *Mānava Dharmaśāstra*, or Law Code, under whose name there exist heterogeneous legal views from different ages.

In the law books women are classified with the lowest class, irrespective of their social class or origin, and are stripped of their ritual and social status. They are considered ritually impure and therefore not entitled to study or recite the sacred *mantra*s (Manu 9:18).[10] Increasingly, marriage came to be equated with initiation into religious studies, and devotion and service to one's husband came to be equated with the period of study under a *guru* or spiritual teacher. Women's domestic duties were equated with rituals performed by men in the stage of householder (see p. 62).

AMBIVALENT ATTITUDE TOWARDS WOMEN

The authors of the legal texts reflect a profound sense of ambivalence in their attitude to woman. On the one hand, she is elevated to the status of a goddess, but on the other, she is seen as a temptress and seducer. A woman's love and devotion to her husband are extolled but at the same time she is seen as incapable of these virtues (Manu 2:213–14).[11] Women are both deified and de-humanised. As mother she is most revered, but as sexual partner she is seen as an obstacle to man's spiritual quest. Sexual love has mystical connotations in Indian art, but in the legal texts it is a hindrance to man's religious pursuits. While in the stage of a householder, a man is considered incomplete without a wife. In the third and fourth stages of life he is free to withdraw from the world of senses and take up the life of an ascetic. There are references to women ascetics such as Sulabhā in the *Mahābhārata* and Sramaṇī and Śabarī in the *Rāmāyaṇa*, but the legal texts restrict women to domestic roles.

FREEDOM AND SUBSERVIENCE

In the law books women are accorded dependent status. A woman is seen in relation to her husband and family. She should be guarded by her father in childhood, her husband in youth and her sons in old age (Manu 9:3).[12] But, on the other hand, Manu seems to allow considerable freedom to women in matters of marriage. A woman has the freedom to choose her own partner if her parents fail to arrange her marriage within three years of her attaining puberty (Manu 9:90–1).[13] An ideal wife is one who serves her husband with love and devotion, even if he is lacking in these virtues (Manu 5:154).[14] The ideal of *pativratā*, devotion to husband, came to be seen as the only *strīdharma*, or duty, of the wife. Her individuality was merged in his and she had no separate existence apart from him. This ideal perhaps later gave rise to and commended the practice of *satī* (see pp. 77–8). Even though the authors of the legal texts disapprove of polygamy and men deserting their wives, men are allowed to remarry on the death of their wives but women are forbidden to remarry except in certain circumstances (Manu 9:65 & 69).[15]

As mother, a woman is more venerable than the teacher or the father (Manu 2:145).[16] She is seen as the best spiritual teacher of her children, but as wife she is expected to do the will of her husband. Furthermore, motherhood is seen as enhancing the value of a woman even more if she gives birth to a male child. This preference is rooted in the Hindu belief that a male child ensures the salvation of the father and the family. Hindu folk tales and myths are replete with the imagery of motherhood and maternal love.

Since women have been led to believe that to be mothers is their prime duty, any departure from it produces guilt and anxiety. Pregnancy delivers a woman from the fear of infertility and establishes her adult identity. It is interesting to note that it is men who idealise their mothers. There are numerous folk legends and myths about the mother-son relationship. Rāma willingly goes into exile to fulfil his stepmother's promise to his father. The marriage of the five Pāndava brothers to Princess Draupadī is partly the outcome of Kuntī's unwitting declaration that her sons should share what they had won.

Although the law books reflect the social conditions of the times to some extent, they are more a description of what society ought to be like. The commentators of later periods formulated rigorous laws to ensure the protection of women from foreign tribes who entered the country in the early centuries of the Common Era. With the advent of Islam in the tenth century, the status of women underwent further changes in North India where Islamic culture was dominant.

The Islamic custom of purdah, or the seclusion of women, was adopted by upper-class Hindus in North India. This further intensified the seclusion of Hindu women who were already segregated from men. Although it restricted the freedom of women, it came to be seen as a mark of high status and prestige.

In a traditional North Indian family, especially in a village, women observe purdah to some extent. The daughter-in-law veils her face in the presence of male members of the family and in public, though in her parental home she is not required to cover her face. Purdah restricts a woman's involvement in social activities, but, on the other hand, it offers a new bride some privacy and protects her from the close scrutiny of her in-laws and neighbours. In the domestic sphere she may gain power and authority as she gets older. In South India, where Islamic influence was not strong, the relationship between the two sexes is more relaxed, especially among the lower sections of the community. It is also more informal between men and women in matrilineal families in certain parts of South India. Today, in urban India, purdah is rarely observed by Hindu women.

Feminine images of the Divine

The Divine is conceived of in both masculine and feminine categories. In the *Upaniṣads*, one finds the idea of male and female as equal halves of one divine substance, each completing and fulfilling the other (*Bṛhadāraṇyaka Upaniṣad* 1.4.3.).[17] From the ultimate philosophical point of view, the Divine is neither male nor female as it transcends both without negating them. Furthermore, the concept of *ātman* (the deeper or inner self in man and woman) being the 'sexless self', the question of gender does not arise. On the contrary, it affirms the spiritual equality of both male and female.

The feminine dimension of the Divine is exalted in the tantric tradition (500–1800 CE) and in popular worship. The Divine is primarily seen in feminine categories such as *śakti*, or the divine energy, from which all forms of life emerge and by which they are sustained. Since *śakti* is latent in both the masculine and feminine, she is not dependent on anything outside herself. Without the activating power of *śakti* (feminine principle), Śiva (masculine) is powerless. In Tantrism, the male principle is subordinated to the feminine, which has an independent status, and in which all contradictions are resolved in interaction with the male (see Kālī and Durgā below).

Goddesses in myths appear in both traditional and unconventional roles. Goddesses relate to gods in a variety of ways – as consort, lover, mother – and they also appear in dominant roles or as equals who are fiercely independent. Although the goddesses Sarasvatī, Lakṣmī and Pārvatī figure as consorts to male deities, they are worshipped in their own right. They are associated with knowledge, wealth and power, which are traditionally male preserves.

Pārvatī (consort of Śiva) has many forms. In the form of Pārvatī she represents the domestic ideal. She figures as a benign and devoted wife. Her role is to lure Śiva from his ascetic ideal into the worldly life of a householder. In the forms of Durgā and Kālī, however, she departs from the traditional model of an ideal wife. Durgā was created by the male gods to subdue the demon Mahiṣāsura, who was immune to all opponents except woman; however she does not depend upon their support to defeat the demon. Durgā's role, despite being married to Śiva, is not in the home but in the battlefield. Standing outside the fringes of civilised society, she challenges the traditional norms of womanly behaviour and yet is regarded as a benevolent mother. Although inseparable from Śiva, in the myths she has an autonomous function and freedom.

In Tantrism Kālī is seen as the dominant force or śakti, from whom all else evolves. Kālī's role is to draw Śiva into the world of dynamic activity – of destroying evil in all its forms. Although Kālī is terrible and blood-thirsty, she is also maternal and compassionate. She creates and destroys, nourishes and starves, comforts and challenges the traditional norms of Hindu society. She reverses the traditional norms of purity and pollution. She reminds us that death, being part of life, cannot be dissociated from birth or creation.

Although Durgā and Kālī are not typical examples of ideal womanhood, they nevertheless help to put things into perspective. All notions of gender-based ideology and assumptions are called into question. They indicate that feminine roles need not necessarily be confined to being a daughter, wife, sister or mother. Contemporary Hindu women have found in Kālī a hope for liberation from various forms of oppression. The publishing house Kali was set up in Delhi by two women for women. Ritu Menon and Urvashi Butalia say: 'Kali stands for the destruction of ignorance in order to recreate. . . .

This positive aspect of Kali is what we are all about' (Sarin 1985:20).[18] Hindu women can look to these dynamic models to resolve the conflict between conformity and individuality.

In contrast to the orthodox tradition, where menstruation is seen in terms of pollution, it is not a taboo in Tantrism. In fact, a menstruating women is accorded a special place in the ritualism of Tantrism. Furthermore, Tantrism does not subscribe to patriarchal conceptions and standards of feminine beauty and conduct. Any woman, irrespective of age, status and looks, is regarded as the representation of *śakti*. Evidence of this can be seen in the high-priest and poet called Chandidas of Bengal (fifteenth century); he loved a maid called Rumi despite society's disapproval.

While at the philosophical level the spiritual equality of male and female principle is acknowledged, there is tension between the two at the mythological level, which is finally reconciled in a higher principle. Śiva, in the representation of *Ardhanārīśvara* (half man and half woman), symbolises harmony and the union of all opposites. At the social level the relation between the two is highly ambivalent. In myths, goddesses are associated with knowledge, wealth and power; in society, a woman's power or *śakti* is largely confined to the domestic sphere. While women's *śakti* is recognised, it is also believed that it should be controlled. Female children are less desired for religious and economic reasons. The oppressive social custom of dowry continues to affect all classes of women, including educated women with professional careers. The status of a girl in her husband's family in some cases depends on the amount of dowry she brings with her. It is a status symbol among some urban middle-class families. Although forbidden by law, the practice continues, and it affects badly parents who have daughters. But there are also a few enlightened families who are against this dehumanising practice.

Of all the feminine images of the Divine, the mother image is the most significant. The worship of the Divine as Mother dates back to the prehistoric period of the Harappan civilisation. India is known as *Bhārat Mātā* or Mother India, and the river Ganges, sacred to Hindus, is known as Gaṅgā Ma (Mother Ganges) – all that is nourishing and sustaining is seen in feminine categories. The image of mother goddess became a focus during the Indian freedom struggle. India's political liberation was tied up with the concept of *śakti*. Both men and women were involved in recovering the feminine principle which was violently abused both by foreign powers and Indian social structures (see pp. 76–77).

While the Hindu literary tradition is predominantly male-dominated, worship at the popular level is centred on the feminine dimension of the Divine, especially in the form of Mother. Another feminine principle closely linked with *śakti* is *prakṛti* (nature), which has both philosophical and popular connotations. Nature, in all her forms, both animate and inanimate, evolves from the feminine principle (*prakṛti*) in interaction with the masculine principle (*puruṣa*). Women in rural India affirm their links with *prakṛti* through their veneration of nature in all her varied forms.

On the ecological front, rural women in India have played a significant part in protesting against the cutting of trees which are venerated as *Vana devatā*s (forest deities). Forests are venerated as the Earth Mother – one who creates, nourishes and sustains life. Some three hundred years ago the followers of a Hindu sect called Bishnoi in Rajasthan, led by a woman, Amrita Devi, protected the trees by embracing them and thus allowing the wood-cutters to harm them instead of the trees. Women sacrificed their lives to prevent the abuse of nature in the name of development. This event was the beginning of the Chipko movement (hug-the-tree) which later became an ecological and feminist movement (Shiva 1988:67).[19]

Women's ecological movements in rural India challenge the conventional categories of patriarchy which do not make any ontological link between humanity and nature. From the standpoint of Hindu ontology, violence to nature implies violence to women, as all forms of life are seen as evolving from the feminine principle.

Women in modern Hinduism

Women's issues in the last two centuries have been tied up with Indian political resistance to British imperialism and social reform movements which aimed at rectifying oppressive social practices. Women became the focus of attention in the nineteenth century, initiated by British colonial attitudes to issues such as child marriage, infanticide, polygamy, widow remarriage, women's property rights, and especially the socially oppressive custom, *satī* (self-immolation of widows). Hinduism came under severe attack from Christian missionaries and others when it was at a low ebb. Some Hindus, although supportive of reformatory measures, felt that they should come from within. While seeing merit in reform, they also saw reflected in the attack attitudes of cultural and moral superiority of British ways.

Both colonialism and nationalism brought into sharper focus the status of women in Hindu society, thus giving it a significant place in the national struggle for freedom. Indian social reformers and nationalist historians tried to show that women had a high status in ancient India. They challenged the advocates of *sati* and condemned corrupt practices by going back to ancient texts to justify the need for reforms. The historical reconstruction of the image of women, however, was largely based on the ancient religious texts that had to do with the upper strata of society.

Indian reformers were actively involved in women's issues, ranging from *sati* to property rights. For example, Raja Rammohan Roy (1772–1833), the founder of the reform movement Brāhmo Samāj, along with other progressive thinkers, created a favourable climate for the abolition of *sati* and other corrupt practices which affected women. Ishwar Chandra Vidyasagar (1820–91) and others campaigned for the right of widows to remarry, which resulted in legalising the marriage of Hindu widows in 1856. Dayananda Saraswati, the founder of the Ārya Samāj, opposed caste and child marriage and spoke in favour of women's education. Bengali writers, playwrights and reformers denounced polygamy. The Property Act of 1874 allowed women a share of their husband's property.

Indian reformers had to contend with British imperialism, the colonial portrayal of Indian women, and Hindu traditionalists who resisted change. Although in favour of women's education, they saw it in terms of producing good mothers and efficient wives. In their view, social evils affecting women could be effectively tackled by revitalising family structures and according women a respectable place within the family. Education should, therefore, reinforce women's role in the home. English-style education did, however, prepare the ground for women's participation in the national movement. By the late nineteenth century there were a good number of educated middle-class women who, alongside political leaders, fought against imperial rule. Women like Sarojini Naidu (a well-known poet and orator), Tagore's sister Swarnakumari Devi (co-editor of a Bengali journal), and Kamaladevi Chattopadhyaya , were active members of the Indian National Congress. Women from various backgrounds (urban and village) responded enthusiastically to Gandhi's call to participate in the national struggle for freedom. They organised marches and political demonstrations, boycotted foreign goods and gave generously of their time and energy.

Gandhi himself saw a link between women's capacity for self-sacrifice and endurance, and the non-violent resistance (*satyāgraha* or 'soul force') against the British. He was well aware of the traditional orientation of women in Hindu society. The *strīdharma* (duty of a wife) involved steadfast devotion to her husband, and a woman committed to this goal undertook fasts and vows for the welfare of her husband and family. In the domestic sphere she was well-versed in the art of self-denial, self-sacrifice and suffering. This kind of single-minded devotion and commitment was essential for engaging in the non-violent struggle against imperial rule. Gandhi was able to divert women's *śakti* from the domestic to the national sphere. This is described in Kathleen Young's essay 'Hinduism' in *Women in World Religions* (1987).

Although Gandhi was using traditional categories to encourage women to take part in the national movement, it had important implications. It called for the redefinition of roles within the family. Both men and women became equal partners in a common cause. Women were able to come out in the open and thus break the barriers of caste and sex. Since then women have played a significant role in Gandhi's ashrams and in the secular sphere. Women availed themselves of educational opportunities and qualified for professions such as law, medicine, teaching, social work and the like. There are colleges exclusively for women in Indian towns and cities, and the teaching staff are mostly women. Men hardly figure in women's institutions except in non-professional roles, such as laboratory technicians, porters or caretakers.

Satī

The word *satī* means a 'virtuous woman'. One does not 'commit *satī*' but can only become a *satī*, i.e., a virtuous one – sometimes through immolation on the funeral pyre of one's husband. It is possible that this act, which was symbolically performed by a widow during the vedic period, may have paved the way for the actual practice of *satī* in later centuries.

Despite minimal warrant or justification for the rite in the *smṛti* literature, *satī* seemed to have gained ground in certain parts of India, particularly Rajasthan and Bengal. It was largely confined to the women of high castes, particularly *kṣatriyas* (warrior class) and Brahmans (priestly class). *Satī* is different from the *Jauhar* custom prevalent among Rajput (martial class) widows, who opted for collective widow-burning on a mass scale to save their honour rather than submit themselves to the Mughal conquerors.

While Lord Bentinck deserves the credit for abolishing *satī* (1829), the efforts of various opponents of the custom created a favourable ground for the effectiveness of reforms. Among Hindus there were both upholders and critics of the rite. It was denounced by Bana, a well-known Sanskrit scholar (600 CE), *tāntrikas* (who hold women in high esteem), *bhakti* poets such as Ramananda, Kabir and Sikh *gurus*. In the early nineteenth century, reformers like Rammohan Roy challenged traditionalists' view that the woman who became a *satī* was assured of a place in heaven. Arvind Sharma[20] shows that he refuted such statements by quoting the *Gītā*, which sets a high value on the concept of *niṣkāma karma*, actions performed without any desire for their fruits or reward. According to the *Gītā*, women are entitled to salvation, and to subject them to an inferior mode of action ('reward-oriented act') therefore smacks of male superiority.

Religious dimension of *satī*

The wife who chose to become a *satī* on the death of her husband was considered auspicious, and the widow by contrast was inauspicious, though they both sought the same goal – reunion with their husbands. While *satī* was glorified, the widow was looked down upon despite her self-disciplined life. Whether women chose to become *satī*s or widows, their sexuality was controlled by their dead husbands. Total fidelity to their husbands was expected of women and this could be established by becoming a *satī* or a widow. Women's salvation came to be seen in terms of being reunited with their husbands and hence rebirth-oriented. Men's salvation came to be seen in terms of release from the cycle of births and deaths.

Widows

In orthodox families a widow was required to shave her hair, wear a white sari and give up her ornaments (toe and ear rings, bangles and the red dot in the middle of her forehead), which symbolise auspiciousness (*subha*). Her economic well-being and status were those of dependence on her sons. Despite a widow's austere life and religious orientation (fasts, vows and prayers) she was not favourably looked upon. Her presence at festivals, social and religious ceremonies was considered inauspicious. It is therefore not surprising that women placed in these circumstances might prefer *satī*. Although the practice is now banned, there are a few advocates of *satī* even today. It is ironic that a tradition that reveres the feminine aspect of the Divine should consider the widow inauspicious.

Although some degree of inauspiciousness may be associated with widows today, attitudes have changed to some extent. India had a Prime Minister (Indira Gandhi) who was a widow, and then had an Environment Minister (Menaka Gandhi), also a widow. Indira Gandhi participated in social functions and sought the advice of *guru*s, and she was given a grand funeral ceremony.

Two earlier women who did not conform to the traditional orientations of a widow were Pandita Ramabai (1858–1922) and Kamaladevi Chattopadhyaya (born in 1903). Widowhood did not stop Pandita Ramabai (who later converted to Christianity) from being involved in women's education and rights. Kamaladevi became a widow soon after marriage and later married the Bengali playwright, Haridranath Chattopadhyaya, and she was actively involved in the national movement for Indian Independence.

Widow remarriage

The remarriage of widows was not uncommon in earlier times. The custom of *niyoga* which allowed a widow to be married to her husband's brother is mentioned in the vedic and post-vedic literature but went out of vogue in the early centuries of the Common Era. Although a Hindu widow can remarry today (The Hindu Widow Remarriage Act was passed in 1856), very few opt for it, for reasons such as family honour and social acceptability. Moreover, since marriage is seen in broader categories, involving not merely two individuals but two families, remarriage poses problems. There have been few cases of widow remarriage among the upper castes whereas it is more socially acceptable among the lower castes.

Devadāsīs

In the *Kāmasūtra* (The Book on the Art of Love), composed in the early centuries of the Common Era, women are neither idealised nor held in contempt. Courtesans in ancient India were women of great artistic accomplishments and cultural refinement. They were to a great extent independent and not bound by the norms that applied to upper-class women.

To the class of courtesans belong *devadāsīs* (female servants of god), who were dedicated to the temple at a very early age. *Devadāsīs* in South India were associated with both royal and village temples. They enhanced worship by their repertoire. They also functioned as ritual specialists in the village temples. The female village deities were both malevolent and benign. Since a *devadāsī* was associated with the female aspect of the goddess, she was seen as specially qualified to deal with the ambivalent Divine.

In later years the *devadāsī* tradition came to be associated with prostitution. The practice of dedicating a female of any age as a *devadāsī* was declared illegal in 1947. But the artistic dimension of the tradition was revived by Balasaraswati, who belonged to a *devadāsī* family. She was one of the best exponents of the South Indian classical dance, *Bharatanatyam*. With her dance performance in Varanasi, the centre of Hindu orthodoxy, it gradually gained favour with upper- and middle-class Hindus. The ritual and folk songs of the *devadāsīs* are still sung in South Indian temples.

Women in religious practice

The question of women priests has not been an important issue in Hinduism. Few women aspire to officiate at public religious ceremonies and they do so out of personal interest. Women do not see priesthood in terms of a full-time profession as men do. However, priesthood not being a remunerative profession, Brahman men tend to choose it only if there is a strong family tradition. Even male priests have only a marginal status outside the ritualistic context.

As with other traditions, women's menstruation is seen as making them impure and therefore unfit for the role of a ritual specialist. At the popular level women have relatively greater freedom and authority, and they can function as religious specialists. Women exorcists and shamanesses are prominent in the oral traditions.

Despite strong opposition, a group of Brahman women in Pune have set up a school for women priests. The Thatte school charges no fees and is open to non-brahman students. It was the result of the efforts of an elderly couple, Pushpa and her husband, Shankarrao, who were disenchanted with the quality of service offered by male priests who often have to officiate at various places on the same day.

Women are important in religious practice in a more fundamental sense. The home is the centre of religious practices such as daily worship, life-cycle rituals, festivals and fasts. The temple, almost wholly the domain of male priests, is not central to Hindu religious practice. The daily worship (*pūjā*) is usually performed by the mother on behalf of the family. It is mostly the women in the family who take care of the religious education of children. As well as daily *pūjā* and numerous festivals in which women take leading roles, there are rituals for women's welfare. Pre-natal rituals such as *sīmanta*, performed during the early months of a woman's pregnancy, are meant to ensure the emotional and physical well-being of the child. Gujarati women perform a special rite called 'inviting the Mata' or goddess during a woman's first pregnancy. It is also performed on other occasions. The rite involves honouring a *goyani* (an unmarried woman or a married woman whose husband is alive) who is treated as if she were a goddess. In identifying a woman with a goddess, this rite affirms the creative energy or *śakti* which is inherent in woman.

Hindu women can look to the concept of *śakti* (latent in both the masculine and the feminine) to challenge the patriarchal images of women and thus recover the feminine principle in both woman and man.

NOTES

1. Griffth, R.T.H. (trans) (1920) *Hymns of the Rig Veda* (3rd edn), vol. I, Benares, E.J. Lazarus, p. 158.
2. Griffth, R.T.H. (trans) (1926) *Hymns of the Rig Veda* (3rd edn), vol. II, Benares, E.J. Lazarus, p. 438.
3. Panikkar, R. (1989) *The Vedic Experience: Mantramañjarī* (2nd edn), Pondicherry, All India Books, p. 265.
4. Shastri, S.R. (1954) *Women in the Vedic Age*, Bombay, Bharatiya Vidya Bhavan, pp. 17–18.
5. Panikkar, *The Vedic Experience*, p. 265.
6. Zaehner, R.C. (trans) (1966) *Hindu Scriptures*, London, J.M. Dent & Sons, pp. 45–6.
7. Zaehner, *Hindu Scriptures*, p. 52.
8. Griffth, R.T.H. (trans) (1963) *The Rāmāyaṇa of Valmiki* (3rd edn), Varanasi, Chowkhamba Sanskrit Series Office, p. 496.
9. Rajagopalachari, C. (1978) *Mahābhārata* (21st edn), Bombay, Bharatiya Vidya Bhavan, p. 92.
10. Bühler, G. (trans) (1886) *The Sacred Books of the East*, vol. XXV, edited by F. Max Müller, Oxford, Clarendon Press, p. 330.
11. Bühler, *The Sacred Books of the East*, vol. XXV. p. 69.
12. Bühler, *The Sacred Books of the East*, vol. XXV, p. 328.
13. Bühler, *The Sacred Books of the East*, vol. XXV, p. 343.
14. Bühler, *The Sacred Books of the East*, vol. XXV, p. 196.
15. Bühler, *The Sacred Books of the East*, vol. XXV, p. 339.
16. Bühler, *The Sacred Books of the East*, vol. XXV, pp. 67–72.
17. Zaehner, *Hindu Scriptures*, p. 35.
18. Sarin, R. (1985) 'Kali's crusade against ignorance', *Sunday*, vol. 13, no. 7, December 22–28, Calcutta, p. 20.
19. Shiva, V. (1988) *Staying Alive: Women, Ecology and Development*, London, Zed Books, p. 67.
20 Sharma, A., Ray, A., Hejib, A. and Young, K.K. (1988) *Satī: Historical and Phenomenological Essays*, Delhi, Motilal Banarsidass, pp. 67–72.

FURTHER READING

Altekar, A.S. (1959) *The Position of Women in Hindu Civilization* (2nd edn), Delhi, Motilal Banarsidass.
Gupta, B. (1987) 'The masculine-feminine symbolism in Kashmir Saivism', in B. Gupta (ed.) *Sexual Archetypes: East and West*, New York, Paragon House, New Era Books.

Kakar, S. (1989) *Intimate Relations: Exploring Indian Sexuality*, Delhi, Viking.

Kersenboom-Story, S.C. (1987) *Nityasumaṅgalī: Devadasi Tradition in South India*, Delhi, Motilal Banarsidass.

King, U. (1989) *Women and Spirituality: Voices of Protest and Promise*, Basingstoke, Macmillan.

Knott, K. (1987) 'Men and women, or devotees? Krishna consciousness and the role of women', in U. King (ed.) *Women in the World's Religions: Past and Present*, New York, Paragon House, New Era Books.

Kingsley, D. (1987) *Hindu Goddesses: Visions of the Divine Feminine in the Hindu Religious Tradition*, Delhi, Motilal Banarsidass.

Leslie, I.J. (1980) *The Religious Role of Women in Ancient India*, Oxford University, unpublished MPhil thesis.

Mookerjee, A. (1988) *Kali: The Feminine Force*, London, Thames and Hudson.

Mukerjee, Prabhati, (1978) *Hindu Women: Normative Models*, New Delhi, Orient Longman.

Parikh, I.J. and Grag, P.K. (1989) *Indian Women: An Inner Dialogue*, New Delhi, Sage.

Swami Ghananda and Stewart-Wallace, J. (1979) *Women Saints: East and West*, Hollywood, Vedanta Press.

Young, K.K. (1987) 'Hinduism', in A. Sharma (ed.) *Women in World Religions*, Albany, State University of New York Press.

4. Islam

Leila Badawi

The views presented here are intended to be within the framework of orthodox Sunni Islam. Some eighty-five per cent of Muslims worldwide are Sunni, the Shi'ah make up about ten per cent, and a number of small groups make up the remaining five per cent. All Muslims are in direct personal relationship to God. For Muslims every thought and every action has both spiritual and ethical consequences, and thus has religious significance. The spiritual dimension is therefore crucial to all institutions of society in Islam, and to every public and private act. Consequently, Muslim religious law embraces every aspect of life and, in principle, law and theology are conflated in Islam.

The theologian-jurists of Islam, the *'ulama'*, are an open class of scholars. Any Muslim, man or woman, with the requisite scholarly qualifications, may become an *'alīm*[1] (singular of *'ulama'*), but an *'alīm* is not spiritually privileged over any other Muslim. The *'ulama'* are not priests, or guardians of souls, but merely guardians of religious knowledge – knowledge which is, in principle, freely available to all.

Islam is a religion founded on the revelation of a text, in Arabic – the Qur'ān, which addresses men and women equally. The 6th–7th century Makkan merchant, Muhammad, whom Muslims believe to be the last Messenger of God, received the revelation of the Qur'ān in stages over many years. The Arabic word, *islām*, signifies 'self-surrender to God', and a Muslim, in Arabic, signifies 'one who surrenders the self to God'. This applies to all communities and creeds. The word for God in Arabic is *Allāh*, which has a grammatically feminine ending, although it is treated as grammatically masculine. The effect is to suggest a vision of God that transcends the masculine and the feminine.

84

The principal institution of Islam is the *ummah*, the Muslim community itself. *Shari'ah* – that is the divinely instituted law interpreted by the *'ulama'* on behalf of the Muslims – governs the Muslim community. Muslim orthodoxy is capable of great sensitivity to social context. In Muslim societies generally, it is orthodoxy that demonstrates suppleness and adaptability, allied to a spiritual and moral egalitarianism that proclaims all believers equal before God: women are the equals of men, the poor are the equals of the rich and there are no hereditary privileges.

The Shi'ah offer an exception to this principle. Although Sunni and Shi'i Muslims can and do pray together, there are fundamental differences in their sources of religious authority. The Shi'i hold that Ali, the Prophet Muhammad's cousin and son-in-law, was his rightful successor, and that only the descendants of the Prophet through Ali and the Prophet's daughter, Fatima, may exercise religious authority. Each Shi'ite Muslim is obliged to follow a particular legal authority. Personal decision on matters of law is considered to be the prerogative of the senior legal authorities alone, all of whom must be descendants of Ali and Fatima. For the Shi'ah, each legal question is regarded as unique regardless of precedents, and the decision of the legal authority is considered binding only on his own adherents. In theory, this allows for greater flexibility in the development of Shi'ah Muslim law than in the Sunni law.

There has always been tension between folk religion and the text-based orthodoxy of the Muslim world. This tension has stimulated repeated renewals of Sunni Islam, for Muslim religious orthodoxy combines iconoclasm with a relaxed acceptance of unfamiliar traditions, and individual behaviours, which offer no discernible harm. Far from being excluded from the literate and scholarly discourse of Sunni Islam, women, and ideas of the feminine, are central. There is a profound distinction between social conservatism and religious orthodoxy in Islam; while local custom may be endorsed by orthodox scholars, and incorporated into Muslim law, it was often repudiated with great vigour.

Sunni Islam rests on the broad consensus of the *'ulama'* on the interpretations of the Qur'ān, and on their learned deduction of general moral principles from the exemplary behaviour, or *sunnah*, of the Prophet Muhammad himself, and of his Companions. For the purposes of this chapter, the four major Sunni schools of law described below, embody the Islamic legal system.

Women at the foundation of Islam

Strong women are keystones in the foundation of Islam. The first person to hear of Muhammad's revelation and become a Muslim was Khadijah, a middle-aged businesswoman, wife and mother. Muhammad himself nominated a young girl, A'isha, as a religious authority for the Muslims, and she remains an important source of authority. Khadijah, a wealthy merchant, first employed Muhammad as her agent. Although she was forty, to his twenty-five years, she proposed to him and they married. Her initiative was profoundly significant. Muhammad received the first revelation when he too reached forty, after fifteen years of marriage. Khadijah was his most intimate companion and his closest friend. She was the first one he told of that terrifying visitation with which the revelation began. Khadijah, covering him with her cloak, reassured Muhammad, in his terror, that God had blessed him as his messenger. There is a tradition, admittedly one that is neither well-known nor widely accepted, that *Jibrā'īl*, the Angel of Revelation, once visited Muhammad in Khadijah's presence, saying only, 'Give Khadijah greetings of Peace from her Lord', and waited for her reply before departing. Khadijah died when she was about sixty-five years old, after twenty-five years of marriage.

After her death Muhammad married again, and the most redoubtable of his wives in a now polygamous household, was A'isha. When A'isha jealously dismissed Khadijah as 'that toothless old woman whom God has replaced with a better', Muhammad rebuked her saying:

> Indeed God has not. I was rejected, but she believed in me. I was called a liar, but she proclaimed me truthful; she shared her wealth with me when I was poor; and God granted me children with her.

The qur'anic account of the Creation and Fall emphasises the common origin of men and women, and does not privilege men in any sense:

> O mankind! Reverence your Sustainer Who created you from a single soul and from it created its mate and from the two spread abroad a multitude of men and women.

> (*Sūrah* 4:1 Asad)

It is a consequence of Arabic grammar that the first created human being is feminine because the word *nafs*, translated here as 'soul', is a feminine noun. *Nafs* also denotes mind, spirit, human being or inner self, roughly corresponding to the Latin *anima* and the Greek *psyche*. *Nafs* is often pejorative, as 'the soul that incites to evil', but it is also able to evolve. It is the *nafs* that matures to become the conscience or 'reproachful soul', and the 'soul at peace' that returns to the Garden of the Lord, paradise (*sūrah* 89:27) is the *nafs* in its final fulfilment.

Eve, known in Arabic as *Ḥawwā'*, is not named in the Qur'ān. However, both Adam and Ḥawwā' are equally responsible for the Fall. There is no suggestion in the qur'anic text that Adam's wife seduced him away from obedience to God, and therefore no implication that either woman or sexuality is accursed:

> But Satan made them both slip from the Garden and so deprived them of their previous felicity. And We said: Fall down all (people), as enemies of each other. Earth shall be your dwelling and your livelihood for a time . . .
>
> (*Sūrah* 2:36–37)

The biology of womanhood is not, in any sense, accursed in orthodox views. However, ritual ablution is necessary to establish a state of physical and spiritual preparedness for prayer. The 'greater ablution', *ghusl*, is necessary after the following: childbirth, menstruation, ejaculation, sexual intercourse, and, according to some *'ulama'*, after touching a corpse; the 'lesser ablution', *wuḍū'* is required after calls of nature, deep sleep or unconsciousness, minor bleeding (slight pricks and grazes excepted), and touching the genitals. The *ghusl* requires the formal dedications: 'I take refuge in God' and, 'In the name of God, the merciful, the compassionate', followed by a shower of clean water over the whole body. The *wuḍū'* is a more limited ablution' necessary as a preparation for prayer, but dependent on a state of *ghusl*. Ablution symbolises the rededication of the spirit to worship, honouring and transcending the body, and the life of the body. A person who is not in the state of *wuḍū'* does not perform the ritual prayers.

For the classical authorities of Islam, the experience of giving birth is honoured, not as suffering in expiation of original sin – a notion

87

repudiated by Islam – but as a form of witness. Despite the necessity for *ghusl* after giving birth, childbirth itself was never viewed as a regrettable pollution.[3] A woman who dies in childbirth is honoured as one who is *shahīd*; the word *shahīd* has some of the connotations of the word 'martyr', as one who dies, or endures great suffering in bearing witness to Islam. However, while motherhood is an honoured role, it neither defines, nor confines women in Islam.

Despite the high honour attached to motherhood, a mother is not obliged to breastfeed if she does not wish to do so, and it is the responsibility of the father to find and pay for alternative care (*sūrah* 2:233). Moreover, some of the most influential classical *'ulama'*, in certain circumstances, permitted both contraception and abortion before the fourth month of pregnancy;[4] for Muslims, both men and women, are entitled to the enjoyment of sexuality within marriage – and such sexual enjoyment is distinct from the right to have children. Muslims in enemy lands (*Dār-ul-harb*), or in times of great trouble, such as pestilence or famine, were commonly advised to practice contraception. It is apparent that, for the classical *'ulama'*, there were religious responsibilities greater than, and incompatible with, parenthood. Indeed, motherhood itself was highly valued by the classical *'ulama'*, partly because it was acknowledged to be physically, morally and spiritually arduous.

For Muslims, motherhood is understood as a metaphor for the loving guidance and authority of compassion in Islam. Indeed, the word for 'compassion', *rahīm*, one of the attributes of God, is derived from the same root in Arabic as the word for womb.

'Mother' was used as an accolade in the first Muslim community and did not merely describe a family relationship. The widows of the Prophet Muhammad were all honoured with the title 'Mothers of the Believers'. A'isha was the most famous and important of these 'Mothers', although she never bore a child; her authority rests upon her personal qualities of intelligence and honesty, and on the love and respect she inspired in her husband, Muhammad. Muhammad advised the Muslims: 'Take half your religion from this one', indicating A'isha, and nominated her as an authority on all religious matters during his absence. Many, if not most, of the reports of the Prophet's private life come from A'isha; for example, when asked what Muhammad did at home, A'isha replied, 'He helped his wife. He swept the floor and mended his own clothes'. A'isha, rather than her older brother Abd al-Rahman, was nominated by the first *khalīfah*, her father, Abu Bakr, as the executor of his will. The Prophet received revelations in her presence, chose to die in her arms, and was buried in the earthen floor of her apartment.[5]

Although celibacy has no place in Sunni Islam, the Prophet Muhammad's widows, honoured as 'Mothers of the Believers', lived as a community of celibate women who exercised great political influence and participated in public affairs in the period of the early *khalīfah*s. Because Sunni Islam has no clergy, and no hierarchy of believers, it has no 'church'. The Muslim community itself, the *ummah*, is the ultimate God-ordained institution of Islam (see *sūrah* 2:143).

Two versions of the pious life for women in Islam

For all Muslims, men and women, the first duty is to God. The love of God and obedience to him supersede all other duties and responsibilities. For most Muslims the practice of Islam demands only a life of conventional goodness as an expression of personal dedication to God. Such conventional goodness demands constant attention to the rigorous ethical demands of Islam; mere performance of the formal expressions of faith is not enough for salvation. Nevertheless, in the history of Islam, there have always been women for whom the conventional was not enough.

One of the most famous of these exceptional women was the historical figure, Rabi'ah al-'Adawiyyah. She was a revered and highly influential Muslim mystic – a ṣūfī – and religious poet born in eighth-century Iraq and enslaved as a child. Although she became famous for her religious poetry, Rabi'ah was not one of the highly-educated and sophisticated slave-women in the service of the ruling élites; by all accounts she began as an ordinary and very humble field-hand. Legend has it that she was freed by her master only because he saw a holy light shining about her as she prayed alone in the fields one night.

Dedicated to a life of poverty and celibacy, Rabi'ah asserted that she was so filled with the love of God that there was no room in her heart for love of any other, although she was famously a vegetarian, and a tender friend to wild animals. One of her most famous poems is:

O God, if I worship Thee for fear of hell, burn me in hell, and if I worship Thee in hope of Paradise, then exclude me from Paradise, but if I worship Thee for Thine own sake, then grudge me not Thine everlasting beauty.[6]

Zeinab al-Ghazali is a lesser known and very different figure. Born in Egypt in 1918 she was a prominent supporter of the Muslim Brotherhood, a revivalist movement dedicated to the introduction of an Islam 'purified' of extraneous innovations. Al-Ghazali believed herself to be a leader of Muslim society, and modelled herself on the prominent women of the Prophet Muhammad's own community. The daughter of an *'alīm* from Al-Azhar university, she was extremely knowledgeable about Sunni Muslim law. Under Muslim law all marriages are contractual, and, within limits, the terms of a marriage contract may be negotiated by the partners. In her own marriage contract Zeinab al-Ghazali designated her husband as her assistant in her mission as a political activist within the Islamic revivalist movement. This role took precedence over her duties as a wife and mother. However, her husband clearly failed to fulfil his part of the contract to her satisfaction, and she divorced him because he 'took up all my time and kept me from my mission'. She embarked on another marriage with the same contractual stipulations, and it appears that her second husband was better able to serve her purpose.[7]

This is all the more noteworthy because the provisions of Sunni Muslim law used by al-Ghazali co-exist in Egypt with the institution of 'The House of Obedience'. Under the rules of 'The House of Obedience', a wife who has left the marital home without her husband's permission, may be returned to him both forcibly and unconditionally. 'The House of Obedience' is not part of the legislation revealed in the Qur'ān, the *Sharī'ah*. It is, however, based on social norms which the *'ulama'* held to be consistent with the *Sharī'ah* in promoting the common good. This is true of much of the positive law developed by the *'ulama'*. There is enormous latitude in Muslim law for individually tailored legal contracts, such as Zeinab al-Ghazali's, which may be highly unconventional, and yet be upheld as valid expressions of the possibilities within *Sharī'ah*. Without a 'made to measure' contract, such as that worked out by Zeinab al-Ghazali to suit her own aspirations, the *'ulama'* apply contractual terms which they consider to be in the best interests of the parties involved, and of society as a whole – of which more below.

Rabi'ah al-'Adawiyyah and Zeinab al-Ghazali personify two poles of Muslim thought. Despite their exceptional characters and circumstances, they also represent some of the possibilities available to women within Muslim society. A woman, as much as a man, may be a learned interpreter of the law, for others as well as herself, or pre-eminent as a contemplative honoured for profound religious meditations. However, Rabi'ah, as a popular saint, also represents the magic-based, myth-making, essentially non-literate culture of folk religion. The idea of the saint endowed with miraculous powers is profoundly inimical to the most rigorous interpretations of Sunni Islam. The Sunni hold that God hears all believers equally and that none may mediate for another. In Sunni Islam neither men nor women may be empowered as saintly figures able to mediate with God on behalf of supplicants. Faith is a source of spiritual empowerment, but it is Muslim law, as the expression of faith within the *ummah*, which is the only legitimate source of empowerment in Muslim society.

The nature of Muslim law

Although Muslim law is partly based on social convention, it is not limited by it. Because there is no ultimate authority in Sunni Islam, interpretations and evaluations may differ substantially. This is so even with *'ulama'* contemporary with one another and of the same school. The Qur'ān, as the revealed Word of God, and the *Sunnah*, as the exemplary practice of God's Messenger, Muhammad, together form the *Sharī'ah*, the foundation of Muslim ethics. The interpretation, elaboration and application of the principles of *sharī'ah* is *fiqh*, usually translated as jurisprudence. *Fiqh* is the tool with which the *'ulama'* constructed Muslim law on the foundations of the *Sharī'ah*.

There are, currently, four orthodox schools of Muslim law. They are named, in honour of their founders, the Hanafī, Mālikī, Shafī'ī and Hanbalī schools. Briefly they evolved in different geographical and cultural regions of the Muslim world and crystallised in the tenth century, the end of the classical era of Muslim law. Although they concur on the broad principles of legislation, they differ in their rulings on specific issues, including the rights and responsibilities of men and women in the family. One of the reasons for this is that

91

'urf, translatable as custom, precedent or mores, was one of the supplementary sources used by the classical 'ulama' in their creative elaboration of Muslim law from the foundations of the Sharī'ah.

There are also acknowledged to be regional differences within each school of law, so that a Hanafī 'alīm from Damascus follows a slightly different tradition from that of his Hanafī colleague in Delhi. This follows the practice of the Prophet, who discontinued traditions which he considered to be harmful, but maintained customary practices which he judged either positively good, or effectively harmless.

The Sunni orthodox schools of law are limited in their authority over individual Muslims because each believer, man or woman, is free to choose his or her own school of law, although frivolous chopping and changing is discouraged. This has important personal consequences given the differences of thought between schools, and it emphasises the distinction between the authority of the Sharī'ah itself, and its human interpretations – the different schools of law.

All schools of law hold that all Muslims, men or women, are equally competent to perform all Muslim rites, and that all believers are equal before God and in direct personal relationship with God. The Qur'ān proclaims:

> Let there be no coercion in matters of faith. The way of truth is now distinct from the path of error.
>
> (Sūrah 2:256)

The Arabic word dīn, here translated as 'faith', denotes religious or moral law, according to context. Freedom of conscience is thus a principle of sharī'ah.

Muslim law is intended to be a guide for moral action. It is in the area of moral choice that legal paradoxes may appear, because moral behaviour is beyond the conventional limits of legal scrutiny. Muslim legislators stopped short of inquiring into the consciences of litigants, but, to a large extent, Muslim law assumes that all members of the community act according to conscience. This creates an obvious problem.

The classical jurists, the 'ulama', warned that those who manipulate Muslim law, failing to observe its moral and spiritual integrity, imperil their souls, but may escape earthly punishment, because jurists are limited by the letter of the law even where they observe its spirit being flouted. In practice, and during all eras of Islam, Muslim law was applied in parallel with the indigenous civil law of the local rulers. Such indigenous customary law made no comparable assumptions about individual probity and moral seriousness, and frequently was in frank conflict with Muslim law. Ibn al-Qayyim, a prominent Hanbalī *'alīm* of the classical era claimed that:

> ... pioneering interpreters of the law felt no necessity to formalize family regulations for early Muslims were conscientious enough to implement the moral teachings of their religion without the need to be reminded that such was a legal duty.

> (Reported in 'Abd al 'Ati 1977: 156)

He was thus clearly conscious of the distinction between the letter and the spirit of the law. This is interesting particularly because the Hanbalī school of law, in principle, considers its role to be limited to codifying the practice of the first Muslim community and restricts itself to the most literal interpretations of the Qur'ān and *Sunnah*.

Relatively new developments in Muslim law include the legal ruling by *'ulama'* in Saudi Arabia that women are forbidden to drive any kind of motorised vehicle. The Saudi *'ulama'* are of an extremely puritanical and socially conservative school, the Wahābī school of law. They view reason with extreme suspicion as a tool in the development of religious practice, although Wahabism is, in effect, a branch of Hanbalī thought. It is interesting that the Wahābī rule that women may not drive in Saudi Arabia, although they may still follow the example of the first Muslims, and ride camels! In the Wahābī view, driving is such a dangerous innovation that men may drive only out of necessity, while women must be protected from all the risks of corruption it entails.

There is a great wealth of Muslim law and Muslim tradition governing the relationship between women and men, and the roles of women within the *ummah*, the community of Muslims. The classical authorities offer divergent views on many key issues of great personal importance. Divergence of opinion, albeit within limits, is an acknowledged and institutionalised feature of Sunni Islam. The *'ulama'*, the scholars of the *Sharī'ah*, have always agreed to differ, and respected diversity of learned opinion as characteristic

93

of Muslim law itself. However, it is not unusual for customary law to be mistaken for Muslim law, even when, in reality, they are wholly at odds.

The 'sleeping foetus' and the 'crime of honour': Muslim law versus customary law

There is one particularly arresting example of the divergence between customary law and Muslim law in the Middle East. This is the vast moral gulf between the orthodox legal fiction (*hilah*) of the 'sleeping foetus' (*ar-raqid*) and the customary 'crime of honour': the designation awarded to the 'execution' by male kin of a woman suspected of illicit sexual behaviour. Hanafī and Mālikī rulings on the 'sleeping foetus' are slightly different. Under Mālikī law, which is dominant in the Arab West and in West Africa, human pregnancy may be claimed to last as long as five or even seven years; Hanafī law, the most geographically extensive of all, covering most of the former Ottoman Empire and most of India, accepts claims of gestation of up to two years.

The notion of 'the sleeping foetus' has important legal consequences for widowed or deserted women: it shields them from the penalties for illicit sex despite pregnancy, and establishes the child as the legal heir of the dead or absent husband. For unmarried mothers, who cannot plead 'the sleeping foetus' as a defence, the conventional legal formula attributed pregnancy to a visit to a public bath shortly after the men's hour. There, it was claimed, a woman might accidentally sit on a little pool of semen and thereby conceive.

The Muslim world is so culturally varied that these particular legal ruses must have been at odds with prevailing attitudes in many regions. It is difficult to know how far folk-belief influenced the development of the law in this instance, and how much the law stimulated changes in folk-belief. Certainly, *'urf*, or customary practice, was one of the supplementary sources of the law for the *'ulama'*. While the *'ulama'* offered 'the sleeping foetus' as a compassionate legal stratagem, folk-belief often embraced it as a reality. In much of the Arab Middle East contemporary customary law is vigorously opposed to the forgiving excuse of *ar-raqid*, 'the sleeping foetus', offered by the *'ulama'* of the classical era.

The 'crime of honour', in the penal codes of Syria, Lebanon and other Arab countries, refers to the killing of a woman by her father, brother (or husband) for suspected sexual misconduct. It is punished by a token six months' imprisonment for the killer. The 'crime of honour' has no basis in Muslim law and is in stark contrast to the classical judgements, in all four Sunni schools of law, creating a legal excuse for illicit pregnancy. However, an excuse which claims that pregnancy is potentially dormant for years is wholly at odds with the qur'anic institution of the *'idda*. The *'idda* is a three-month delay (four months plus ten days in the case of widowhood) for a woman between the end of one marriage and the beginning of another; its purpose is to confirm the paternity of any child she may bear – and a pregnant woman may not remarry until the child has been delivered. Given the acceptance of 'the sleeping foetus', however, it is always open for a woman to claim that she is pregnant by her ex-husband, or other nominee, for as long as the law allows, that is for two years or more, depending on the school of law she follows. There are interesting possibilities for conflict between ex-partners of different schools of law. All schools hold that an ex-husband and father is responsible for maintenance of both mother and child, although he may remarry as soon as he likes.

There are many tensions evident in the development and application of Muslim law. Such tensions are particularly striking in the contrast between qur'anic legislation and the *fiqh* rulings on sexuality.

The *'ulama'* and sexuality in Islam

Sexual behaviour is not merely a matter of private choice. The creation of a family is one of the consequences of sexuality, and sexuality itself is an expression of spirituality in marriage. Men and women in the partnership of marriage are addressed by God, saying:

> . . . they are as a garment for you, and you are as a garment for them . . . you may lie with them skin to skin, and avail yourselves of that which God has ordained for you . . .
>
> (*Sūrah* 2:187 Asad)

Modesty is enjoined upon all Muslims, both men and women:

> Tell the believing men to lower their gaze and be modest. . . . And tell
> the believing women to lower their gaze and be modest, and to display
> of their adornment only that which is apparent, and to draw their veils
> over their bosoms. . .

> (*Sūrah* 24:30–31)[8]

Because the verse commands 'believing women' to cover the bosom
in public, some *'ulama'* have interpreted it further as implying that
'believing women' should also cover their heads in public. Other
'ulama', however, consider that there is no specific ruling about head
coverings and so Muslim women may please themselves on this
matter. Several of the earliest Islamic scholars interpreted this verse
as one commanding modesty in dress according to the standards
prevailing. The arch-traditionalists viewed only the face and hands
of a woman as suitable for public display, and sometimes not even
these; nevertheless, a woman must not veil her face on the
pilgrimage to Makkah, the *ḥajj*.

Because sexual behaviour is more than a matter of private
indulgence, the Qur'ān offers considerable guidance and imposes
certain penalties for transgression. The qur'anic penalty for gross
indecency (*fahishah*) is house arrest for the guilty, applicable equally
to men and women, until repentance ensues (*sūrah* 4:15–18). The
Qur'ān imposes a hundred lashes on men and women found guilty
of illicit sex (*zina*, often translated as 'adultery' although it includes
fornication) (*sūrah* 24:2–5). However, conviction requires four
Muslim eyewitnesses to the illicit sexual act, that is to the act of
penetration itself. The eyewitness must be not only Muslim, but of
unquestionable virtue. This is inherently unlikely, and is recognised
as such. The penalty for falsely accusing anyone of *zina* is eighty
lashes and loss of legal capacity as a witness. The burden, as in all
areas of moral choice, lies principally on the conscience of the
individual Muslim.

There is no sexual double standard in the Qur'ān.

> Both are equally guilty: the adulterer couples with none other than an
> adulteress – that is a woman who accords (to her own lust) a place side
> by side with God; and with the adulteress couples none other than an
> adulterer – that is a man who accords (to his own lust) a place side by
> side with God: and this is forbidden to believers.

> (*Sūrah* 24:3 Asad)

Some of the classical *'ulama'* hold that partners in adultery or fornication may not marry one another.

Remarkably, however, despite the unambiguous qur'anic rulings on the penalties for illicit sexual behaviour, these are completely ignored in Sunni Muslim law. Sunni law follows the biblical law of Moses which decrees stoning to death for adultery. The *khalīfah* 'Umar, a Companion of the Prophet and second *khalīfah* of the *ummah*, introduced this Mosaic punishment. Although the qur'anic rules of evidence still apply, the Mosaic, rather than the qur'anic, penalty persists as a feature of orthodox law. There are *hadīth* which claim that the Prophet enforced stoning to death for adultery, even though this is contrary to the Qur'ān. The Kharijites, members of a minority Sunni school of law, rejected this as wholly unjustified since the Qur'ān itself abrogates all earlier works of revelation. This application of the Mosaic law to sexual transgressors is a very early example of civil or customary law prevailing over qur'anic legislation. It may be that the moral and spiritual tensions so created within the consciences of the legislators stimulated the development of legal stratagems such as that of the 'sleeping foetus' described above. It was one of the avowed intentions of the major jurists to maintain equity between men and women; 'the sleeping foetus' permitted women the same freedom as men by excusing and regularising pregnancies which would otherwise be incriminating, for, in the Qur'ān, Muslim women are the equals of Muslim men in their power to exercise moral choice.

The Qur'ān addresses the problem of freedom of choice for the enslaved. The classical *'ulama'* held different views on the permissibility of extra-marital sex between Muslim men and their unmarried slave women. Their difficulties were compounded by the fact that all but four of the Abbasid dynasty of *khalīfah*s were the sons of concubines, that is slave women without the status of legal wives. There are three extracts from the Qur'ān which are particularly relevant here:

And let those who cannot find a spouse keep chaste until God give them independence by His grace. And those of your slaves who seek emancipation, award it them if ye are aware of any good in them, and share with them the wealth which God hath bestowed upon you. Do not compel your slave-girls to whoredom that ye may enjoy the life of the world, if they would preserve their chastity. And if one compels them, then, for them, after their compulsion, Behold! God will be Forgiving and Merciful.

(*Sūrah* 24:33, after Pickthall, Ali and Asad)

And all married women are forbidden to you except those whom your right hands possess. . . . so that you solicit them with your wealth in honest wedlock, not debauchery. And those with whom you seek marriage, give them their marriage portions as a duty. And there is no sin for you in what you do by mutual agreement after the duty is fulfilled. . .

(*Sūrah* 4:24)

And whoever is not able to marry free, believing women, let them marry from the believing maids whom your right hands possess. . . . You come from one another; so marry them by their people's leave, and give them their marriage portions[9] fairly, they giving themselves honestly in marriage, and not in fornication nor as secret lovers. And if when they are honourably married, they are guilty of immoral conduct, they shall incur the half of the punishment incurred by free women. Permission to marry slave women is for him among you who fears to commit sin. But patience and self-restraint would be better for you. . .

(*Sūrah* 4:25)

The legality of concubinage was a source of dispute even among the Companions of the Prophet. The 'rejectionists' included some of the most outstanding commentators or exegetists of the Qur'ān. They asserted that the expression *ma malakat aymanukum* (here rendered as 'those whom your right hands possess') denotes 'women who you rightfully possess through wedlock'. Thus the tenth-century historian and *'alīm*, author of a definitive commentary on the Qur'ān, at-Tabari, argued that the Qur'ān sanctions sex only within marriage. In support of his view at-Tabari cited the Companions of the Prophet 'Abd Allah ibn Abbas, and Mujahid among others (reported in Asad 1980: 106, note 26). The expression *muḥsanah* (plural *muḥsanat*, translated in *sūrah* 4:24 above as 'married women'), suggests three possible interpretations: (1) a married woman, (2) a free woman, (3) a chaste woman. Almost all authorities agree that in the context of this verse it should be taken to mean 'married woman'.

The great twelfth-century authority, Fakhr ad-Din ar-Razi, an 'alīm of the Shafi'i school, points out in his authoritative qur'anic commentary, *Mafatih al-Ghayb* (The Key of the Unseen), that the reference to 'all married women' (*al-muhsanat min an-nisa*), is made after a list of the degrees of relationships precluding marriage (*sūrah* 4:22). As such, according to ar-Razi, the verse emphasises that sex is prohibited with any woman other than the lawful wife (reported in Asad 1980: 106, note 26).

There are greater moral and spiritual hazards for the slave-owner in this context, than there are for the slave. Forgiveness and mercy are clearly not on offer to the man who forces, or otherwise induces, his slave woman into either sex or marriage:

> And do not, in order to gain some of the fleeting pleasures of this worldly life, coerce your (slave) maidens into whoredom (if they desire protection against unchastity) . . . and if anyone should coerce them, then, after they have been compelled (to submit in their helplessness), God will be much forgiving, a dispenser of grace!
>
> (*Sūrah* 24:33, after Asad)

This kind of sexual coercion would have been almost impossible for the courts to deal with. As in much of the qur'anic legislation, the issue is effectively beyond the scrutiny of the courts. It is worth noting that the 'slave girls' also have some moral responsibility as the comment, 'if they desire protection against unchastity', makes clear. Slave women in the classical era of Islam were often married. A slave woman who married her master, or who bore him a child, automatically became free. There were also many instances where slave women were married to free men of other households. Slaves are not only more easily coerced than the free, but also more easily enticed. Freedom of action, and thus moral responsibility is acknowledged to be limited for the enslaved:

> And if when they are honourably married, they commit lewdness they shall incur the half of the punishment (prescribed) for free women (in that case).
>
> (*Sūrah* 24:25)

Sexual harassment, or any other exploitation, remains a risk in any relationship with a marked imbalance of power. Under Sunni law, the courts grant, or deny, emancipation to an enslaved person. The

99

slave-owner may be compelled to free the slave for appropriate recompense, either from the public purse, or from the slave's own earnings. However the Qur'ān re-iterates that to free a slave voluntarily, is one of the routes to salvation (see *sūrah* 9:60). According to all authorities it is therefore a moral obligation to free bonded servants, or any person enslaved to their own detriment.

Rulers blithely ignored the gap between the praiseworthy and the merely permissible. The Abbasid *khalīfah*s preferred concubinage to marriage because the rights of a wife are substantial in Muslim law, and a *khalīfah*'s in-laws were invariably importunate. Concubines, of course, had no relatives worth bothering about, and rights which were both limited and easily ignored.

Marriage and divorce

The founder of the Abbasid dynasty, al-Abbas, who ruled from 750–754 CE as the *khalīfah* Saffah, the Shedder of Blood, was once a penniless youth. Although poor, he was handsome, and a rich aristocrat called um-Salama was so taken with him that she proposed marriage, which he gladly accepted. She was careful to stipulate in her marriage contract that he was forbidden to take either another wife, or a concubine. When he became the *khalīfah* Saffah, al-Abbas took as his adviser a Persian nobleman called Khalid ibn Safwan. In the view of this representative of an ancient and cultured realm, a collection of concubines was obligatory as a resource for kingly recreation. He therefore urged the unsophisticated Saffah to equip himself with a suitable array of slave girls. Um-Salama's response was to send servants to beat Khalid to within an inch of his life. Khalid escaped the beating, but the matter was never raised again, and the marriage continued monogamously.

The next in the dynasty was the son of a concubine, al-Mansur (ruled 754–775 CE). The succession was disputed by another dynasty, the 'Alids, descendants of the Prophet's daughter Fatima. They claimed that the mere son of a concubine was not entitled to the khalifate. Al-Mansur riposted 'that a woman can neither inherit nor acquire supreme power and that, therefore, she cannot transmit it'. Al-Mansur's wife, um-Musa, had also married him on the terms of a monogamous contract. The *khalīfah* vigorously and frequently petitioned the *sharī'ah* courts to have this marital contract set aside in favour of a new one permitting him both polygamy and concubinage. The courts repeatedly rejected his applications, and the marriage survived until um-Musa's death ten years later. It is interesting that al-Mansur does not seem to have attempted to divorce um-Musa, and that although, after her death, he took many wives and concubines, he considered only her two sons for the succession, and not any of his sons by other women (Abbot 1946: 16).

In the orthodox view, marriage is the principal arena for the spiritual growth of both men and women. This opinion is founded on the qur'anic declaration:

> O our Sustainer! Grant that our spouses and our offspring be a joy to our eyes, and lead us to be among those who are most conscious of Thee.
>
> (*Sūrah* 25:74)

According to the '*ulama*', the purpose of marriage is thus joy and the growth of faith and nearness to God. In consequence, the classical '*ulama*' held that the principal duties of a wife towards her husband are the sharing of joy and the comforts of companionship, and sharing the love of God. These duties are reciprocal, but a husband has the added responsibilities of maintaining and protecting his wife, according to the guidelines of the '*ulama*'.

Many of the classical jurists held that the duties of a wife do not include housework, and that housework falls within the husband's responsibilities of maintenance and protection. Accordingly, husbands may not insist that their wives attend to household chores, and therefore husbands may be obliged to organise household management themselves.

> And among His Signs
> Is this, that He created
> For you mates from among
> Yourselves, that ye may
> Dwell in tranquillity with them
> And He has put love
> And mercy between your (hearts):
> Verily in that are Signs
> For those who reflect.
>
> (*Sūrah* 30:21, after Pickthall)

101

Although it is of prime spiritual significance, a Muslim marriage may be dissolved if it fails in its principal purpose of spiritual growth, although the Qur'ān warns:

> . . . live with them on a footing of kindness and equity.
> If ye take a dislike to them
> It may be that ye dislike
> A thing, and God brings about
> Through it a great deal of good.

> (*Sūrah* 4:19, after Yusuf Ali)[10]

There are wide differences of opinion among the classical '*ulama*' on the liberty of women, and in some circumstances men, to contract marriages independent of a *walī*, or legal guardian. The Sunni canon encompasses a complete spectrum of views. The most restrictive opinion is that women are not legally competent to contract a marriage without the permission of a *walī*, and that a virgin may be coerced into marriage by her father or grandfather. The most liberal viewpoint is that a woman, of sound mind, may freely negotiate her own marriage contract(s) and that no other person whatsoever has any legal right to intervene. These views, and the four or so inter-mediate opinions, depend on interpretations of the Qur'ān and *Ḥadīth*, and illustrate the possibilities available to learned interpreters of the relevant texts. (For a more complete discussion see 'Abd al 'Ati 1977: 72.)

All schools of thought agree that there is no community of property between spouses and that a wife's property, and income, is under her control and for her use alone, and that it may not legally be acquired by her husband. A wife retains her own family name (that is her father's or clan name), her independent legal personality and allegiance to her own school of law. A wife is also entitled to appropriate maintenance from her husband and to the *mahr*, or marriage gift, from husband to wife, which is usually a matter of private agreement. Spouses inherit from one another, if they are both Muslim. The marriage contract comes into force immediately upon consummation, and the full *mahr* is due. Unpaid *mahr* constitutes a debt which must be cleared before a Muslim man may undertake the *ḥajj*, the pilgrimage to Makkah.

Polygamy is possible, although conditional in Sunni law (see *sūrah*

4:3 and 4.129), polyandry is not. Opinions range from the claim that only monogamy fulfils the criteria for a Muslim marriage, through the notion that polygamy is possible, but only with the permission of the women in question, to the assertion that Muslim marriage necessarily includes the possibility of polygamy and that this is fundamental to its nature. Such a view does not, however, demand that all, or even most, Muslim marriages be polygamous, only that they are potentially so.

Marital problems which do not end in divorce are the subject of some interesting classical legal analyses, based on the following verses from the Qur'ān:

> Men shall protect and maintain women because God has made some of them excel others, and because they support them from their means. Therefore the righteous women are obedient, guarding the intimacy which God would have them guard. As for those women whose rebellion you justly fear, admonish them first; then leave their beds; then beat them. Then if they obey you, seek no harm against them. For God is most High, Exalted, Great.
>
> (*Sūrah* 4:34, after 'Abd al 'Ati)

> And if a woman reasonably fears ill-treatment from her husband, or desertion, it is no sin if they make terms of peace between themselves. Peace is better. But selfishness is ever present in human souls. If you do good and practice self-restraint, God is ever aware of what you do.
>
> (*Sūrah* 4:128, after Pickthall, Ali and Asad)

In one classical minority school of law, the courts act for the wife who justly fears the covert 'rebellion' of her husband against his marital obligations, or possibly covert rebellion against any other religious obligation, in a reciprocal fashion. That is, the court first admonishes the husband. If this fails the court then forbids him his wife's bed, without compromising any of her other marital rights (for sexual satisfaction is a legal right within marriage), and if this too fails, the court finally executes a symbolic beating on the wife's behalf.[11] Some scholars also hold that the husband acts only as an instrument of the courts in the punishment of a 'rebellious' wife, and that he is not free to act without the sanction of the courts.

The 'rebellion' referred to in *sūrah* 4:34 above is interpreted by most *'ulama'* to mean covert breaches of marital obligations. Overt

103

infringements are automatically the province of the courts. All Sunni schools agree that the 'beating' is a symbolic humiliation, and that if any physical harm is inflicted, then the executioner of the punishment is himself legally punishable. However, *sūrah* 4:34 cannot be interpreted without further reference to verses on divorce (e.g., see *sūrah* 65:1), on mediation between spouses and on the value of the legal testimony of spouses in a dispute about such private matters.

There are situations, particularly in intimate relationships, where the legal testimony of a woman is not only equal to, but actually overcomes the testimony of a man, *sūrah* 24:6–9 for example; while in matters of commerce, the testimony of one man is equal to that of two women (*sūrah* 2:282). The Qur'ān recommends that two women may replace one man witness 'so that if one of them errs, the other can remind her'. It is therefore remarkable that the second *khalīfah*, 'Umar, saw fit to appoint a woman as inspector of markets; as an officer of the law her testimony cannot have been judged inferior to a man's. It seems clear that the issue is one of competence and experience, rather than any inherent feminine incapacity.

Legal symmetry and reciprocity between men and women are justified in a verse from the Qur'ān on divorce:

> And concerning each other, wives shall have rights equal in justice to the rights of husbands, although men have precedence over them in this respect.
>
> (*Sūrah* 2:228)

The '*ulama*' agree that 'precedence' here refers to the legal protocol that a husband has the first option to rescind a provisional divorce. Although a wife may refuse to resume the marriage after a provisional divorce, even if her husband wishes to do so, he has the legal, if not the psychological, initiative in repairing the relationship.

The issue of the 'precedence' of husbands over wives and, in *sūrah* 4:34, the implication that men 'excel' women, was the source of much discussion as jurists considered how to reconcile these verses with the equity between men and women proclaimed elsewhere in the Qur'ān. The tenth-century '*alim*, al-Jassas, considered that men 'excel' women because men are the 'guardians and protectors' of women, and a man is legally obliged to support his wife and female relatives with whatever wealth he has.[12] In other words, men 'excel' women in their economic responsibilities. Economic responsibility is a moral trust and men excel women in the extent of their economic obligations and therefore in the extent of their moral obligations. Al-Jassas inferred from this verse that because a husband must maintain his wife, a wife is therefore obliged to obey her husband without dissent in such matters as fall within a husband's rights. The Qur'ān and the *Hadīth* repeatedly commend wives who reject their husband's wrongdoing (see *sūrah* 66:11); thus wifely obedience must not extend beyond the limits allowed by religious conscience, and of course a wife retains her independent legal personality and does not necessarily share her husband's school of law.

It is interesting that there are extensive classical legal discussions of a wife's rights to maintenance when her husband becomes destitute. The Zahiri school of law, a minority and 'literalist' – or perhaps 'fundamentalist' – school, holds that a wife is obliged to use her own lawful means to provide for her destitute husband, and that he incurs no legal debt to her for this. It is not considered what duty of obedience exists between spouses in this situation, although the legal grounds for a wife's obedience of her husband depend on the maintenance, guardianship or trusteeship (*qawwāmīyah*) he provides for her. The majority schools of law, that is the four Sunni schools, do not explore the implications of a husband depending on the financial support of his wife (see *sūrah* 65:5–7). However, should a husband refuse to support his wife, the Hanafīs recommend that he should suffer imprisonment until he resumes his obligation, while the three other schools hold that a wife may freely obtain a divorce under these circumstances.

A fundamental principle reiterated in the Qur'ān is the moral and spiritual equality of men and women, husbands and wives, sons and daughters. The realisation of this principle in society depends on the cultural assumptions which Muslim legislators bring to their interpretations of the *Sharī'ah*. For the classical jurists, a husband was within his rights to prevent his wife from leaving the marital home without his permission. This view persists in contemporary legislation in some Muslim countries where a wife of the most senior professional standing, a government minister or an academic head of department for example, may not leave the country without her husband's written permission. The classical jurists recommended that a husband should be generous in the exercise of his rights and strive to preserve marital harmony. Nevertheless, under Sunni law a husband may divorce his wife without the intervention of the courts, whereas a wife must petition the courts to obtain a divorce on her own account. Such legislation is based on deductions derived from interpretations of the Qur'ān and Ḥadīth, and the avowed intention of all such asymmetry and unequal treatment before the law is the preservation of social order and the protection of women.

The legislators of the classical era were often open to legal reform. The great tenth-century 'alīm of the Hanbalī school, Ibn Taymiyyah, opposed the rulings on divorce instituted by the great and much honoured khalīfah 'Umar, even though he was a Companion of the Prophet, and one of the four Rashidun, or rightly guided, khalīfahs. Under Muslim law, a man may divorce his wife by pronouncing the formula: 'I divorce you'; if said three times the divorce becomes irrevocable. Until 'Umar intervened, men who said 'I divorce you thrice' were considered to have pronounced only one revocable divorce. However, the khalīfah was incensed by the careless use of this formula and with the counsel of his companions declared that the declaration 'I divorce you thrice' must count as an irrevocable divorce in order to discourage its careless use. However, some two centuries later, Ibn Taymiyyah observed that angry men would utter the triple formula for divorce as freely as a commonplace imprecation or expletive, or merely as an empty threat. He argued that the casual use of the oath of divorce could not be atoned for in the same way as other imprecations or dishonoured oaths, by the freeing of a slave or a gift of alms sufficient to feed or clothe ten of the poor. The words signifying divorce were in the nature of a solemn undertaking before God and entailed the destruction of a family. He therefore ruled against the khalīfah 'Umar's judgement and declared that the casual use of such a powerful formula was void and without effect on the legal status of a marriage. However, he stopped short of ruling that men, like women, must obtain divorce only through the courts. Ibn Taymiyyah intended to protect women against the capriciousness of men, just as the khalīfah 'Umar had intended. The 'alīm judged that the changes in Muslim society in the intervening centuries had rendered the great khalīfah's ruling a license to victimise women rather than protect them. He therefore changed the letter of the law in order to uphold its spirit.[13]

Parent and child

There is a very famous tradition according to which a man asked the Prophet Muhammad: 'Whom should I honour most?' The Prophet replied, 'Your mother'. 'And who next?' asked the man, and again the Prophet replied, 'Your mother'. 'And again who after my mother?' inquired the man, and the Prophet for the third time rejoined, 'Your mother!' 'And then who?' asked the man and the Prophet replied, 'Your father'. This tradition has a rather interesting legal consequence.

The question of obedience within the family is one of the issues discussed at length by the classical jurists. All agree that a husband and father is the head of the family, and therefore is to be obeyed by both wife and children, within the limits of religious conscience. But this is not necessarily viewed as the best option according to the classical 'ulama', as the following illustration reveals. A young man, torn between his parents, asked for the advice of Imām Malik, the founder of the Mālikī school of law. His father was far away in the Sudan and had written asking his son to join him; his mother, however, refused to let him go. Malik advised him to go to his father and disobey his mother, but he is in the minority. All three of the other majority schools of law hold that the young man owed greater devotion and obedience to his mother, and that he should have stayed with her.

A parent may not 'divorce' or disown his or her child. Under sharī'ah it is every child's right to know the identity of both parents, whether living or dead, and in law no child may be kept in ignorance of its origins. It is reported that the Prophet warned that a mother who conceals the true identity of the father of her child has committed a great sin. Likewise, a father who denies paternity of his child has earned universal disgrace and committed a great sin. It is possible that a child be conceived and born out of wedlock, but without breaking the law; such a circumstance could arise in a case where one person is mistaken for another in the dark and when half asleep. If such a child, although guiltlessly conceived, is not acknowledged by the father, then according to all four major schools of law, only the mother will have any rights concerning the child and it will belong to her line of descent; the father is punished by complete exclusion from any family relationship with the child, and has no claims on it. This is also the case where a husband denies paternity of his wife's child – such a denial is always succeeded by an irrevocable divorce. Thus, a man who wrongfully impregnates a woman is punished for his wrongdoing by the denial of any rights to the child, and the woman is also punished by the denial of any support or maintenance from the father.

There is some latitude in the rulings of the various schools which, to some extent, mirror the reasoning behind the idea of the 'sleeping foetus', that is compassion for human failings and an attempt to limit moral damage. The care and upbringing of a child is considered a great privilege and honour. A man who carelessly and illicitly causes the conception of a child is not worthy to be a father. All schools agree, however, that a mother's rights cannot be denied and that her claims on the child cannot be terminated, although the care and protection of the infant is the principal consideration.

Where there is a dispute between parents over the custody of a child the 'ulama' agree that the parent who seems to have the child's best interests at heart is to be preferred. Ibn al Qayyim held that the mother is to be preferred, citing the views of Companions of the Prophet in his support. Nevertheless there are different approaches in the different schools of law. In principle, all schools of law agree that children are better off with their mothers until they are about seven years old, the notional age of reason. The Shafi'is assert that a boy or girl is free to choose which parent to live with as soon as they are capable of making a choice, at about seven years old. Some Mālikī 'ulama', and those of the Hanafī school, hold that a girl should continue to stay with her mother at least until puberty, because a mother will be more concerned about a daughter's upbringing. The Hanbalīs disagree; they claim that a father will be more concerned about a daughter's upbringing and that therefore he should have custody of a daughter over the age of seven. The Hanafīs consider that from the age of seven, boys are better off with their fathers.

Conclusion

Although there is a variety of interpretation and expression among Muslim scholars and jurists, the 'ulama' all agree that the family, and marriage and motherhood as the foundations of the family, are the most important institutions of the *ummah* – the 'extended family' of Muslims. On this foundation it is possible to build a variety of different family structures, all of them equally viable under *sharī'ah*. Marriage and blood relationships define the family in Islam, but Muslim families may take many forms. They may be nuclear, or extended, polygamous or monogamous, patrilocal or matrilocal – none of these is prescribed or proscribed under Muslim law. What is prescribed are the rights and obligations of partners in a marriage, parents and children – both infant and adult – and brothers and sisters. Other relationships, such as cousin, uncle or aunt, grandparent and suchlike, entail different rights and duties according to different '*ulama*'.

The place of women in Islam is, for many people, symbolised by their place in the mosque. By tradition men pray in the main hall, while, in accordance with conventional views of modesty, the women pray in the section set either behind the men or in a gallery to the rear of the main hall. The classical authorities assert that women may lead the prayers only for other women and only in the absence of a man. However, according to both at-Tabari and ibn Sa'd, two generally reliable reporters of *ḥadīth*, the Prophet Muhammad appointed a woman, one um-Waraka, to lead the prayers for both the men and women of her household.

Sunni legislation on the place of women in Islam draws on a rich and complex tradition. This tradition embraces many differences of authoritative opinion on a number of issues. Such differences emphasise the personal moral and spiritual responsibilities of all Muslims, men and women equally, in making their own choices within a living tradition. Religious orthodoxy permits a far wider range of choice than is generally allowed by social convention within any one society. Where the '*ulama*' consider that conventional norms are in accord with *sharī'ah*, they uphold convention. Conventions, however, change and the leading '*ulama*', such as Ibn Taymiyyah, amended the legislation in response to this for *sharī'ah* is God-given and immutable, but Muslim law was developed by Muslim jurists in response to the needs of individuals and the community. Because an '*alim* is not a priest, nor in any sense a consecrated person, for there are none in Islam, any Muslim, man or woman, may become an authority on Muslim law – an '*alim*. In this sense there is perfect spiritual and intellectual equality between men and women under the laws of Sunni Islam.

However, the relationship between Muslim society and Muslim law, and thus the status of women in society and under the law, is complex and subtle. In part this is because Muslim law adapted to endorse some of the conventions or norms of the societies in which it developed; this is the usual Sunni practice, but this does not mean that the social conventions themselves are intrinsic and necessary features of Muslim law. The range of opinion, outlined above, on the degree to which women are free to contract marriages independent of any legal guardian, including their fathers, is a case in point. A further difficulty is that Muslim law is identified with cultural tradition, often quite wrongly. For example, many Muslim women are denied education, their legal inheritance and their entitlement to economic independence because they, and their families, are ignorant of the law and assume that conservative local tradition is identical with Muslim law when in reality such traditions are inversions of the law. Muslim religious law is not the same as social conservatism. The life of Zeinab al-Ghazali, a Sunni Muslim revivalist, was highly unconventional and yet wholly in accord with traditional Sunni thought and with the letter of Muslim law.

The action of Ibn Taymiyyah (see above) in changing the letter of Muslim law on divorce to preserve the equity between men and women intended by the revered *khalīfah* 'Umar in fulfilment of *sharī'ah*, demonstrated the essential purpose of Muslim law: that as an expression of the *Sharī'ah* it must respond and adapt to different social contexts to maintain its purpose. The central purpose of Muslim law is to establish and preserve social justice and to proclaim the equality of all individuals before the law as an expression of the equality of all before God. With greater freedom comes greater liability – as illustrated in the lesser penalties enacted for the enslaved than for the free. However, not all the *'ulama'* agreed that women were more volatile and prone to error than men. Two of the greatest, at-Tabari, cited above, and Ibn 'Arabi, an Andalucian religious thinker and arguably the greatest mystic of the classical era, asserted that personal qualities could not be limited by gender, and that great minds and great spirits were as likely to be found among women as among men. This view is also part of Sunni legal heritage.

NOTES

1. The feminine of *'alīm* is *'alīmah*. While an *'alīm* is a religious scholar, an *'alīmah* popularly signifies a disreputable female entertainer. The connotations of the English words master and mistress offer the closest analogy.
2. The Maliki school institutes a more detailed ritual for *ghusl*. The dedications in Arabic follow the *niyyah* or the expression of intention that precedes every voluntary act of spiritual or ethical significance. Other *'ulama'* merely recommend *ghusl* (as *sunnah*) after touching a dead body, and it is not obligatory.
3. Ghunaim, Ahmad (1980) *Al-Ma'ah Mundhu an-Nash'a Baina At-Takrim*, Cairo, Al-Kailani, p. 144.
4. Musallem (1983) *Sex and Society in Islam*, Cambridge, Cambridge University Press.
5. Although she is honoured by the Sunni Muslims, the Shi'ah execrate her because of her opposition to Ali, the fourth caliph and son-in-law of the Prophet.
6. M. Paul (1975) *Loving God for Himself Alone. An Appreciation of the Prayers of a Muslim Mystic, Rabi'ah of Basrah*, Oxford, SLG Press, p. 7.
7. Ahmed, L. (1992) *Women and Gender in Islam. Historical Roots of a Modern Debate*, Yale University Press, p. 200.
8. *khumor*, (sing. *khimar*) here translated as 'veils' as is usual, according to most commentators, were more or less ornamental scarves worn by the women of pre-Islamic Arabia. They commonly covered the top of the head and flowed over the back; they were worn with a tunic which exposed the breasts.
9. 'portions' refers to *mahr*, the marriage gift from the groom to the bride.
10. See also S. 4 v19–21 and notes 17–21 in the Asad translation.
11. Zahra, Abu M. (ed.) (1963) *Usbu al Fiqh al Islami*, Cairo, al Majlis al A'la li Ri'ayat al Funun, p. 66.
12. Jassas, Al (1927) *Ahkam al Quran*, 3 vols, Cairo, Abd al Rahman Muhammad, vol. 1, p. 443.
13. Zahra, Abu (ed.) (1963) *Usbu al Fiqh al Islami*, Cairo, al Majlis al A'la li Ri'ayat al Funun, pp. 683–4.

FURTHER READING

Abbot, N. (1946) *Two Queens of Baghdad. Mother and wife of Harun al-Rashid*, republished Al-Saqi Books in 1986.

'Abd al 'Ati, Hammudah (1977) *The Family Structure in Islam*, American Trust Publications.

(A valuable study using primary classical sources. Professor 'Abd al 'Ati was an *'alīm* trained at the University of Al-Azhar, the most important centre of Sunni Muslim scholarship.)

Ahmed, L. (1992) *Women and Gender in Islam. Historical Roots of a Modern Debate*, Yale University Press.

Asad, Muhammad (1980) *The Message of the Qur'ān Dār al-Andalus*, Gibraltar (distributed by Dār Al-Taqwa Ltd, 7a Melcombe St., London N.W.1).

(The most convincing English language translation of the Qur'an, with superb explanatory notes. Most useful to read in conjunction with another translation such as: Ali, Abdullah Yusuf (1946) *The Holy Qur'an. Text Translation and Commentary*, The Islamic Education Centre, P.O. Box 6720, Jeddah, Saudi Arabia.)

Musallem, B. (1983) *Sex and Society in Islam. Birth Control Before the Nineteenth Century*, Cambridge, Cambridge University Press.

Paul, M. (1975) *Loving God for Himself Alone, An Appreciation of the Prayers of a Muslim Mystic, Rabi'ah of Basra*, Oxford, SLG Press.

Pickthall, M.M. (1977) *The Meaning of the Glorious Koran. Text and Explanatory Translation*, Muslim World League.

Schleifer, Aliah (1986) *Motherhood in Islam*, Cambridge, The Islamic Academy.

(This text was approved by the Islamic Research Academy of Al-Azhar and is a thorough study using primary classical sources.)

5. Judaism

Alexandra Wright

Introduction

Judaism is the religious culture of the Jewish people. The central religious teaching of Judaism is the belief in one God and the duty to love God. This affirmation is found in the Hebrew scriptures (Deut. 6:4–5) and repeated in the Jewish liturgy in the daily morning and evening service:

> Hear, O Israel: the Eternal One is our God, the Eternal God is One. And you shall love your Eternal God with all your heart, with all your soul and with all your strength. . .

Belief in and love of God are borne out by another teaching essential to Judaism: 'You shall love your neighbour as yourself' (Lev. 19:18). Love of God and love and respect for one's fellow human beings characterise the religion of the Jewish people. The laws, practices, rituals and customs that have evolved over a very long period of time, are considered to be the means whereby one strives for the ideal relationship with God and with God's creatures.

The Hebrew Bible

The earliest stage in the history of the Jewish people is told through a collection of narratives found in the Hebrew Bible. It is the story of the migrations of a family and its descendants. That family, and later community, had entered into a covenant with God, obedience to which gave the Israelite community a special status in the eyes of

113

their God (Exod. 19:5–6). The essence of the covenant was its laws: prescriptions governing all aspects of the life of the individual, the family and the community of Israel.

The women of the Hebrew Bible are both the subjects of legislation, for example on slavery or divorce, and they are, themselves, subjects of narratives or historical accounts. While it is difficult to generalise about the position of women in such a diffuse work of literature, it is perhaps possible to say that the women of the Hebrew Bible enjoy a particular status both privately and publicly in the domains which they inhabited. The matriarchs of the book of Genesis, Sarah, Rebekah, Leah and Rachel, are portrayed not only in their domestic roles as wives and mothers, but also as individuals whose lives contributed to the course of Jewish history. Deborah, in the Book of Judges, and the prophetesses Miriam and Huldah represent women who occupied important leadership roles in ancient times, while the 'virtuous woman' in the Book of Proverbs (chapter 31) represents the idealisation of a woman who works hard for her household, who enters into negotiations to buy and sell, who is charitable, kind, wise and respected because of the work she undertakes.

There are, too, other role models in the Hebrew Bible, from whom contemporary women have drawn inspiration: Hagar, the single mother who is made homeless by the father of her child and his wife; Tamar, the daughter of King David, who is raped by her brother (2 Sam. 13); Yael, in the Book of Judges, whose courage and fearlessness are imitated by Judith in the Apocrypha; and Ruth, whose loyalty to her mother-in-law, Naomi, is held up as an example of a woman who forsook her own people to join the culture and religion of her new family. The five daughters of Zelophehad (Num. 27) provide an interesting example of women whose influence brought about a change in the inheritance law, which subsequently allowed women to inherit property from their father if there were no sons. In the mythical narrative of the Garden of Eden, the first woman, Eve, plays a crucial role in Jewish tradition, not as catalyst of a 'fall' – a concept which is foreign to Judaism, but as a woman who desired wisdom (Gen. 3:6) and whose role in these chapters is somehow inevitable, if not ordained in the divine scheme of things.[1]

The heterogeneity of the Hebrew Bible, its contradictions, the diversity of its literary genres and the different stylistic uses of the

Hebrew language, reflect a wide variety of portrayals of, and attitudes to, women, not to mention the constantly changing circumstances of Israel's history.[2]

Intertestamental literature

It is not possible to say with any certainty at what point the corpus of books of the Hebrew Bible became canonised, that is to say, a recognised, authoritative collection which excluded other literature. There is a little evidence that suggests this might have begun happening as early as the second century BCE. From this period and earlier, until the second century CE, the Jewish literature of the Greek and Roman world, the non-canonical literature of Judaism, conveys the developments that were taking place in the Jewish community. Again, it contains different literary genres: apocalypses, narrative fiction, testaments and history, not to mention the works of Josephus and Philo. The centuries that spawned this literature witnessed great religious turmoil and upheaval, and culminated tragically for the Jewish people in the destruction of the Temple in Jerusalem in 70 CE and the end of the Jewish commonwealth and independence. Some of the narratives and Wisdom literature of this period reflect an attitude to women and their position in society, but there are, too, epitaphs and inscriptions and other archives that offer us a more reliable source for a picture of women's lives in the diaspora world of late antiquity.

Excavated inscriptions from this period demonstrate that women held titles of leadership and seemed to take a more active part in synagogue life than they were destined to do at a later date. Certain women are described as *archisynagogissa* ('head of synagogue') and *presbytera* ('elder' or 'member of council').

The Dead Sea Scrolls provide a remarkable insight into community life and biblical interpretation during this period. Indeed, some of the interpretation by the parties of the Pharisees, Sadducees or Essenes is decidedly idiosyncratic. For example, the Pentateuch gives no direct ruling on whether a niece may marry her uncle. Pharisaic and rabbinic Judaism legitimises this union on the basis of the silence of the Torah, and even praises it as a particularly generous act comparable to the lovingkindness shown to the poor and needy (*Yevamot* 62b). However, the Qumran Essenes regarded the union as 'fornication':

> Moses said 'You shall not approach your mother's sister [i.e., your aunt]; she is your mother's near kin' (Lev. 18:13). But although the laws against incest are written for men, they also apply to women. When therefore a brother's daughter uncovers the nakedness of her father's brother, she is (also his) near kin.[3]

Rabbinic Judaism

Until the Pharisaic revolution had marginalised almost completely expressions of non-rabbinic Judaism, Jewish life in the ancient Hellenistic and Roman world was characterised by its heterogeneity. The destruction of the Temple, the centre of almost continuous Jewish worship and sacrifice since the days of King Solomon, was a catastrophe for the Jews, but it was not unmitigated. The Pharisaic movement, hardly a new movement within Judaism, was to determine the pathway of Jewish history. In the last decades of Jewish independence, the Pharisees, a scholar class of Jews, had lived side by side with other sects within Judaism, notably the Sadducees, the men of the Temple. Yet there was hardly consonance in the views of these two movements. Even as the Temple was going up in flames, Pharisaic leaders, such as Johanan ben Zakkai, were suggesting that service to God could be performed as effectively in the synagogues or houses of study as within the Temple.

The Pharisees saw themselves as guardians and interpreters of the teachings of the Torah (the Five Books of Moses). But those teachings did not derive exclusively from the Pentateuch. By the side of this body of written teaching, there evolved a corpus of oral teaching. These prescriptions were more detailed, defining how the written law was to be carried out and enforced. Its authority was considered to be as great as the authority of the written Torah, for it was believed to be part of the revelation that had been received on Mount Sinai. The Oral Torah expands and defines, it resolves conflicts inherent in scripture, provides for new situations and interprets the Written Torah.

The teachers of the first and second centuries (Tannaim), notably

R. Akiva and R. Meir, had begun the work of codifying the Oral Law, but it was left to R. Judah the Prince, towards the end of the second century CE, to complete their labours. The completed work of codification is known as the Mishnah (teaching). It contains six orders, each order being concerned with a different aspect of Jewish life. One complete order is devoted to the legal status of women (*Nashim*).

Pharisaic literature is not exclusively legislative or prescriptive. Its counterpart is richly interpretative, containing legendary embellishments on the narratives of the Torah, and different theological preoccupations and viewpoints. The generic terms that are used to classify these two kinds of literature are *halakhah* (literally 'the way', law) and *aggadah* (lore).

Both genres are found in the literature of the Talmud. Discussions about women in the Mishnah and Talmud are numerous. Both deal with the legal status of women in the private and public domain, but both also deal with attitudes to women. One of the difficulties in studying this material is that the discussions are recorded by the rabbis and teachers of Jewish colleges of learning in Palestine and Babylonia. There is sparse mention of individual women, and such allusions are scarcely corroborated in other material. Mostly, we find references to women generally, and occasionally a caustic or indeed affectionate remark from one man about his mother, or his wife or daughter.

The Talmud is a very diffuse work. It does not present discussion systematically as does the Mishnah, on which it is based. It presents discussions in the form of a stream of consciousness. Its exponents pick up allusions and frequently introduce a different branch of discourse. For this reason, it was always necessary for the scholars of subsequent generations to make further clarifications of the law and to respond to new situations.

The Gaonic period (from the seventh century), and certainly the middle ages of the Islamic world and central and northern Europe, offer us further evidence for the life of women and their domestic and public roles. It is clear that Jews were often influenced by the cultures in which they lived, so that there sometimes existed a wide disparity between women in the Islamic world, for example, and more independent women of central Europe.

The discovery of a *genizah* (literally 'storing') in Cairo at the end of the nineteenth century has provided scholars with remarkable historical information concerning the preoccupation of Jews of Israel and Egypt from the ninth to the twelfth centuries. Again we are fortunate to learn more about the status and position of women in this period from some of the documents preserved.

The major literary sources of this period are medieval codes of Jewish law, reflecting both Sefardi and Ashkenazi practices, and the responsa literature, a genre of literature which has continued until the present day. The responsa literature addresses itself to individual questions posed by different communities concerning the daily religious life of individuals. Entire sections are devoted to the laws concerning women: their education, betrothal and marriage, their occupations, their duties and responsibilities towards their families and the boundaries that were set around their religious involvement in the community.

Rare are the testimonies of women themselves until the modern period. A notable exception is Glueckel of Hameln (1646–1724), whose autobiography offers a rare insight into the personal lives of women. Glueckel, a widow, had considerable commercial success and we learn that women were certainly not excluded from the world of economics or commerce.

Emancipation

The emancipation of European Jewry in the early nineteenth century had an immense influence on the intellectual and social life of the Jewish people. Women and men were faced with two choices: to retain the traditional practices and beliefs of Judaism, or harmonise their religion with their civic emancipation and thus gain from their compatriots recognition as full citizens. In response to this choice, two distinct religious movements arose in the nineteenth century: Orthodoxy and Reform. Attitudes towards women and the extent to which women are accorded full equality within these movements are shaped by the theological premise on which each movement is based, and in particular by the attitude to the authority of Written and Oral Torah.

The role of women in Judaism today is largely determined by the religious and intellectual environment in which one has grown up. The progressive Jewish movements of Israel and the diaspora accord equality to women in religious life, which means that women are permitted to lead services, become rabbis and assume those rituals that have been regarded as being exclusively for men. The Orthodox movements do not restrict women in their choice of secular career, but draw a distinction between secular and religious life. The nature of equality is different. While women may conduct services, read from the Torah and accept as binding certain obligations that were traditionally perceived to be exclusively male obligations, they may do these things for themselves and for each other, but not for a mixed congregation.

Contemporary scholarship, dealing with the place of women in Jewish life, has been enhanced considerably by feminist studies of all periods of Jewish history. The student today is beginning to claim an easier access to the lives of Jewish women of the past than has hitherto been possible. We no longer need to rely on the andro-centric sources that offer us only one insight into women's lives. The work of scholars such as Bernadette Brooten and others is offering us a completely new way of looking at women and their place in Judaism.

Beginnings

The commandment to seek out a partner for companionship and procreation derives from the Book of Genesis.

> Therefore shall a man leave his father and his mother, and shall cleave unto his wife and they shall be one flesh.

> (Gen. 2:24)

> And God blessed [the man and the woman] and God said to them: 'Be fruitful and multiply, and replenish the earth. . .'

> (Gen. 1:28)

The birth of female children is not mentioned at all in the Hebrew Bible, whereas the importance of securing a male heir is given great emphasis. While the narrator of the Book of Genesis mentions the birth and naming of each of Jacob's sons, the arrival of Jacob's daughter, Dinah, is not mentioned at all, and we learn of her existence only later. During the slavery in Egypt and the multiplication of the Israelites there, the Hebrew midwives are instructed by Pharaoh to kill all male babies and allow female children to survive. These details are indicative of the attitude towards, and position of, women in ancient near eastern society. The woman does not appear to be important to Israelite lineage. Cultic and national identity is passed through the male line.

The biblical laws surrounding childbirth also indicate that the boundaries in which women existed were materially different from those defined by and for men. A woman was rendered ritually unclean after the birth of her children, seven days and then a further thirty-three days for her male child, and for a female child fourteen days and then a further sixty-six days (Lev. 12:1–5).[4] Like many other primitive religions, the ancient form of Judaism surrounded pregnancy, birth and menstruation with many taboos and a system of strict order which defined what was considered ritually clean and ritually unclean. This was not an isolated system, but part of a larger definition of margins connected with what was considered to be holy or polluting, whether of the body or to do with the sanctuary or other areas of holiness and defilement.

A minority of Jewish women today observe these laws of isolation. For others, the emphasis is laid upon the act of welcoming the child into the covenant. For boys, this is done with the ritual of circumcision at eight days old, at which ceremony the boy is also given his Hebrew name. For girls, the ceremony is combined with an act of thanksgiving by the parents in the synagogue at no specifically defined time after the birth of the child. The elements of such a service include both the mother's and the father's expression of gratitude and thanksgiving that they have been brought through an anxious time:

> I love the Eternal One who has heard my supplications.
> Who has heeded me and whose name I will call upon all my days.
> How can I repay the Eternal One for all the divine benefits wrought unto me?
> I will offer You the sacrifice of thanksgiving and call upon the name of the Eternal One.
>
> (From Psalm 116)

The child is then given her Hebrew name. The hope that she will grow up to become a full and loyal member of the House of Israel is expressed, and God's blessing is invoked upon her life. In synagogues where women cannot be called up to recite prayers aloud, the father alone is called up without the child and given the honour of reciting the blessing over the Torah on the Sabbath following his daughter's birth.

Education

The study of the Torah is considered to be the most important of all the commandments incumbent upon the Jewish individual. The Torah here indicates the whole of Jewish tradition as transmitted through the great works of Jewish literature – the Bible, the Mishnah, the *Gemara*, medieval codes, and so forth. This commandment derives from Deuteronomy 6:7, in which each generation is commanded to teach diligently to their children the words of the *Shema*: 'Hear O Israel: The Eternal One is our God, the Eternal God is One'. Study is considered to be a form of worship leading to the observance of the commandments, and it is with that aim in mind that the rabbis made *talmud torah* (study of the Torah) central in the life of the Jew.

In traditional Jewish law (*halakhah*) the obligation to teach one's child falls on the father. Furthermore, the obligation is binding if the child is a son, but it is not binding if that child is a daughter. Women's exemption from study derives from a passage in the Mishnah and the talmudic commentary on it (*Kiddushin* 29a). The exemption of women does not mean that women may not study. Indeed, in another discussion from the Talmud (*Sotah* 20a), there is a disagreement between the second-century Tannaitic teacher, ben Azzai, and his contemporary, R. Eliezer. While ben Azzai is of the opinion that a man is under the obligation to teach his daughter Torah, R. Eliezer counters with the statement, 'Whoever teaches his daughter Torah, teaches her nonsense'. While R. Eliezer's statement received some modification in the *Gemara* (*Sotah* 21b), it was to be responsible for perpetuating the ignorance of women until more enlightened scholars realised the importance of rearing women in Jewish classical texts.

Rachel Biale makes this point in relation to an interesting paradox which emerges from the legal obligation of the father to teach his

121

son Torah and the more popular image of the mother's influence in the home:

> It is interesting to contrast the text of Kiddushin 29a which places the responsibility of preparing a child for a proper Jewish life as an adult on the *father*, with the popular image of the traditional Jewish woman. The image one encounters time and again in literature, memoirs, and sentimental and polemical writings glorifying the role of women in traditional Judaism points to the woman as the bearer of tradition in the home, and as the one who passes the heritage to her children. The relation between the image and the historical reality is an elusive problem . . . but it is important to note that the image is grounded in popular ethos, perhaps magnified by sentimentalism, and is not based on the requirements of the Halakhah.
>
> (Biale 1984, p. 30)

Just to underline this dichotomy between the *halakhah* and the experiential reality, one should record that the talmudic period knew of a number of exceptionally learned women who were singled out for their piety and knowledge. Beruriah, the wife of the second-century teacher, Rabbi Meir, is one example; Imma Shalom, the wife of Eliezer ben Hyrcanus and sister of Rabban Gamaliel of Yavneh, is another. Rachel, the wife of Akiva, valued learning in her husband and was said to have sold her hair to allow her husband to go and study.

These women follow in the footsteps of earlier examples of learning and leadership. Deborah's role as judge and prophetess is an important one in the Hebrew Bible (Judg. 4–5). She is the only one of the twelve judges in the book of that name, of whom it is said that she presides as a judge over the people. Her male counterparts all appear to be local military heroes and leaders. Her role as prophetess is not explicated, but we do know that it was a prophetess, Huldah, whom King Josiah consulted at the time when a book of law was found in the Temple in the sixth century BCE.

Observance of the commandments required knowledge of the commandments. Some practical knowledge of the basics of Jewish law was inevitably necessary. *Halakhah* prescribes three positive commandments to be undertaken specifically by women and, of course, women were obligated to observe all negative prohibitions, such as the observance of the Sabbath and the dietary rules. The three positive commandments are: the lighting of the Sabbath candles, the separation of the dough of the *hallah* (the Sabbath bread) and *niddah* (the laws of menstruation). Knowledge of these laws prepared a girl for the domestic role she was to undertake in adulthood. They symbolised her responsibility for the household and as regulator of sexual relations between her and her husband.

The difference of opinion that existed among talmudic scholars over the subject of women and learning has continued right into the twentieth century. While R. Eliezer's opinion that in teaching a woman Torah one is teaching her nonsense, is certainly not adhered to, there has, until recently, been an inequality between the education of women and that of men. It is very much the social and economic status of a family that determines whether a woman is to receive either secular or religious education. Pomona Modena, a member of the eminent Modena family of Ferrara in seventeenth-century Italy, is a model of female scholarship. She was well-versed in the Talmud. On one occasion, Rabbi David of Imola addressed a detailed responsum to her, on a point of Jewish law which only a scholar could have understood.

Bathsheba Modena, a relation of Pomona and an ancestress of the famous Leone da Modena, was an inspired poetess. She was, according to one of her grandchildren, constantly engaged in study, had considerable acquaintance with the *Zohar*, the medieval mystical commentary on the Torah, was an expert in the writings of Maimonides and undertook regular study each week. There is also some evidence to suggest that she had considerable influence on the intellectual development of the *conversa* Dona Gracia Nasi. Another outstanding woman of this period was Benvenida Abarbanel, the niece of Isaac Abarbanel, whose family had left Spain in 1492 to live in Naples. She was an educated woman who had established a good relationship with the Duchess of Tuscany and had managed to postpone a decree of expulsion of the Jews from southern Italy in 1541. After the death of her husband, Samuel, she took over his business concerns, attained important trade privileges and lived the life of a pious and charitable woman, whose home was a centre of study and culture. Immanuel Aboab, the chronicler, described her as 'one of the most noble and high-spirited matrons who have existed in Israel since the time of our dispersion; such was the Senora Benvenida Abarbanel – pattern of chastity, of piety, of prudence and of valour'.

Not all Jewish women benefitted from such a fine education. In Eastern Europe, there existed certainly among the more wealthy Jews a view which endorsed secular education for girls but which neglected Jewish learning at such an advanced level. Such learning was certainly valued, but for men, not for women. It was not unusual for a wealthy man to consider a match for his daughter to a young talmudic scholar whose breadth of knowledge would hardly match his own daughter's accomplishments in language and the arts.

Contemporary Jews agree on the importance of education for both girls and boys. In the United States of America, where the majority of Jews reside, and in Israel, universities provide programmes for men and women who wish to undertake Jewish studies at a higher level of learning. The training of women for the rabbinate in the progressive tradition, and the importance ascribed to religious education within Orthodoxy today, have also ensured a high level of learning and Jewish scholarship among women. In addition, women scholars are throwing new light on traditional subjects and unearthing new topics for discussion which reveal a higher degree of involvement by women in public Jewish life than was hitherto imagined. The influence of women's research on the contemporary practice of Judaism, particularly among women, has been far-reaching.[5]

Courtship and marriage

THE HOME

The institution of marriage and the establishment of a family have played a crucial part in ensuring the survival of Judaism. While the synagogue plays a critical role in safeguarding the institution of communal prayer and observance, and adult study, the home is the place in which the child first experiences and learns about his or her Jewish heritage. The Sabbath is welcomed every Friday evening in the home with the lighting of the candles, traditionally performed by the woman of the household. Several festivals are marked prominently in the home – notably *Pesach* (Passover), with the *seder* (a service and meal taking place round the table at home), and *Sukkot*, where a *sukkah* (booth) is built. Food and meal times play an important part in helping the Jew to define his or her identity.

Blessings both before and after the meal make the Jew conscious of the people's relationship to God and obligations to their fellow human beings; and the dietary laws remind the Jew of both the principle of *tza'ar ba'aley hayyim*, the ethical principle that prohibits cruelty to animals, and the distinctiveness of the Jewish people. These major observances all take place within the confines of the home. Though marriage may not be considered ideal for everyone in today's society, it has the potential to provide a safe context in which to bring up children and to teach them the moral values of truth and compassion which Judaism prizes so highly.

MONOGAMY AND POLYGYNY

Curiously, the Bible furnishes no prescriptions regarding the actual ceremony or act of marriage. There are plenty of accounts of marriages and partnerships, but no record of how such unions were performed. We learn from the stories of Abraham and Sarah and Hagar, Jacob, Leah and Rachel, David and Solomon, that it was not unusual in biblical times for men to acquire more than one partner and to father children through those partners. Polygyny was permitted even during the talmudic era, though women were permitted to have only one husband. However, though the Talmud goes as far as speculating on the maximum number of wives a man may have, the legislation as well as the speculation seems to have been academic. We do not know of one rabbi in the entire Talmud (out of approximately 2,800 mentioned) who was polygynous.

In the middle ages, Christianity forbade polygyny, and Jews living under Christian rule developed an aversion to, and embarrassment about, the law permitting it. The ban against polygyny is attributed to Rabbenu Gershom (960–1028), though there is evidence that such a ban had already been accepted in many communities even before his time. The ban was introduced in the form of a *takkanah*, a new ruling, which was a departure from biblical and talmudic law. It was backed by the threat of excommunication by the community and its leading rabbis. Not all Jewish communities accepted this ban. In Islamic countries, where polygyny was permitted, some Jews still married more than one wife. Indeed, when the Jews of Yemen were brought to the newly formed State of Israel in 1948, some men arrived with more than one wife. Even though Israel prohibited polygyny, these Yemenite Jews were permitted to maintain their polygynous marriages.

FAMILY LIFE

The narratives of the Hebrew Bible possess a tangible, human dimension. We do not see the portrayal of an ideal state of marriage. The conflicts and jealousies as well as the happier aspects of family life are portrayed in the narratives about Jacob and his family and many others. The account of the courtship and marriage of Isaac to Rebekah shows us that the woman possessed a certain degree of freedom in deciding whom she was to marry. Indeed, the consent of the bride remained an important principle in rabbinic Judaism. Rebekah's role is clearly as companion to her husband – we are told that Isaac was comforted by her after the death of his mother. From the story of Jacob and Rachel, we learn about the affection and devotion that can exist between a husband and wife. Jacob laboured for fourteen years, the price he paid for Rachel to become his wife, and we are told, 'it seemed but a short time for the great love he had for her'.

While lineage was passed down through the patrilineal line in biblical times, the role of the woman in marriage is not wholly a passive one. The matriarchs, Sarah, Rebekah, Leah and Rachel, are spirited individuals in their own right. Both Sarah and Rebekah are instrumental in pushing forward the younger of their husband's two sons, Isaac and Jacob, who are to occupy the centre of the stage in the unfolding biblical drama. In other words, these women are used as instruments of the divine plan. In Genesis 38, the story of Tamar, daughter-in-law of Judah, one of Jacob's sons, interrupts the narrative of Joseph to illustrate the institution of levirate marriage and to underline the prominence of the tribe of Judah in the history of Israel.

YIBBUM (LEVIRATE MARRIAGE)

The law of *yibbum* is prescribed in Deuteronomy 25:5–10:

If brethren dwell together and one of them die, and have no child, the wife of the dead shall not be married abroad to one not of his kin; her husband's brother shall go in unto her, and take her to him to wife, and perform the duty of a husband's brother unto her [*v'yib'mah*]. And it shall be, that the first-born that she bears shall succeed in the name of his brother that is dead, that his name be not blotted out of Israel. And if the man does not wish to take his brother's wife, then his brother's wife shall go up to the gate to the elders, and shall say: 'My husband's brother refuses to raise up unto his brother a name in Israel; he will not perform the duty of a husband's brother to me.' Then the elders of his city shall call him, and speak to him; and if he stand and say: 'I do not wish to take her'; then his brother's wife shall draw near to him in the presence of the elders, and undo his shoe from his foot, and spit in his face; and she shall answer and say: 'So shall be done unto the man who does not build up his brother's house.'

What lies behind the principle of levirate marriage and other institutions which were preserved by rabbinic Judaism, such as *agunah* (see below p. 135)? Under Jewish law, a girl belonged to her father. Marriage represented, on one level, the acquisition of a bride by the groom from her father. The only way she 'acquired herself', i.e., gained her independence, so to speak, was through divorce, which had to be granted to her by her husband, or on the death of her husband. Although a husband 'acquired' a wife, by 'taking' her, using the biblical and mishnaic vocabulary, she was not his property. He could not sell her, for example. The act of acquisition was to forbid her to all other men. She was to become exclusively the wife of her husband.

THE DEVELOPMENT OF MARRIAGE LAWS

How did a man 'acquire' a wife? The opening pages of the mishnaic tractate, *Kiddushin*, provide us briefly with the fundamental laws of marriage:

A woman is acquired in three ways and acquires herself in two. She is acquired by money, by deed, or by intercourse. . . . And she acquires herself by divorce or by the death of her husband. A childless widow is acquired by intercourse and acquires herself by *halitzah* (taking off the shoe) or by her brother-in-law's death.

The sum of money involved in this transaction was negligible; the act was symbolic rather than real. Its function was to designate one particular woman to be the wife of her husband. The Mishnah also cites a second way of effecting marriage: 'by deed'. This 'deed' actually refers to the bill of divorce which releases a woman from marriage. The *Gemara* deduces that since a divorce document can release a woman from marriage, it must also effect her marriage. The third way to effect the marriage was simply through intercourse.

However, though both the Mishnah and Palestinian Talmud (*Kiddushin* 1:1) state the validity of any of these three ways of marriage, the talmudic discussion that follows on the mishnaic passage reveals certain changes, and a level of disapproval of betrothal simply by intercourse. There is a measure of discomfort, as well, with the idea that betrothal can be effected through the almost negligible sum of a *perutah*. Eventually, these simple requirements developed and became more demanding, to the extent that the third-century Babylonian *amora* would punish anyone who became betrothed 'in the market place, or by intercourse, or without prior engagement, or who annulled a divorce. . .' (*Kiddushin* 12b).

The talmudic literature reflects, therefore, a change from a fairly simple code of sexual morality to a much stricter one. The biblical code consists of primary rules relating to incest (Lev. 18), perversion and adultery, laws concerned with rape and seduction and a few others.[6]

MODESTY

Rabbinic morality reflects a preoccupation with a woman's modesty. The practice of a minority of very pious married women today of covering their hair stems from the belief that a woman's appearance in public with uncovered head constituted immoral behaviour. The Palestinian Talmud (*Sotah* 16b) records that the School of Shammai, who recognised no cause for divorce other than adultery, believed that a wife's appearance in public without a head covering constituted legitimate cause for divorce. In other words it was compared to unfaithfulness.

In the sixteenth century, women started wearing a *sheitel* (wig) to cover their hair. It was worn by the bride at her marriage and throughout her married life. However, the practice was not universal. Many women rebelled against what was now an out-moded fashion and went bare-headed. Oriental Jewish women continued to use a veil, as had been used since ancient times. Although the wig is still used by pious women today, for example by the Hasidic sects, the majority of women do not cover their hair.

Rabbinic standards of modesty with respect to exposure and dress were extremely rigorous, though it was frequently the prevailing cultural attitudes that influenced Jewish responses. In the ancient Orient, for example, women wore a veil over the head and a woman of dignity would draw it down over her face. The Palestinian tradition of covering one's face continued through the middle ages. However, this practice was not widely accepted among the Jews of Babylonia, and the legislators during the Gaonic period in Babylonia and later on in Europe speak of the veiling of a woman's face as unusual.[7]

SEXUALITY AND *NIDDAH*

Two responses characterise the classical Jewish attitude towards women's sexuality. One is governed by the laws of *niddah* (menstruation). Contact with a menstruant woman was taboo, not only in Judaism, but also in other ancient cultures. Marital sex is strictly regulated by the laws of *niddah*, forbidding husband and wife contact during and after the period of a woman's menstruation and intensifying sexual contact during a period which is conducive to conception. The second attitude is characterised by legislation which prescribes what might be permitted in terms of sexual relations between a husband and wife. While *Halakhah* might permit relative freedom in sexual practices, this often created a tension with a more ascetic general attitude towards sexuality. Maimonides summarises this tension clearly:

> A man's wife is permitted to him. Therefore, whatever a man wishes to do with his wife he may do. He may have intercourse whenever he pleases and he may kiss any organ he wishes. And he may have intercourse in a natural or unnatural manner as long as he does not expend semen to no purpose. And nevertheless, the pious way is not to act lightly in this matter, and to sanctify himself during intercourse, as we have explained in the Laws of Knowledge. And he ought not to

129

deviate from the common practice, for this thing [intercourse] is really only for procreation.

(Maimonides, *Mishneh Torah*, *Issurei Bi'ah* 21:9)

What Maimonides recognises is a certain latitude in the practical aspects of the *Halakhah*, while demanding a certain degree of piety in a man's sanctification of the act of sexual intercourse. There is little doubt that this kind of legislation was directed towards the male partner, whose 'extroverted sexuality' required harnessing to the sexual rhythms of his wife. Biale points out the contrast in perceptions of male and female sexuality:

> Male sexuality is seen by the rabbis as the greater threat to familial and social structures. Male sexuality is active and egocentric, and always in danger of 'running wild'. It must be restrained through the controls of marriage, procreative duties, responsibility towards the woman, and a powerful taboo on male homosexuality and masturbation.
>
> Female sexuality is seen very differently. . . . Women are portrayed as sexually introverted and passive. . . . Though her sexuality is hidden, it is as powerful as a man's obvious eroticism, or even greater: 'A woman's passion is greater than that of a man'. (*Bava Metzi'a* 84a)

(Biale 1984, p.122)

The biblical laws of *niddah* required a woman to remain 'unclean' for seven days, to correspond with her menstrual discharge. At the end of that period she was to bring a burnt offering to make expiation for her discharge (Lev. 15:19–33). Post-biblical *halakhah*, however, required her to remain impure for up to fourteen days, a maximum of seven of menses, and a subsequent period of seven 'white days', free of bleeding. The end of this period was marked by *tevilah* (immersion) in a *mikveh*, which indicated permission to resume sexual relations between husband and wife.

After the destruction of the Temple in 70 CE, a shift took place in the laws of *niddah*, from a focus on purity and impurity to a sexual prohibition. Originally, it appears that the laws of *niddah* were designed to keep a woman away from the Temple and from sacred objects only. The laws were not intended to interfere with her daily life and work. Later on, however, the restrictions of the *niddah* applied to the private realm of husband-wife relations. The laws of *niddah* do not exclude a woman from attending the synagogue or taking a part in communal life, though some women voluntarily used to exclude themselves from the community during menstruation. The separation of husband and wife during the period of a woman's menstruation and immersion in a *mikveh* can be a powerful affirmation of a woman's sexuality. Though not all Jewish women observe these laws, many regard them as a way of renewing the marital relationship and preserving the purity of the family. Other women have evolved new rituals to mark the onset of menstruation or menopause, placing these important events in women's lives in a religious context.

VIRGINITY

Virginity was always highly esteemed and marriage required chastity of both sexes. During the Second Commonwealth we are told of specific times of the year when courting took place:

> There never were in Israel greater days of joy than the 15th of Av and Yom Kippur. On these days the daughters of Jerusalem used to walk out in white garments, which they borrowed in order not to shame anyone who had none. The daughters of Jerusalem came out and danced in the vineyards exclaiming at the same time, 'young man, lift up your eyes and see what you choose for yourself.' The beautiful among them called out, 'set your eyes on beauty for the quality most to be prized in woman is beauty'; those of them who came of noble families called out, 'Do not set your eyes on beauty but set your eyes on [good] family.' For 'Grace is deceitful and beauty is vain; but a woman that fears the Eternal One, she shall be praised.' (Proverbs 31:30) 'Look for [a good] family, for woman has been created to bring up a family.' The homely ones among them called out, 'Carry off your purchase in the name of Heaven, only on one condition – that you adorn us with jewels of gold.'
>
> (m. *Ta'anit* 4:8)

THE MARRIAGE CEREMONY

The marriage service today combines what were originally two separate ceremonies; betrothal and marriage. These two rituals were separated, usually by a year, the marriage being established when

131

both husband and wife came to live together. Some time in the middle ages the two ceremonies were combined into one for different reasons. The waiting period provided a number of problems. Betrothal was not engagement; it required an annulment through divorce to cancel it. The problem of the waiting period was dealt with in different ways by different communities. In Alexandria, for example, it was common to add a clause to the *ketubah* (the marriage contract) which was written during the *kiddushin* (the betrothal). If the groom did not take the bride home to begin their married life within a year, then the betrothal would be void. Other practices were to write an agreement making the *kiddushin* dependent on the *nissuin* (marriage) taking place, usually within a year. In Babylonia, no such conditions were attached to the *kiddushin*; instead the family took great care to protect the bride during the waiting period. Eventually the two ceremonies were merged into one.

The ceremony reflects both the contractual element of a marriage between a man and a woman, not, as already stated, in the sense that a man acquires the woman as his property, but in the sense that marriage mirrors the divine covenant that exists between God and the Jewish people. In non-Orthodox marriages, both bride and groom declare their intention to be loyal to each other and recite the betrothal formula: Behold you are betrothed to me [by this ring] according to the law of Moses and Israel. In Orthodox marriages only the man recites this formula.

Marriage is a profoundly solemn and religious occasion. It takes place beneath the *huppah* (wedding canopy), which symbolises the new home and family unit of the couple. The essence of marriage is the holiness of the union between a man and wife. Each is, so to speak, dedicated to the other, and yet they are at the same time, part of a larger family, of the community of Israel.

Post-biblical Judaism made a number of provisions protecting a woman's rights. One was a clause in the *ketubah* in which the groom promises to make substantial payments to his wife in the event of a divorce. This only partly mitigated, and mitigates, the fact that under Orthodox Jewish law, men possess the unilateral power to divorce their wives. We have already mentioned the ban attributed to Rabbenu Gershom, against polygyny and, in addition there was another ban which forbids a man to divorce a woman against her consent.

What is interesting to note, once again, is the dichotomy that exists between the prescriptive position of woman, and the historical and experiential reality of women. The status of women as defined in Jewish legislation, their characters and beliefs about them, as collected in the counterpart of *halakhah*, *aggadah* (Jewish lore), reflect the preoccupations of men rather than of the women themselves. Though to be married was considered an ideal to the extent that a man without a wife was thought to live without blessing, the overriding concern of legislation is both to protect and to control the woman, particularly in the public domain – which was reserved for men.

Women and Work

Much of women's work took place indoors, where they could be relaxed, hiding in their own apartments. Spinning, weaving, washing, cooking, baking, and grinding flour were the jobs undertaken by women in the seclusion of their homes. One remark reflects this cloistered existence, saying of the woman, that 'she is banished from people and confined to prison' (*Eruvin* 100b). However, there was cultural progress, and as the rabbis raised the level of cultural awareness in their own generations, so the position of women improved. Sometimes a wife supported her husband and worked for the family; she farmed or traded, she attended public lectures, visited the house of study, participated in synagogue services, attended weddings and funerals and could have her own social life.

In the sphere of the home, women did possess, and still do possess, a certain degree of knowledge and authority. Though legislation often marginalises the status and position of women in religious life, it does not often reflect the reality of the woman's position in the home, or indeed in the community. The three positive commandments of lighting the Sabbath candles, separating the dough from the Sabbath bread and the law of the *niddah*, do symbolise the traditional woman's role in the home and the power that she possesses in relation to her domestic and private life.

It is not surprising to note that the position of contemporary women – their freedom to work, to express themselves, to take a full part in the public sphere – has been adopted by many Jewish women. Though there remains a minority for whom traditional

Jewish law is divinely ordained, by far the majority see their Jewish tradition as engaging in a dynamic dialectic with contemporary society and its influences. The influence of modern movements such as feminism has been considerable in recent years and has played a particularly important part in helping to educate women to take an equal role in synagogue life, as we shall see.

Divorce and *agunah*

While irretrievable breakdown of marriage is recognised in Judaism and divorce permitted, the rabbis of the Talmud acknowledged the tragic aspect of divorce in the statement that when a man divorces his first wife, the very altar sheds tears (*Gittin* 90b). Biblical laws of divorce are not systematic or detailed :

> A man takes a wife and possesses her. She fails to please him because he finds some indecency about her, and he writes her a bill of divorcement, hands it to her, and sends her away from his house; she leaves his household and becomes the wife of another man, then the second man rejects her, writes her a bill of divorcement, hands it to her, and sends her away from his house; or the man who married her last dies, then the husband who divorced her first shall not take her to wife again, since she has been defiled – for that would be abhorrent to the Lord. You must not bring sin upon the land which the Lord your God is giving you as a heritage.
>
> (Deut. 24:1–4)

These verses appear to characterise that tension in Judaism which, on the one hand, accepts divorce, but on the other, sees it as profoundly regrettable. A man and a woman who have become divorced from each other are not permitted to remarry each other, because they have been 'defiled' – or rather the woman has been 'defiled' by a second man. This ambivalent attitude towards divorce is also borne out by legislation that forbids a priest to marry a divorcee (Leviticus 21), though they were not forbidden to divorce their wives.

Despite these vestiges of anti-divorce legislation, post-biblical *halakhah* accepts divorce as legitimate. The *get*, which is the bill of divorcement given by a man to his wife, essentially releases her from the marriage and permits her to another man should she wish to remarry. The grounds for a divorce to take place are given in the Bible as 'some indecency' (*ervat davar*), but inherent in this simple formulation are multiple problems which are the subject of this discussion in the Talmud (*Gittin* 90a–b):

> The School of Shammai held that a man should not divorce his wife unless he has found her guilty of some sexual misconduct, while the School of Hillel say that he may divorce her even if she has merely spoiled his food. Rabbi Akiva he may divorce her even if he simply finds another woman more beautiful than she.

Each of these opinions is substantiated by a scriptural verse, quoted in support of each of the three opinions.

However, the legislation on divorce does not stop there. Two important factors were introduced to protect a woman from being divorced against her will and leaving her without any financial support. One was the medieval ban, traditionally ascribed to Rabbenu Gershom, which was introduced as a counter to the talmudic statement that a woman may be divorced with her consent or without it (*Yevamot* 112b). The new law made a divorce given to a woman against her will, null and void. The second factor was the *ketubah* (the marriage document), introduced much earlier, which outlined the obligations of the husband towards the wife and included financial arrangements in case the marriage ended through divorce or the husband's death.

Despite the complexity of divorce legislation which developed in the post-biblical period, a woman remained vulnerable. She still could not initiate a divorce, and, more seriously, if her husband refused to grant her a divorce, she could find herself in the position of being an *agunah* (chained woman).

The *agunah* is a woman who is not free to remarry. If her husband has disappeared, or is presumed dead, or if he refuses to grant her a religious divorce, if she remarries she is deemed to be an adulteress and her children will be *mamzerim* (offspring of an illicit union). This is the most serious problem that confronts Orthodox Jewish courts today. Particularly in the wake of the *Shoah* (Holocaust), the position of *agunot* is an intolerable and tragic one. Non-Orthodox Judaism has found methods to circumvent this law and permit *agunot* to remarry.

Synagogue, prayer and the commandments

Judaism teaches that God guides humanity. This guidance is presented in terms of the *mitzvot*, the commandments. Orthodox Jews understand the *mitzvot* to have originated at Mount Sinai. Progressive Jews see the *mitzvot* as the religious responses of individuals and generations to the economic, social and political conditions of their era. They see those responses continuing even today, with the need for a certain elasticity in the way they respond to the changing circumstances of their time. However, the principles of Judaism do not change – the strict search for truth, the need for justice to be tempered by compassion, absolute equality for men and women of all races, creeds and nations – these are the certainties with which one starts when formulating an answer to the question: What is it that God requires of us?

Traditional Judaism acknowledges a structure of 613 commandments which are variously derived from the Torah. Several attempts were made, especially in the middle ages to list these commandments, 365 negative commandments and 248 positive commandments. The great majority of the *mitzvot* apply equally to both women and men. This is especially true of the negative commandments. But there were exceptions, and these fall into two categories: those *mitzvot* which are specifically linked to gender, such as circumcision for a man and the laws of menstruation for a woman; and commandments which are not directly related to biological differences, but which are, nevertheless, gender based.

Women's exemption from certain laws derived from a principle which was laid down in the Talmud (*Kiddushin* 33b). Women were exempt from all positive commandments that are time-bound. Exemption here does not mean prohibition; it means that women are permitted to observe those positive commandments which are linked with a specific time if they wish to take the duty upon themselves, but they do not have to. So, for example, women are exempt from the obligation to dwell in the *sukkah* on the Feast of Tabernacles. They do not have to hear the *shofar* on the New Year and Yom Kippur; they are exempt from the obligation of wearing *tzitzit* ('fringes') or *tefillin* ('phylacteries'). This is not a general rule, for there are exceptions. Women must observe the commandment to eat unleavened bread at *Pesach*, even though this is a positive commandment linked to a specific time. Also there are certain commandments which are positive and not time-bound from which women are exempt, such as study of the Torah (see above), procreation[8] and redemption of the first-born son. Though women were permitted to perform all these commandments, the reality was that they did not take on these *mitzvot* until recently, when the *halakhah* began to be studied by women who discovered a range of observances that had been closed to them for a variety of reasons.

Mostly the reasons justifying female exemption from these laws were domestic. David ben Joseph Abudarham, a medieval commentator, explains the reason for the exemption of women from time-bound positive *mitzvot* as due to a basic conflict between the commands of God and the demands of a husband:

> The reason women are exempt from time-bound positive *mitzvot* is that a woman is bound to her husband to fulfil his needs. Were she obligated in time-bound positive *mitzvot*, it could happen that while she is performing a *mitzvah*, her husband would order her to do his commandment. If she would perform the commandment of the Creator and leave aside his commandment, woe to her from the husband! If she does her husband's commandment and leaves aside the Creator's, woe to her from her Maker! Therefore, the Creator has exempted her from his commandments, so that she may have peace with her husband.

It would appear that women were exempt from commandments which fell outside the domestic sphere; commandments to do with prayer, study, reading from the Torah are all duties which fall within the realm of a man's religious existence, according to the *halakhah*. Therefore, the exemption of women is not a legal-logical principle, according to Rachel Biale, but a social-cultural one. Biale's commentary to the passage from *Sefer Abudarham*, quoted above, shows an astute understanding of the position of women in relation to their men-folk:

> The rivalry between God and husband over female obedience is not merely a picturesque way of explaining the exemption of women from certain *mitzvot*. Indeed it seems to underscore a profound point, though I am not sure it was one intended by the author of *Sefer Abudarham*. The halakhic and religious position of women is strained by a tension between two views of women. God, in the "rivalry" of our text, holds a fundamental theological and ethical position which recognizes no

137

stratification of human beings, no inferiority of women to men. All persons are of equal value, spiritually and morally, and all human life is equally sanctified. On the other hand, the husband represents an attitude grounded in daily life and social reality, where there are distinctions of religion, class, learning and of course, gender. Women are inferior to men in economic power, social standing, legal rights, and religious role and importance. While in ultimate moral and spiritual terms a woman's life is equal to a man's, her concrete, day-to-day life is marked by subservience to men. This tension appears in Genesis in the two creation myths. In one account woman is created equally with man "in God's image," and in the other account is created to meet man's needs.

This tension in the woman's position in Jewish law is reflected in terms of her obligation to pray. While women are obligated to pray, they are exempt from reciting the twice-daily recited affirmation of belief, the *Shema*, because it is a positive commandment which is linked to a specific time, namely the evening and the morning. We see here that women shared a secondary role in religious life, together with slaves and minors. The result of this specific exemption was that women exempted themselves generally from the act of public, communal prayer and women's prayer became associated with an act of private, personal worship. Various prohibitions compounded this division between 'men's prayer' and 'women's prayer'. Women were not permitted to be counted in a *minyan* (the quorum of ten men required for any act of public worship). Though they were legally permitted to read from the Torah, they did not do so on account of the 'honour of the congregation'. The fear was that if a woman was called to read she would show up the male members of the congregation who perhaps did not possess the technical skill required to be able to read from the Torah. The segregation of women from men in synagogue was another factor in reducing the participation of women in synagogue services.

Orthodox scholars today are divided in their response to the question of whether women may take a full part in public ritual and prayer. In the United States of America, Orthodox rabbis do allow women to conduct their own services, read from the Torah and assume those responsibilities which were originally in the domain of male worship. However, women are still not permitted to undertake those duties on behalf of men. In Great Britain, the role of the women is greatly restricted. Women are not allowed to conduct their own services on the premises of a synagogue, but only in a private home.

The non-Orthodox movements do permit full participation of women in services, with a few exceptions. Women may don *tefillin* if they so wish, they may wear a *tallit* for morning services, they pray equally with men and can lead the services on behalf of a mixed congregation. Women have been ordained as rabbis since 1972 in the United States of America and since 1975 in Great Britain. Women are also permitted to assume roles of leadership and act as witnesses, which Orthodox *halakhah* prohibits. Such changes are a classic example of Judaism responding to the religious needs of the Jewish woman in contemporary society, without losing sight of those prophetic principles of strict justice and truth which are the pillars on which the religion is founded and which sustain its existence.

NOTES

1. I am grateful to Rabbi Rachel Montagu who underlined this point in a sermon in which she said that the work of a gardener is not as long-term as the work of *tikkun olam* (repair of the world).
2. For further reading on women in the Bible see Trible, Phyllis (1976) 'Depatriarchalizing in Biblical Interpretation', in *The Jewish Woman*, Elizabeth Koltun (ed.) New York, Schocken; Trible (1984) *Texts of Terror* and (1978) *God and the Rhetoric of Sexuality*, both Philadelphia, Fortress.
3. Cairo Damascus Rule v, 7–9; Temple Scroll LXVI, 16–17. For a clear description of the Jewish sects in this period and the historical context see Maccoby, Hyam (1989) *Judaism in the First Century*, London, Sheldon Press; Vermes, Geza (1987) *The Dead Sea Scrolls in English* (rev. edn), Harmondsworth, Penguin, which provides helpful introductory essays on the history and religious ideas of the Qumran community.
4. Rachel Biale in (1984) *Women and Jewish Law*, New York, Schocken, suggests that 'the birth of a female, who will one day herself menstruate and give birth is seen as "doubly bloody" and doubly impure'.
5. For a discussion on the subject of literature for women from the middle ages onwards, and in particular pious paraphrases of the Hebrew Bible into Yiddish, see Brayer, Menachem M. (1986) *The Jewish Woman in Rabbinic Literature, A Psychohistorical Perspective*, vol. 2, New York, Ktav, pp. 114–19.

6. See Epstein, Louis M. (1948) *Sex Laws and Customs in Judaism* (rep. 1967), New York, Ktav.
7. Epstein, *Sex Laws and Customs in Judaism*, Chapter 2.
8. While one might assume that the biblical injunction 'Be fruitful and multiply' (Gen. 1:28) is addressed to both men and women, since both participate in the procreative act as equal partners, the *Halakhah* makes procreation the duty of the man only. Rachel Biale's explanation for this rabbinic exegesis that goes against the plain meaning of the Torah is helpful here: 'Why do [the rabbis] go to such lengths to exempt women from the duty of procreation? I believe that there are two primary reasons. The first is a general sentiment regarding procreation. It seems that the rabbis took it as self-evident that women had a natural desire to bear children. Men, on the other hand, were seen as torn between familial "instincts" and other powerful motivations such as learning and economic activity. For men it was necessary to mandate procreation as a duty to assure that other activities did not take precedence. For women it was seen as unnecessary, and perhaps "unnatural". The second reason may have been to allow contraception in some circumstances.' (pp. 202–3).

FURTHER READING

Biale, Rachel (1984) *Women and Jewish Law*, New York, Schocken.
Brayer, Menachem M. (1986) *The Jewish Woman in Rabbinic Literature*, New York, Ktav.
Epstein, Louis (1948) *Sex Laws and Customs in Judaism*, New York, Ktav.
Heschel, Susannah (ed.) (1983) *On Being a Jewish Feminist*, New York, Schocken.
Koltun, Elizabeth (ed.) (1976) *The Jewish Woman*, New York, Schocken.
Trible, Phyllis (1978) *God and the Rhetoric of Sexuality*, Philadelphia, Fortress Press.

6. Sikhism

Kanwaljit Kaur-Singh

Sikhism is one of the youngest of the world religions, being a little over five hundred years old. Guru Nanak, the founder of Sikhism, was born in 1469 CE at a particularly difficult period of history for women throughout the Indian sub-continent, an age when women were not considered fit for independence at any stage of their lives. They were tied by the shackles of such customs as purdah, *satī* and female infanticide. The plight of women had been made even more miserable by the invaders who took women away as slaves and sold them as cattle in foreign markets.

Guru Nanak and the other nine Gurūs who followed him advocated equal status for women with men in all spheres of life. They condemned the then prevalent customs which perpetuated the inferiority of women. The Gurūs felt the need to rehabilitate women to a place of honour if Indian society as a whole was to be saved. Guru Nanak honoured women by saying:

> In a woman, man is conceived,
> From a woman he is born
> With a woman he is betrothed and married.
> With a woman he contracts friendship.
> If one dies another one is sought for,
> Man's destiny is linked to woman.
> Why denounce her, the one from whom even great people are born?
> From a woman, a woman is born,
> None may exist without a woman.

> (Gurū Granth Sāhib: 473)

Guru Nanak asserted that men and women shared the grace of God

141

equally and were responsible for their deeds before him. He said: 'All (women as well as men) acknowledge the same God as their own. Point out who does not. Each person is responsible for his/her account him/herself' (Gurū Granth Sāhib: 474). According to Bhai Gurdas,[1] 'Woman is one half of the complete personality of man and is entitled to share secular and spiritual knowledge equally' (*Gurdās Jī Vār 5, Paurī* 16:59). Guru Amar Das, the third Gurū, respected woman for her creativity and said, 'Blessed is the woman who creates life' (Gurū Granth Sāhib: 32). The Sikh Gurūs not only taught equality of women with men, they took steps to implement those teachings in real-life situations. The Sikh congregation, *saṅgat*, was opened to both women and men, and women took part in the prayers, leading them and reading and reciting the scriptures. *Saṅgat* is a group of persons, men, women and children, who gather together in a gurdwara or any other place to read or listen to the recitation of the Gurūs' hymns in praise of God. The Gurūs' *bāṇī* or *śabad*s (hymns) are in poetry and are sung in deep devotion.

Since the days of Guru Nanak the Sikh congregation has comprised male and female disciples of Sikhism. Hari Ram Gupta wrote in his *History of the Sikhs* (Gupta 1973: 162) that Guru Nanak allowed women to attend his sermons along with men and all joined in the chorus in singing hymns. No social custom was ever to hinder women from joining the congregation along with men. Out of twenty-two *maṅjī*s[2] established by the third Gurū for the preaching of Sikhism, four were held by women. He also appointed fifty-two women missionaries to educate women in the 'three Rs' and to spread the message of Sikhism.

Guru Nanak also welcomed women to *paṅgat* (*laṅgar*) and offered them a seat side by side with men. This Sikh institution of *laṅgar*, or community meal, symbolises the equality of humanity. Men and women worked together in the *laṅgar* – drawing water from the well, grinding corn, collecting fuel, cooking food, distributing food and cleaning the dishes. This food, prepared by men and women of mixed backgrounds, was eaten by all, inmates and visitors alike, sitting in rows affirming their new sense of community which was founded on the equality of humanity.

The Sikh institutions of *saṅgat* and *paṅgat* inculcated a strong sense of community links, and women felt for the first time that they were an integral part of the community. They became active participants and worked for the betterment of the community. The

142

Sikh Gurūs placed great importance on the institution of *langar* in the *dharamsālā*s (places of religious worship that provided food and lodging; later on the Sikh *dharamsālā*s became known as gurdwaras), and by encouraging male Sikhs to work in the *langar*, the Gurūs gave dignity to household chores and broke the myth that cooking and cleaning are menial tasks fit for women only.

The Gurūs, by emphasising that the Sikhs should give food and shelter to the needy in their own homes as well as in the gurdwaras, and by involving males and females in cooking and cleaning, not only inculcated brotherhood but also showed the importance of woman's contribution to the welfare of society. S. Harbans Singh (1984: 182) wrote:

In a way the Guru (Guru Nanak) advocated and allowed much more equality for women in the fifteenth century than the freedom and equality which has existed in the twentieth century. He wanted to build a nation of self-respecting men and women with equal dignity. He considered that without the active participation of women in all walks of life, the social structure was not only weak but incomplete.

When, on *Baisākhi* Day in 1699 CE, Guru Gobind Singh was preparing *amrit* (baptismal water) with the double-edged sword, his wife, Mata Sundri (also known as Jito), added sugar crystals (*patasa*s) as her contribution. The Gurū received this gratefully and remarked, 'We filled the *Panth* (community) with *bīr ras* (heroism) and you have mixed with it *prem ras* (love).' The *Panth* would be not only strong but sweet-tempered as well. The Gurū gave equality to women, and this spontaneous act of the Gurū's wife made the initiation whole. Had it not been the Sikh Gurūs' teachings of equality of women with men, the action of the Gurū's wife would, according to the existing rites, have polluted and defiled the ceremony.

The tenth Gurū, Guru Gobind Singh, gave *amrit* (Sikh initiation) to men and women alike. There is no distinction made in the injunctions about the maintenance of the five Ks – the symbols of Sikh faith. At the time of *amrit* a man is given the name Singh, meaning lion, the woman is given the name Kaur, meaning princess – a positive discrimination in woman's favour to enhance her position. A Sikh woman is an individual in her own right; she does not have to take her husband's name.

143

Family life

The teaching of the Gurūs exalted the status of woman by regarding her as indispensable for man's spiritual growth and morality, and they gave the highest dignity to married life. Those who seek salvation need not keep themselves aloof from women, or treat their company as a sinful barrier to spiritual effort. He repudiated the prevalent notion that a woman was 'inherently evil' and rejected the idea that she was a 'temptation'. She was not a hindrance in the way of a man aspiring for communion with God, but a helping hand in the achievement of salvation. A.C. Bannerjee (1978: 29) wrote that 'the concept of woman as man's helpmate became one of the distinctive features of Sikh society. This was the first step towards the liberation of women from crippling social restraints'.

The Gurūs abhorred the prevalent custom of a male leaving the home and sometimes even renouncing his wife and children and going to the forests and monasteries for spiritual attainment. Guru Nanak said: 'Living within the family life, man can obtain salvation' (Gurū Granth Sāhib: 661). Again he said: 'God himself infuses His devotion, in family life persons remain unattached. . . . Who is the family man and who is the detached one? . . . he alone is approved as a householder or renouncer, who accepts him' (Gurū Granth Sāhib: 1329).

The Gurūs honoured woman by giving a new sanctity to marriage. If completeness of life were taken as a unit, a woman was one half and a man was the other. Guru Nanak described the escapist celibate as escaping from social responsibilities. He did not regard celibacy as a passport to heaven and marriage as a barrier. The Gurūs, by preaching equal partnership of man and woman in married life, gave a higher value to renunciation – the real renunciation of selfish motives – which would produce actions of self-denial, love and sacrifice. Men and women living in the world ought to be above worldly pettiness. Guru Nanak said:

As the lotus thrusts upwards and does not drown in water,
As the duck swims and does not become wet while swimming,
so can we cross,
safely and naturally,
the ocean of existence

144

by attuning our minds to the word of the Guru
and repeating the holy name of God.

(Gurū Granth Sāhib: 938)

The Gurū laid stress on ascetic virtues without the need to renounce
family life: abide pure, amid the world's impurities. The Sikh Gurūs
pointed out that those hermits and mendicants who renounced the
world and considered themselves holy and pious, came back to the
family man's door for food. Guru Nanak wrote:

> For their food and clothes,
> they run from door to door.
> Without the support of householders,
> who are dubbed by them [*Yogis*] as
> ensnared in the nooses of worldly attachment,
> they cannot pursue their
> spiritual aspirations.

(Gurū¯Granth Sāhib: 879)

Celibacy is redefined in the framework of chastity. Bhai Gurdas (*Vār*
6, *Paurī* 6:65) wrote: 'He is celibate who is married to one wife only
and treats all other women as mothers, sisters or daughters'. Guru
Nanak emphasised the importance of self-restraint and self-control.
Stress is laid on moral values without having to renounce the family
and society.

> A paper with salt on it, if treated with ghee [clarified butter] dissolves
> not in water. So do the Lord's devotees abide in the midst of worldliness
> and yet remain detached.

(Gurū Granth Sāhib: 877)

Every Sikh is commanded to lead a married life and all the Gurūs
with the exception of Guru Har Krishan, the eighth Gurū, who died
at the tender age of eight, set up homes and led married lives with
their families. Although Guru Nanak came into contact with many
ascetics, Hindu and Muslim, during the two decades of his travels,
he resumed his family ties when he settled down at Kartarpur.

Guru Nanak's renunciation of asceticism was not only an original
idea, but also a significant breach with the Indian religious tradition.

145

Religion for householders had been distinguished from religion for *sannyāsis*. Many religious teachers were ascetics, guiding their followers from a distance. Guru Nanak's preference for the life of a family man was also indicated by his choice of Angad, a family man, as his successor. It was a revolutionary and also a decisive step. By barring the door to asceticism for the Gurūs, he made Sikhism a householder's religion. Guru Amar Das expressed his feelings in the following verse:

> By contemplating truth,
> light dawns,
> then amidst sensual pleasures one remains detached.
> Such is the greatness of the true Guru
> that living with his wife and children,
> one obtains salvation.

(Gurū Granth Sāhib: 661)

Because the Sikh Gurūs believed in the equality of men and women, they urged that both men and women should be taught a sound knowledge of their religion, so that, by having common religious knowledge, the couple would be better able to cultivate the same basic aims in life and thus achieve harmony of outlook. The Sikh marriage is the joining together of two equal partners, a spiritual opportunity mutually to support and enrich one another's lives. The Gurūs taught that the highest and most ideal purpose of marriage is to fuse two souls into one so that they become spiritually inseparable. The couple is expected and urged to strive after this ideal state of marriage.

The Gurūs were fully aware of the evil effects of family entanglements:

> Entanglements are mother, father and the whole world,
>   Entanglements are sons, daughters and women . . .
> By entanglements of worldly love and sin man perishes.

(Gurū Granth Sāhib: 914)

Instead of advocating escape from such entanglements, through renunciation, the Gurū asked his Sikhs to live pure among the impurities, and thus enhanced and gave dignity to the status of women who were an integral part of family life.

Monogamy

Guru Nanak's view was that marriage was monogamous. On his return home from his tour of the East after twelve years, he stayed in the jungle five kilometres away from his home town, Talwandi. His father and mother waited for him, and tried their best to persuade him to stay at home and to stop from wandering any longer. Nanak refused all the imploring of his parents, because comfortable living was not his idea of what life demanded of him. In the course of argument it was suggested that they would get him another wife, more attractive and younger. Nanak replied, 'Father dear, it is God who arranges marriages. He makes no mistake and those whom He has once joined, He joins forever' (Gupta 1973: 92).

Guru Gobind Singh refused to marry Sahib Devi, the daughter of Ram Basi, who had vowed to be the Gurū's wife from childhood. When she was brought to the Guru by her father, the Gurū explained that he was already married to Sundri and could not marry again. On her refusal to go back, the Gurū accepted her on condition that she would not have any conjugal relationship, and she was declared the Mother of the *Khalsa*.

Conjugal fidelity

Sikhism lays great stress on mutual conjugal fidelity. The Gurū said, 'He is blind who deserts his own wife and commits adultery in the meanness of his conscience' (Gurū Granth Sāhib: 1163). And again, 'Those who indulge in illicit sexual intercourse shall be punished' (*Dasam Granth*: 842). Guru Gobind Singh gave instructions on sexual matters, which were to serve as a guide to the Sikhs. These were similar to the instructions given to him by his father, Guru Tegh Bahadur. He said:

O son, as long as there is life in your body, make this your sacred duty, ever to love your own wife more and more. Approach not another woman's couch either by mistake or even in a dream. Remember that the love of another's wife is fatal, like the blow of a sharp dagger. Believe me, death enters the body by making love to another's wife. They who think it great cleverness to enjoy another's wife, shall in the end die the death of dogs.

(*Dasam Granth*: 842)

147

Visualising women in the noblest relationship, the Gurū assigned to them the role of a loving wife and companion. He advised them to cultivate the qualities of fidelity and sweet temper to bring happiness to the family. All these qualities enhance the woman's charm. Guru Nanak said: 'Go and ask the happy wives by what merits did they enjoy their spouse. They reply, by the decorations of divine knowledge, contentment and sweet discourse' (Gurū Granth Sāhib: 71). Thus, in the Gurū's eyes, only the good wife is commendable. Any sex relationship outside marriage is both unnatural and immoral. The Gurū frequently used the words *suhāgaṇ* and *duhāgaṇ*. She who practises fidelity to her husband is a queen among women, a *suhāgaṇ*, and *duhāgaṇ* is one who wanders away from her husband in dishonourable pursuits or evil ways.

Guru Nanak idealised the love of a wife for her husband by holding it up as an example for a devotee of God:

> My beloved Lord is not distant when my soul was reconciled to the word of the Guru, I found God the prop of my life. In this way the bride met God, the bridegroom, and became his beloved.
>
> (Gurū Granth Sāhib: 1197)

To uplift the social status of women was in the forefront of the Gurūs' reforms. They raised their voice against the system of *satī*. The Gurūs regarded the burning of a woman with the dead body of her husband as unnecessary and sinful. Here was a challenge to her courage and virtue. Guru Amar Das said:

> Call them not satis, who burn themselves on the pyre of their husbands. Rather they are satis who feel the shock of separation from their husbands. And they are satis, who abide in virtue and contentment.
>
> (Gurū Granth Sāhib: 787)

Guru Amar Das, the third Gurū, even persuaded Emperor Akbar to stop this practice, and succeeded in having a directive issued, banning the custom.

Widow marriage

Widows in India at that time led a miserable life. As the custom of child marriage was quite common, sometimes girls in their teens became widows. They had to observe certain restrictions, not to be well dressed and well groomed. Guru Amar Das felt keenly the miserable condition of widows, and encouraged widow remarriage among his Sikhs. Guru Arjan arranged the wedding of his disciple, Bhai Hema, with a widow. A Sikh widow is allowed to marry a man of similar age.

Purdah

Sikh women are not to wear the veil to cover their faces or to live in seclusion. The *Rahit Maryādā* states, 'It is contrary to Sikhism for women to wear Purdah' (Kaur and Singh 1971: 9), as the purdah system suppressed the personality of women and reflected their inferior status.

Female infanticide

Sikh Gurūs pleaded the cause of the emancipation of Indian womanhood and did their best to ameliorate the sordid condition of women. They challenged practices and customs that stood in the way of their emancipation. Guru Gobind Singh prohibited the practice of female infanticide. Bhai Chopa Singh's *Rahit nāmā*[3] says that Gurū's Sikhs should neither indulge in, nor have any social dealings with anyone who practises, female infanticide. Bhai Desa Singh wrote, 'According to the teachings of the Sikh Gurus the daughter has an equal status with the son, so a Sikh should not have any social dealings with anyone who indulges in female infanticide.' Newly baptised Sikhs are told not to associate with those who practise female infanticide (Kaur and Singh 1971: 15).

Dowry

The Gurūs also spoke against the custom of giving bride price or dowry. Where bride price was taken, the woman became the bought property of the husband's family, and was usually treated like a slave. Where the custom of giving dowry was prevalent, the birth of a girl was seen as a liability. (The practice has, unfortunately, since become the accepted custom among Sikhs.)

Guru Gobind Singh criticised the custom of acceptance of money by the groom's parents from the parents of the bride. He considered it a highly irreligious practice. 'He who giveth his daughter in marriage to a Sikh and taketh no money for her, is a Sikh of mine and may after his death reach my abode' (Macauliffe 1909, vol. 5: 158). Guru Amar Das discouraged the dowry system by asking his Sikhs to refrain from the egoistic practice of public display of dowry. He wrote, 'Any dowry which is displayed by the perverse for show is false pride and worthless display' (Gurū Granth Sāhib: 79).

These views of the Gurūs, and the steps they took to accord equality to women, revolutionised the tradition of a society which was steeped in prejudice against them. Woman was not only equal with man in social and religious affairs, but also an equal partner in the political matters of war and peace: she was at liberty to join the army to fight for national defence. As a result of the Gurūs' teachings, men began to realise the worth of women as equal partners, and women began to receive the respect and honour they deserved. Relieved from unnecessary and unreasonable customs, taboos and practices, Sikh womanhood played a momentous role in various walks of life within the Sikh community.

Contributions of women

Mata Khivi, wife of the second Gurū, was the manager of the very important institution of *laṅgar*. This institution is fundamental to Sikh religion, as it teaches its adherents the basic Sikh principle, the equality of humanity: no one is higher or lower merely by birth. Because of its importance, Guru Amar Das had said, *pahila paṅgat pīche saṅgat*, meaning that if anybody wanted to see him, they should eat in the *laṅgar*. This injunction was honoured even by Emperor Akbar, who ate in the *laṅgar* before he could meet with the Gurū. To be in charge of the *laṅgar* was a great honour that was bestowed on a woman, which of course was earned by her sheer genius in the field of administration, but it was the Gurūs' views of equality that made it possible for women to come out of the confines of household work and take up a vocation/profession of their choice.

The Sikh Gurūs infused the spirit of self-confidence and self-reliance in woman's secular and religious life. They emphasised that the strength of women should not be confined to the proven area of domestic life, but should be used in nation-building. The Gurūs wanted to develop fully the potentialities of women for leadership in all walks of life. When Mai Bhago decided to take up arms and spend her life as a soldier, there was a seal of approval from Guru Gobind Singh on her decision.

The name of Mata Gujri, the wife of Guru Tegh Bahadur and mother of Guru Gobind Singh, inspires many women. She was a great educationist; she taught her family and everyone around her the teachings of the Gurūs, and infused in them the spirit of courage for their convictions, so that they were ready to lay down their lives for principles. After the martyrdom of Guru Tegh Bahadur in 1675, the responsibility of looking after the education of the nine-year-old Guru Gobind Singh, and the leadership of the Sikh community at that crucial and dangerous time, fell on the shoulders of Mata Gujri. She discharged her duties superbly, and showed remarkable astuteness and farsightedness in dealing with the external and internal dangers to the Sikh community. She showed great courage in dealing with dishonest *masand*s (who misappropriated the offerings collected from the congregation on behalf of the Gurū). It was Mata Gujri's emphasis on the courage of conviction and steadfastness that infused the spirit of sacrifice in the younger sons of Guru Gobind Singh. They accepted death, and sacrificed themselves on the altar of their faith. Mata Gujri holds the unenviable position of being wife of a martyr, mother of a martyr, grandmother of martyrs and herself a martyr.

Mata Sundri, the widow of Guru Gobind Singh, continually provided leadership in the most trying time in the history of Sikhs. She dealt with the pretenders and aspirers of Gurudom very strictly, and maintained the Guruship given to Gurū Granth Sāhib in 1708 by Guru Gobind Singh, the tenth Guru.

Sikh women also exercised strict checks and restraints on the weaknesses of their menfolk. Mai Bhago bravely helped forty Sikh deserters to keep on the right path, when the latter had signed a disclaimer renouncing their allegiance to Guru Gobind Singh. She admonished them for leaving the Gurū, herself leading them back to

151

him, and they fought bravely to defend the Gurū's party against the Moghul troops.

During this period of history (1720–60), when the male Sikhs were persecuted and there were rewards for the capture or killing of Sikhs, the women not only showed undaunted courage in warfare, but also shouldered family responsibilities. They had to work to earn money to keep the families from starvation, as well as looking after the religious and educational needs of the children. They were to teach the children the principles of Sikhism and inculcate courage in facing persecution.

During Mir Mannu's governorship of Panjab (1748–53), hundreds of Sikh women were caught, put into prison and forced to grind corn. They were made to wear 'wreaths' round their necks, made from the flesh of their slain children. These women were tortured, starved and speared alive. They bore all this but did not falter from their religious beliefs.

George Thomas, who was the Rajah of a small state in Panjab, wrote of Sikh women in his memoirs, 'Instances indeed have not infrequently occurred in which they have actually taken up arms to defend their inhabitants from the desultory attacks of the enemy and throughout the contest behaved themselves with the intrepidity of spirit highly praiseworthy'. When Sikhs came out of the period of persecution and had a chance to establish Sikh rule, Sikh women, as and when the occasion arose, took charge of state administration, and their contributions as rulers were creditable. One such great woman was the Rani of Patiala State, Rani Sahib Kaur. She proved to be the saviour of Patiala State more than once. She often commanded armies on the battlefield, and inflicted severe defeats on the invaders. She was an enlightened organiser, a brilliant administrator and a superb commander of her forces.

Rani Sada Kaur, the mother-in-law of Maharajah Ranjit Singh, was the chief architect of his empire. She headed the army many times to assist her son-in-law. The Maharajah was only eleven years old when his father died, and it was Rani Sada Kaur who set him on the road to power and glory. Rani Jind Kaur, the wife of Maharajah Ranjit Singh and the mother of Maharajah Dalip Singh, exerted her influence to keep the state of Panjab independent from the British Raj. But her efforts were foiled by the British politicians and she had to suffer imprisonment. She made persistent efforts to free Panjab and restore the legitimate authority of her son, but in vain.

Today, many Sikh women are serving the community in various spheres. They are performing important tasks as eminent administrators, doctors, educationists, business women, religious leaders, politicians and artists. They have proved their mettle in whatever sphere they have chosen to serve. Even as housewives, the authority of the Sikh woman, among rich and poor, is extensive. She usually controls the purse strings and decides what the family shall eat and how much her husband will spend. Social events, such as marriage or birthday celebrations, are usually settled by women, and the men merely give their consent. The Sikh woman has enjoyed superior status compared with her counterparts in other communities. She has earned this by showing the ability to stand by the side of her husband in difficult times.

Sikh women have come to the fore, and have shown their ability and stamina, in working outside Panjab. In 1966 in Smethwick, in England, a serious dispute arose between the two parties of the gurdwara management committee. The women took charge of the gurdwara affairs, and for a whole year very successfully conducted the affairs until the men cooled down and got ready to work together. Bibi Balwant Kaur, in Birmingham, has contributed greatly to the social and religious welfare of Sikh women by establishing Bebe Nanaki Gurdwara, where it is mostly women who manage all the affairs of the gurdwara. In Kenya she had helped widows to become self-supporting by teaching them tailoring techniques and providing sewing machines. For the recent famine in Ethiopia, she collected funds and personally visited the famine-stricken areas.

Many women have occupied, and are currently occupying, the positions of presidents and secretaries of gurdwaras and other similar Sikh organisations. In almost every gurdwara, women are seen organising functions to collect money for charities. In spite of her active participation in all religious, political, social and cultural affairs, however, the position of the Sikh woman is far from satisfactory. Her status in life is still lower than that of a man. The Sikh Gurūs' teachings of equality are not fully implemented.

The Sikh Gurūs envisaged a society where men and women would be equal partners. They would be 'two bodies and one soul' sharing their responsibilities equally. It should be a society where men and women remember God (*Nām japna*), do honest work (*kirat karni*) and share their fortune with others (*vand chakna*). The honest work

153

is looking after the family, cooking, cleaning and professional duties. Either man or woman, whoever is better suited to perform the household duties, should do so with dignity. There should not be any stereotyping in the roles of men and women.

The Sikh Gurūs initiated the *langar* system where men and women both were to cook and clean and serve food in the gurdwaras, and, incidentally, Sikh men do so quite happily there. But at home, they still think these jobs are for women! Even when women go to work outside the home and earn money, still the man thinks himself the breadwinner, hence worthy of occupying a higher position. If Sikh men were to think seriously about the institution of *langar*, they would realise that the Gurūs believed in the dignity of labour and advocated full participation of men and women in that labour. Sikh men and women must follow the Gurūs' teachings, and not blindly copy the practices of other communities, or give in to the pressure of the tradition of other communities to conform to their way of life.

Despite the Gurūs' teachings of full equality, Sikh women still do not share leadership roles equally with men. The number of women who have been members, secretaries or presidents of gurdwara management committees is very small. In spite of the fact that women perform very competently the duties of the *rāgi*s (who sing hymns in the gurdwaras) and of the *granthī*s (who read the Gurū Granth Sāhib), there are very few women who perform these duties. There is no reason why women should not perform half of all the duties relating to the worship and to the management of the gurdwaras. Sikh women need to make an effort to ensure that they claim the equality given to them by the Gurūs.

This somewhat inferior status of women can be attributed to the fact that Sikhs have been the minority community and have been ruled by either Hindu, Muslim or British traditions. These rulers did not envisage the equality of women and men to the same extent as the Sikh Gurūs. During the British Raj, when Sikhs got the control of the Sikh gurdwaras (1925), and the right to elect the managing committee, only Sikh men were given the right to vote. Despite the Sikh leaders' explanations and pleadings that Sikh women enjoy equality with men and share all the duties in the gurdwaras equally with men, the British Government in India refused to give Sikh women the right to vote. An extract from Master Tara Singh's speech criticising the proposal of the Gurdwara Reform Bill shows how the traditions of the Sikh people were ignored:

A little insight into Sikh history will show what a heroic part [women] have played in it ever since the time of its foundation. They have been taking equal part with their brethren and have on occasions guided the community as leaders. In our religious diwans and conferences their number has been just the same as that of males. There is far more higher education among the Sikh females than in any other community. In this Gurdwara struggle their record has been glorious. I am right in saying that one-half of the community has been debarred from taking part in this management.

(Ahluwalia 1985, 208)

The other major contributory factor is the unwillingness of Sikh males to surrender their dominant role, though if they would turn to their Gurūs' teachings they would recognise the need to practise equality.

Sikh history has been written by men only, who either chose to disregard women's contributions, or did not think their contributions worthy of note. Whatever the reason, women's contributions have been kept out of the record and, as a result, Sikh women have not been able to transmit their achievements to later generations, which have therefore not had positive images to emulate. Sometimes the male historians have even attributed women's contributions to their male relatives. In the case of Mata Gujri, who shouldered the responsibility of looking after the affairs of the Sikh *Panth* during the minority of Guru Gobind Singh, there were *Hukamnāmās*[4] to the *saṅgat*, written by her and accepted by the community, but the credit is given to her brother, Kirpal Chand. Of course, Kirpal Chand was Mata Gujri's adviser, but she was at the helm of affairs. The Gurūs had their advisers, and the names of these prominent Sikhs are mentioned in various history books, but no historian has said that these advisers/prominent Sikhs were running the affairs of the Sikh community rather than the Gurū. Let us take the case of Rani Sada Kaur. She laid the foundation of the 'Khālsā Rāj' of Ranjit Singh. Ranjit Singh was only eleven years old when his father died. By the time he was eighteen years old, he was crowned the Maharajah of Panjab. Who was leading his armies against the enemies, and who administered the affairs of state? It was Rani Sada Kaur. The credit that is due to Rani Sada Kaur has not been given to her by the male historians.

Sikh women should challenge the traditions and customs that put

155

women in a subordinate position. The evil custom of *dahej*, that puts women on a lower level than men, would soon be eradicated if women, as sons' mothers, refused to accept it. There should be women's organisations which use their energies to stop this cancer-like growth in Sikh society.

Women should propagate equality of the sexes within the family unit by welcoming the birth of a daughter equally with that of a son. The celebration of a girl's birthday should be on the same scale as that of a boy's birthday. Girls and boys should both be taught to help in housework, and should not be stereotyped in traditional roles. Mothers should pay equal attention to the health care of both sons and daughters, and should provide opportunities for their daughters and sons to have higher education and challenging careers. Women who have been allocated the duty of bringing up the children have the power to mould and influence their thinking.

The Sikh Gurūs advocated complete equality of woman with man in all walks of life – social, religious, political and administrative – and completely rejected the idea of one being inferior and the other being superior. Sikh women must reclaim the equality that was given to them five hundred years ago.

NOTES

1. Bhai Gurdas was a renowned Sikh theologian at the time of Guru Arjan, the fifth Gurū. He was chosen by the Gurū to be the scribe for the Gurū Granth Sāhib.
2. To meet the need of an expanding Sikh community, Guru Amar Das divided the geographical area into twenty-two groups or *mañjīs*, each under a *mañjīdār* responsible to the Gurū. His main duties were to preach, convey instructions to the congregation from the Gurū, and collect *daswandh* (tithe).
3. *Rahit nāmā* – a manual of conduct laying down the rules by which a Sikh's life should be ordered. They were written in the eighteenth century and are considered to be based on the injunctions of Guru Gobind Singh.
4. *Hukamnāmā*s are letters of instructions issued by the Sikh Gurūs, the mother and wife of the tenth Gurū, and Banda Bahadur. They are regarded as the commands of the Gurūs and are binding upon the whole Sikh community.

FURTHER READING

Ahluwalia, M.L. (1985) *Select Documents Gurdwara Reform Movement, 1919-1925*, Delhi, Ashoka International Publishers.

Bannerjee, A.C. (1978) *Guru Nanak to Guru Gobind Singh*, Allahabad, Rajesh Publications.

Bhai Gurdas (1981) *Vara*, Amritsar, Shiromani Gurdwara Parbandhak Committee (SGPC).

Bhai Kahn Singh (1979) *Gurmat Martind*, Amritsar, SGPC.

Gupta, H.R. (1973) *History of Sikhs* vols 1-4, Delhi, Manohar Lal.

Harbans Singh, S. (1984) *The Message of Sikhism*, Delhi, Guru Nanak Foundation.

Kaur, K. and Singh, I. (trans) (1971) *Rehat Maryada*, London, Sikh Cultural Society.

Khalsa Panth De Rehatname, Amritsar, Chattar Singh and Jiwan Singh.

Macauliffe, M.A. (1909) *The Sikh Religion*, vol. 5, Delhi, S. Chand.

7. Chinese Religions

Stewart McFarlane

Many ambivalent attitudes to women in traditional China can be detected in: textual sources, authoritative statements, domestic and legal arrangements, rites and practices. For example, the *Lun Yu* (*Analects*) of Confucius (sixth century BCE), reflect the values of a patriarchal moralist, and certainly had a formative influence on Confucian thought in China and Japan.

> The Master said, "In one's household it is the women and the small men that are difficult to deal with. If you let them get too close, they become insolent. If you keep them at a distance, they complain".
>
> (Lau (trans) 1979: 17 v13)

It appears that patriarchal values and attitudes were well entrenched in ancient Chinese culture long before the time of Confucius, as the following passage from the 'Book of Songs' (*Shi Ching*), dating from about 800 BCE, testifies.

> The diviner thus interprets it:
> "Black bears and brown
> Mean men-children.
> Snakes and serpents
> Mean girl-children.
>
> So he bears a son, And puts him to sleep upon a bed,
> Clothes him in robes,
> Gives him a jade and sceptre to play with.
> The child's howling is very lusty;
> In red greaves shall he flare,
> Be lord and king of house and home.

Then he bears a daughter,
And puts her upon the ground,
Clothes her in swaddling-clothes,
Gives her a loom-whorl to play with.
For her no decorations, no emblems;
Her only care, the wine and food,
and how to give trouble to father and mother."

(Waley 1960: 283–4)

The traditional Chinese family was, and still is, patrilineal, which means that inheritance and family authority always pass to the eldest son on the death of the father. For a family to be without a son was a serious problem. The lack of a daughter was not so serious. Girls were not seen as permanent members of the family of their birth, and, as newly married, they were marginal in status in their new family. This having been said, women did have an important role in traditional Chinese society; but it is strictly defined and delimited. That role was defined almost entirely in terms of the family they nurture, and specifically, the sons they rear. The family in traditional China was seen as a microcosm of the wider social world. The family and society should ideally reflect and embody the order and harmony of Heaven. Correct relations in the family have social and cosmic significance (see Black 1986: 174–8).

It is through bearing and rearing children that a woman achieves what status she has. But even here there is danger and ambivalence. Apart from the physical risks of pregnancy and childbirth, the traditional Chinese world-view regards these processes as ritually and morally polluting.

Sexuality and fertility: purity and danger

In the feudal period of Chinese history known as the Chou (1000–400 BCE), the king of Chou was theoretically the titular and ritual head of all the feudal states of China. He bore the title 'Son of Heaven'. This did not signify literal divine descent, but meant that the righteous and worthy king carried Heaven's approval and mandate. With the formation of the Chinese Empire, first under the Ch'in (221–207 BCE), then under the Han (202 BCE–220 CE), many of the ritual and symbolic functions of the former Chou kings were applied to the Emperor. This included the title 'Son of Heaven'. The Emperor represented, and had the responsibility for maintaining, the regularity of the cosmic, social and political order. The harmonising of the *yin* (passive, dark, quiescent forces in nature) with the *yang* (active, light, dynamic forces) was partly achieved and symbolised by the Emperor's sexual relations with his consort/s. On a cosmic level this represented the harmonising of the forces of Heaven and Earth. On a practical level the successful outcome of sexual relations between Emperor and consort/s ensured the continuation of the dynasty and the Imperial family.

To a lesser extent, at the level of the ordinary people, sexual relations between any husband and wife also embody relations between these cosmic polarities. The traditional Chinese view was that through correct intercourse males can absorb the *yin* essences of females, and transform them in order to increase their own *yang* essences. Women can more easily absorb the *yang* essences of men to increase their own *yin* essences. The difference is that women's resources were regarded as inexhaustible, while men's were regarded as easily depleted (*Tao Te Ching*, chapter 6). The belief in this unequal relationship, and the ever-present male fear of depletion of vital essence, helps explain some of the traditional Chinese ambivalence towards women and their sexuality. In conventional Chinese terms, women's sexuality and fertility were valued, but also greatly feared by many men. Sex is essential for procreation as well as for physical and spiritual well-being, but women's role in it was seen as potentially dangerous and disruptive. Women's sexuality could deplete and debilitate men, and the birth and menstrual processes were regarded as ritually dangerous for men. Many taboos and ritual mechanisms were developed to cope with the threat. One dramatic and elaborate example is the 'blood bowl' ceremony at women's funerals. In order to remove the pollution and karmic consequences affecting the mother, which are the result of procreation and childbirth, the eldest son acts out the role of the famous monk and disciple of the Buddha, Mu Lien. In this dramatic ritual, he breaks (sometimes drinks) the bowl of birth blood (dyed wine) to free his mother from the 'bloody pond' (Seaman 1983: 381–96; Ahern 1975: 192–214).

The bitter irony of this situation is clear. In order to have status and a role in traditional Chinese society a woman must be a wife and a mother of sons. But the process of becoming a mother ritually and morally reduces her. So, to regain status in ritual or supernatural terms, in the afterlife, her son/s must ritually intervene.

Disjunction and marginalisation

Women's lives in traditional China were disjointed, and their role was seen as a subordinate one. Disjunction occurred through marriage, which involved a change of family, through childbirth, which was necessary but dangerous and ritually polluting, and through their changing roles in childcare. As sons grow up they assume roles and responsibilities defined by Confucian domestic and family ethics, and therefore change from being subordinate to their mothers, to having authority over them. The Confucian 'Book of Rites' presents the idealised model which women were supposed to follow,

> The woman follows (and obeys) the man: in her youth, she follows her father and elder brother; when married, she follows her husband; when her husband is dead, she follows her son. (Legge (trans) 1: 441, quoted in Black 1986: 170)

Because a woman married into her husband's family, her position there prior to producing sons was insecure and vulnerable, both in emotional and legal terms. In Imperial times (before 1911), women could be divorced on any of the following grounds:

1. Barrenness.
2. Wanton conduct.
3. Neglect of parents-in-law.
4. Garrulousness.
5. Theft.
6. Jealousy and ill-will.
7. Incurable disease.

On the other hand, a woman had three conditions defined by law which ensured that she could not be divorced. These were:

1. She had kept the three years mourning for either of her parents-in-law.

2. Her husband's family had become wealthy after she was married into it.
3. She had no home to return to. (Baker 1979: 45).

Such ideas and institutions give some impressions of how women were perceived in official terms in traditional China.

Some anthropologists have identified strategies and institutions, which to some extent reduce the disjunction and marginalisation such conditions produce. Margery Wolf's theory of the uterine family as a culturally engendered strategy for reducing the sense of disjunction and marginalisation is one example (Wolf 1972: 32–7; Wolf 1985: 9–12). The uterine family is the unofficial family which is identified with a mother and her children. The uterine family does not necessarily serve the same interests and endorse the same values as the family as understood in the traditional Confucian and male-orientated Chinese family. It exists in some tension in relation to the patrilineal family. It is, of necessity, an unstable and fragile strategy, because daughters leave it on marriage, and sons, as they mature, are involved in the patrilineal family. Some support for such a theory may also be found in the following passage, taken from the life story of a Chinese servant, told to the author, Ida Pruitt in the 1930s.

Life must go on. The generations stretch back thousands of years to the great ancestor parents. They stretch for thousands of years into the future, generation upon generation. Seen in proportion to this great array, the individual is but a small thing. But on the other hand no individual can drop out. Each is a link in the great chain. No one can drop out without breaking the chain. A woman stands with one hand grasping the generations that have gone before, and the other the generations to come. It is her common destiny with all women.

(Pruitt 1967: 239)

This passage seems to articulate a sense of the power and solidarity of women in traditional China, as well as the tremendous burden of responsibility which their role in the family network imposes on them. Socially and supernaturally, for a woman to die before marriage, or die before producing children was, and still is, a serious and threatening matter. It is not surprising that in Chinese popular religion, the majority of unhappy and troublesome ghosts are women (Potter 1974: 229–30; Harrell 1986: 112). Their more

162

marginal status with its potential for serious disjunction seems to be reflected in the supernatural order. Many of these unhappy ghosts are girls or women who died without marrying, or women whose families have neglected to, or been unable to, make proper funeral and mourning provision. One of the ritual mechanisms for coping with a troublesome or unhappy ghost who has died before marriage, and therefore is without status in a family, is the practice of 'ghost marriage'. This is still practised in Taiwan, Hong Kong and the New Territories. Through ghost marriage, the girl's spirit is married either to another spirit or to a living man. The wedding service is carried out using paper models of the ghosts, and on its completion the girl's spirit tablet is then placed on the ancestral altar of the family into which she is married. It is a purely formal arrangement; if a living man has agreed to act as her partner, usually involving a fee paid by the dead girl's original family, then after the marriage he is free to marry in the normal way, since the girl's status as a member of his family has then been achieved (Jordan 1972: 140–64).

The practice of adoption has always been a solution to the problem of childless families, and to ensure the continuation of a lineage. A particular Chinese refinement was the practice of posthumous adoption, which provided an heir to a man or youth who died without one. Like spirit marriage it was regarded as a formal ritual arrangement. The adopted son was required to make the appropriate offerings to the tablet and grave of his 'father'. Because rights of inheritance were involved in this arrangement, it was usual to seek the adopted son from within the same family or clan. Another arrangement to deal with the problem of childlessness, was for the childless couple to adopt a daughter in order to 'lead on' or encourage the conception of a natural son. This was a mechanism which was widely regarded as effective. It does again suggest something of the lower and more expendable status of women.

An even stronger indicator of the marginal and expendable status of women is the practice of female infanticide. Cases of it have occurred in Chinese history for centuries, and were invariably condemned by Confucian officials. However, little was done by way of punishment or preventive legislation by the administration. There have been some indications that the practice has again reappeared in some rural areas of China where the one-child policy means that the birth of a girl would be seen as a disaster in some peasant families.

Women as religious functionaries

Women did, and still do, have a role in traditional Chinese religious life. But it was a role largely located outside the great institutionalised traditions of Buddhism, religious Taoism, and the State cult of Confucius. Women have long occupied important roles as mediums, shamans, divination experts and fortune tellers in Chinese popular religion. From the viewpoint of the religious élite of Buddhism, Taoism and Confucianism, these functions in popular religion are low level and marginal. But the special powers of female shamans in dealing with *yin* forces and lower order spirits associated with women's illnesses, childbirth and infancy problems, fulfil vitally important ritual and therapeutic roles in the community. Higher forces such as *yang* spirits and gods as well as the important ritual functions at communal festivals, are dealt with by male shamans or Taoist priests, who are seen as more ritually effective and powerful. This delegation of ritual authority to specialisation in the *yin* forces and lower order spirits, can be interpreted as another example of the marginal status of women, seen from the viewpoint of the élite traditions and their representatives. It can therefore be seen as but another traditional mechanism for ensuring the subordination of women. However, the roles of female shamans, diviners and healers, and the way they are performed may also be seen as a way of consolidating the power of women, and ensuring some vital functions, within the constraints of a dominant patriarchal system.

Ritual responsibility for the lives of children in local communities is clearly an important role, and a service which the community sees as important. An example of how this works in practice can be seen in the observations of the anthropologist, Jack Potter, who was working in the New Territories of Hong Kong. He describes in detail the role of female diviners and shamans in identifying and ritually correcting the problem of 'soul loss' in infants. This problem was, and still is, regarded by Chinese peasants in this region as a life-threatening danger. Potter describes in detail the ritual skill, psychological subtlety, as well as detailed knowledge of the family histories of the community which the shaman has to demonstrate in order to perform her role. The shaman's entry into trance and her encounters with different spirits, and her diagnosis of medical and spiritual problems are described in detail by Potter. Once a troublesome spirit has been settled and the immediate threat to the child averted, the shaman may continue to exercise an important protective role by ritually adopting the child, i.e., becoming its ritual guardian or auntie. As Potter observes, a successful and powerful shaman may adopt many children in this way, and the ritual relationship serves to protect the child from the threat of soul loss and other spiritual disorders until it reaches adolescence when it is no longer so vulnerable (Potter 1974: 207–31).

Yin and the Mother Principle in early Taoism

It is clear that there are elements of Chinese thought which do not unequivocally accept the patriarchal values of the Confucian élite. Some of these seem to be apparent in the ancient Taoist classic, the *Tao Te Ching*. This text appears to elevate the *yin* qualities in nature as examples of the qualities which the wise should cultivate in their lives. Some passages in the text describe the concept of *tao* as Mother. The *tao*, which literally means 'way', is the creative but quiescent principle which produces, sustains and pervades all things, without volitional or purposeful action. The wise are recommended to model their behaviour on the *tao*, as a way of non-striving and non-contention. Chapters 10 and 28 of the text specifically recommend taking 'female' and 'infant' or *yin* roles in one's actions. This entails preserving, rather than expending, one's energies, and taking a non-intrusive role in handling one's affairs and not forcefully manipulating situations.

Commentators such as Ellen Marie Chen have seen the positive value in such advice and strongly argue that the elevation of the feminine in the *Tao Te Ching*, both practically and philosophically, is a genuine expression of an authentic tradition within early Chinese culture (Chen 1969: 391–405). She even suggests that this tradition represents a more matriarchal value system, which may actually have existed in ancient China. She therefore sees this tradition and its survival in the *Tao Te Ching* as being older than the assumptions of Confucian thought and the later dominance of patriarchy. This is interesting because the conventional scholarly interpretations see early Taoism itself as a reaction to, and critique of, an emerging Confucian orthodoxy. Many of the passages in the text do read more like the latter than the former. They seem to suggest a known and generally accepted moral and social orthodoxy

165

which the text is seeking to undermine or counter. Sukie Colegrave also supports the theory of an ancient Chinese matriarchal society, though her main interest is in the interpretation of early Taoist thought as an insight into the principles of psychological androgyny (Colegrave 1979). She cites the *Tao Te Ching* in support of the view that the balanced and stable personality must harmoniously combine the masculine (*yang*) aspects of the personality and consciousness, with the feminine (*yin*) aspects. Good support for this interpretation can also be found in the *Tao Te Ching* and other early texts.

However, there are problems with the early Taoist characterisations of the feminine, which are not adequately addressed by either Chen or Colegrave. The concept of the feminine, articulated by the *Tao Te Ching*, does seem to issue from masculine and possibly patriarchal assumptions about the nature of the feminine and the role women play in society. Does the advocacy of yielding, and taking the 'female role' of compliance and subordination simply legitimise the patriarchal system and the assumptions behind it? Notice that most of the advice given in the *Tao Te Ching* is addressed to the Sage Ruler, who still seems to be regarded as necessarily male. It can be objected that despite the attempt undertaken in the *Tao Te Ching* to provide an alternative model and value system to that of Confucian patriarchy, the terms in which that attempt is framed are still largely dictated by those same values. As Alison Black points out, the early Taoist Classics *seem* to offer idealised 'feminine' models, along with images drawn from nature and rustic life, but it remains the male Sage Ruler who learns and benefits from these lessons (Black 1986: 174). A further indication of the strength of this critique is the fact that historically and socially, despite the elevation of the feminine principle, and the *Tao Te Ching*'s influence on so much of Chinese thought and culture, the subordination of, and devaluing of, women persisted as a significant feature of Chinese history.

Against such a critique it may be argued that the radical nature of the Taoist political method was simply never implemented, and that the failure to overcome Confucian patriarchal values was never effectively realised. Therefore the Taoist vision of society cannot be blamed for the errors and oppression of later Chinese history. It could also be objected that the fundamental message of the text is a sophisticated tactical and psychological one, which is teaching that, by appearing to yield and appearing to accept the subordinate role, one actually achieves domination. Chapters 76, 77 and 78 of the text may certainly be read in this way.

But the argument about the persistent low status in traditional Chinese society is an important one. This was particularly noticeable in the perspectives of the Chinese scholarly/bureaucratic élite, many of whom were significantly influenced by the *Tao Te Ching*.

FURTHER READING

Ahern, E.M. (1975) 'The power and pollution of Chinese women', in M. Wolf and R. Witke (eds) *Women in Chinese Society*, Stanford, Stanford University Press.

Baker, H.D.R. (1979) *Chinese Family and Kinship*, London, Macmillan.

Black, H. (1986) 'Gender and cosmology in Chinese correlative thinking', in C.W. Bynum, S. Harrell and P. Richman (eds) *Gender and Religion: On The Complexity of Symbols*, Boston, Beacon Press.

Chen, H.M. (1969) 'Nothingness and the mother principle in early Chinese Taoism', *International Philosophical Quarterly*, pp. 391–405.

Colegrave, S. (1979) *The Spirit of the Valley*, London, Virago Press.

Confucius (1979 edn) *The Analects* (trans D.C. Lau).

Harrell, S. (1986) 'Men, women and ghosts in Taiwanese folk religion', in C.W. Bynum, S. Harrell and P. Richman (eds) *Gender and Religion: On the Complexity of Symbols*, Boston, Beacon Press.

Jordan, D.K. (1972) *Gods, Ghosts and Ancestors*, Berkeley, University of California Press.

Lau, D.C. (trans) (1982) *Chinese Classics. Tao Te Ching*, Hong Kong, The Chinese University Press.

Potter, J.M. (1974) 'Cantonese Shamanism', in A.P. Wolf (ed.) *Religion and Ritual in Chinese Society*, Stanford, Stanford University Press.

Pruitt, I. (1967) *A Daughter of Han: the Autobiography of a Chinese Working Woman*, Stanford, Stanford University Press.

Seaman, G. (1983) 'The sexual politics of karmic retribution', in E.M. Ahern and H. Gates (eds) *The Anthropology of Taiwanese Society*, Stanford, Stanford University Press.

Waley, A. (trans) (1960) *The Book of Songs*, New York, Grove Press.

Wolf, M. (1972) *Women and the Family in Rural Taiwan*, Stanford, Stanford University Press.

Wolf, M. (1985) *Revolution Postponed. Women in Contemporary China*, Stanford, Stanford University Press.

8. Japanese Religions

D.P. Martinez

Introduction

Any attempt to discuss a topic as broad as women in Japanese religion has to begin with the warning that there is no such *simple* thing as Japanese religion. What may have once been a seamless structure combining native beliefs (to which the Chinese characters *shen – tao*, i.e. *shintō*, were applied)[1] with Buddhism, Confucianism and Taoism (which were all imported from China), was torn apart during the Meiji Restoration (1868). The separation of Buddhism from Shinto at that point not only seriously damaged the former, but allowed the latter to be used for the ideological basis of State Shinto, which gave rise to the nationalism of the 1930s.

Furthermore, the separation of the two religions was, in many ways, not successful, and the Japanese continued to practise what had, in the past, been one religious system.[2] Scholars of religion in Japan coped with the problems these practices presented in terms of defining religious life by adding the category of folk religion: a catch-all category into which ancestor worship with its Confucian roots, astrology, Taoism and spirit possession all fell.[3] The picture is further complicated by the success of the so-called 'new' religions in modern Japan. These religious movements, many of which were originally headed by women, often had their roots in pre-Meiji Japan, but became strongly associated with the modernising urban scene. In order to look at women's roles in all these areas of religion, this chapter will be divided into two parts: the first will look at organised religious beliefs and practices, including the new religions; the second will consider women's roles in folk and family religion.

Organised religion

Very little is known about Japanese religious practices before the arrival of Buddhism in the sixth century CE. The *Nihonshoki* and *Kojiki*, which claim to be collections of pre-Buddhist myth and history, are both strongly influenced and shaped by similar Chinese works. However, one thing upon which both the mythology and scholars are agreed is that in the early history of Japanese religion, women were important figures as shamanesses. Not only were women important as mediators for the deities (*kami*), but one of the central deities worshipped in early Japan was Amaterasu, the goddess who is now associated with the sun, and who is called the ancestress of the Japanese Imperial family. Nakamura[4] points out that it is not clear when Amaterasu, originally associated with the sea and rivers, became associated with the sun, but what is most interesting is that in the early mythology Amaterasu seems to be a prototype shamaness as well.[5] Thus it is not certain if she was originally a priestess for the solar deity or the deity herself. Hori,[6] on the other hand, dismisses this as an unimportant distinction. In early Japan, he argues, shamanesses – and in fact all women – were seen to be possessors of great spiritual power with the potential for becoming possessed by deities. On this view, the current distinction between types of shamaness – the shrine shamaness (*jinja miko*) and the spiritualist shamaness (*kuchiyose miko*) – is only an elaboration of the more primitive shamanistic 'child of the deity' (*miko-gami*). *Miko*, then, was the term most often associated with the women who acted as mediators for the *kami*, and is still used today to refer to shrine maidens (who perform dances in Shinto ceremonies) as well as to mediums who speak with the dead.

Blacker[7] refers to the *miko* as ancient sibyls who both advised political leaders and mediated between humble villagers and the *kami*. So important were these women in pre-Buddhist Japan that the Chinese observers of the country, who travelled there during the Wei dynasty (265 CE), referred to this area, which the inhabitants called Yamato, as 'Queen Country'. It is clear, however, that the mythical first 'Empress' (named Pimiko or Himiko) of Queen Country, was actually a shamaness who had a religious but not political function. According to Hori:

She closed herself up in her room and, though of a mature age, would not take a husband. Her younger brother presided over the affairs of state. Into her room only one man was allowed, a man whose job it was to communicate her messages and serve meals to her.[8]

It was through these three people that the land was unified and administered.

The religious role of these early shamanesses must be stressed because some feminists (both Japanese and western) have mistaken their existence – as well as the worship of Amaterasu – as signs that ancient Japan was a matriarchy.[9] There is no evidence of women as actual political rulers in pre-Buddhist Japan, but it is true that Japanese women had higher status in all spheres of life before the feudal era (twelfth–seventeenth centuries). Feminists[10] have argued that Buddhism and Confucianism were responsible for the decline in women's status, but Ackroyd[11] argues persuasively that this decline was the result of constant warfare and growing feudalism. Buddhist and Confucian arguments about the role of women in society, however, were used to support the laws which took away women's rights to inherit property or to divorce their husbands. It is important to be aware that in both Shinto and Buddhist systems of belief women were considered to be polluting because of their menstrual blood.[12] Buddhism, backed up by Confucianism, as will be discussed below, had more elaborate things to say about the unworthiness of women.

BUDDHISM[13]

Buddhism is a broad term for what in medieval Japan comprised eight different sects and today acknowledges several more. (In Japan all sects are Mahāyāna.) With the introduction of Chinese-style government and Buddhist religion, the *miko* lost her central role in Japanese political life. She did not disappear completely from the scene, for in the seventh century CE the institution of an imperial princess who served at the Sacred Shinto shrines was begun (*saigū*). The practice continued until the fourteenth century, and the princess, or *saio*, was to be a virgin whose practices included the worship of the *kami* but not divination. It is interesting to note that the last *saio* retired in 1336 to become a Buddhist nun, demonstrating the way in which various religious practices were intertwined at the time.[14]

170

Hori (1968) also notes that esoteric or tantric Buddhism offered a rationale for men to take over some of the shamanic practices of the *miko*, at the same time that some 'folk' Buddhist practices, such as dancing *sūtra*, became the domain of women. Nakamura[15] links the ancient idea of the spiritually powerful woman with the important role of women in Japanese new religions.

In general, Buddhism did offer a niche for women who wanted to devote their lives to the Buddha; they could become nuns. Unlike the ancient mediating *miko*, the Buddhist nun was to shun all worldly attachments while she was actually governed by stricter precepts and monastic codes than Buddhist monks.[16] The reasoning for this lay both in Buddhist dogma (which taught that women were impure, having a more sinful *karma* than men, filled with evil desires and presenting obstacles to men who were striving to attain enlightenment) and in Confucian ideology, which argued that women should obey first their fathers, then their husbands and finally their sons. In short, nuns still retained the low status with which women in Japan came to be associated during the feudal era. Such was the discrimination against them within the religious system that they were not even allowed to set foot on the sacred places and mountains of Japan.

The women who became nuns in pre-Meiji Japan, as in medieval Europe and in other Buddhist countries, did not do so solely because of their quest for buddhahood. Many aristocratic women 'retired' to nunneries when their fathers, husbands or sons fell out of political favour, and one convent in Kamakura, Tōkei-ji, was famous as a sanctuary for commoner women who were unhappily married.[17] During the Tokugawa era (seventeenth–nineteenth centuries), women who fled to Tōkei-ji and spent a certain amount of time there, could obtain divorces from their husbands. Nuns came from other areas of society as well; there are stories of prostitutes who became nuns in penance for their sins,[18] a practice common to women in traditional Catholic and Buddhist societies.

Modern nuns in Japan, however, must be very committed to the religious life for, until recently, they remained discriminated against. Uchino[19] discusses the arduous process of achieving status elevation for *soto-zen* nuns. The process was complicated by the fact that priests who were forced to marry during the Meiji Restoration could still be priests, but married nuns were no longer considered religious practitioners. Buddhist nuns have thus continued to maintain their ascetic life-styles, although the possibility of marriage remains open to them. A major concern for these nuns had been that in post-Meiji Japan they were not, until the 1970s, allowed equal opportunities in education; they were not allowed to teach, practise meditation on their own, initiate other nuns, or serve as missionaries. A further point of contention is that during the Second World War some *soto-zen* priests' wives, receiving the lowest nun title, took over their husbands' temple duties – which nuns had not been allowed to do – and even Shinto shrines allowed women to act as priests as more men were called to war. Nuns, in contrast, were to remain secluded and unmarried. The situation of Buddhist nuns in modern Japan remains unclear, but becoming a nun remains a possibility for the woman who wishes to leave the secular world.

One other interesting modern phenomenon related to women and Buddhism has been the growth of the cult of *Jizo-sama*,[20] the Japanese protector of children. In the proliferation of *mizuko* (literally water baby), which can be found in many Buddhist temples today, we have interesting evidence of the continued importance of religious beliefs for modern Japanese women. These small *Jizo* statues, which are dressed in children's clothing, are meant to represent foetuses who were miscarried or aborted, and babies who were stillborn; they are carefully cared for and are often offered toys and children's sweets. The comfort this provides women who, in the past, lived in a society where infant mortality was so high that it was believed no child below the age of three was yet a person, is immeasurable.

THE NEW RELIGIONS

In many ways the role of women in the so-called Japanese new religions encapsulates the history of women in Shinto and Buddhism. There are hundreds of 'new' religions today and a noticeable proportion of these sects were started by women who had revelatory experiences. Interestingly, as these religions have become routinised, men have taken over the leadership. Nakamura[21] sees a direct parallel here between the ancient shamanesses and these new religions. Moreover, women predominate as followers of these religions, comprising up to seventy per cent of the congregations. However, as some anthropologists have noted, despite the fact that women make up the majority of members in any new religion, they are often, through the religion's ideology, marginalised.[22] The pre-Meiji Confucian notions of women's status, as well as Buddhist dogma, which argues that women are more prone to sin, means that these new religions re-emphasise women's feelings of inferiority. Paradoxically, in many of these sects women often act as healers and counsellors for others and this gives them a sense of value at the same time that they are quite capable of claiming that they can feel the weight of the dirt of being female.

As a largely urban phenomenon, the importance of new religions for Japanese women points to the fact that religious activity has always been central to what it means to be female. This view contradicts some of the material on the family in Japan which always emphasises the man's role in familial and community ritual and says nothing about women. As will be argued below, we understand little of everyday religious life in Japan if we do not look at women's experience of religion in their day-to-day existence.

Folk and family religion

There is one central issue which must be tackled in this section and that is what is meant by being religious? After the Second World War, many Japanese answered 'no' to surveys on whether they considered themselves religious. Much of this had to do with the perception that in order to be modern a society should be secular. With changes in Japan's economy and self-confidence, these same people are answering 'yes' when asked if they are religious. However, the traditional religion of Japan (actually the mix of religious practices which survived the Meiji Restoration) continues to change, and the discussion here may soon be considered outdated.

One way in which women's role in folk and family religion is changing is that beliefs in the dangerous spiritual power of women seem to be disappearing. This is not to say that women are no longer considered polluting within a religious context, but that the more dangerous aspects associated with womanhood are less often verbalised. Yet, the depiction of women as guilty, jealous, demonic, ghosts, or even were-creatures, themes long found in the literature, theatre and folklore of Japan, still surfaces in modern films, television and fantastic literature.[23] Thus, while Yoshida[24] was able to find fears about women's ability to become foxes or witches, he did so only in remote areas and villages. On the other hand, the notion of women as bearers of spiritual powers, also prevalent in popular culture, is one still found in modern Japan. Women continue to act as healers or mediums for the dead outside of the established religions, often mixing ritual elements from Buddhism, Shintoism and Taoism.

In small, still close-knit rural areas, it is clear that women are often the holders of religious knowledge. They remember how the rituals should be done, organise the food, clothing, and keep an oral record of the implements needed. No large-scale community ritual performed in rural or urban Japan is possible without the work of women. Yet the outside observer will notice only men when the ritual performance occurs in public. The same holds true for studies of ancestor worship in Japan. Ideally, since the ancestors worshipped are the patrilineal ancestors, their worship is the work of the men in the family. On important public occasions, such as O-bon,[25] it is the men who go to the Buddhist temple and play a central role in the rituals of prayer and purification. Yet, more central to the daily well-being of the ancestors is the worship of the women of the household.

Daily care for and worship of the ancestors is, of course, a personal thing. Sugiyama-Lebra[26] noted that it becomes more important to the women involved as they grow older. As young daughters-in-law and strangers to the household, many women do not feel close to their husband's ancestors. As the years go by and they have children, care for their in-laws in their old age, etc., these women begin to feel closer to the dead of the household and often become involved in reciting nembutsu (sūtra) for the dead. This, along with daily offerings of food, drink, flowers and fruit, is the work of the women. In some rural areas nembutsu-kai are still found. These groups of older women, who meet to learn sūtras and who go from household to household on important anniversaries, are, according to Hori (1968), the inheritors of a tradition which in the middle ages was called dancing nembutsu and is related to even older shamanistic practices.

Preparing and making the offerings for the deities on the household kamidana (Shinto altar) are the work of the women of the household, just as making frequent visits to temples and shrines seems to be the province of women in all parts of Japan. It is often mothers and grandmothers who can be found buying amulets for the protection of the household or the car, for good health and for their children's success in school. Various scholars of Japan have noted the connection between Japanese housewives' concern with cleanliness and hygiene, and older religious ideas of purity, pollution and sacred work. The point is that in the arena of the domestic, it is the women who provide for the well-being of the family through their work and worship. I would argue that for every modern Japanese woman who eschews religious practices, there can be found another who not only upholds traditional practices, but who may also belong to a new religion.

NOTES

1. See Toshio Kuroda's (1981) 'Shinto in the history of Japanese religion', *The Journal of Japanese Studies*, 7 (1): 1–21, for the argument that 'Shinto' was originally a Chinese term used for any local or Taoist practices and that it was some time during the Japanese middle ages (twelfth–seventeenth centuries) that the term came to refer to a coherent system of religious belief.
2. See Allan G. Grapard's (1984) 'Japan's ignored cultural revolution', *History of Religions*, 23 (3): 240–65.
3. The huge body of work by the folklorist Yanagita Kunio formed the backdrop to this, and Hori Ichiro's work which is referred to throughout this chapter must be seen in the light of Yanagita's work.
4. Nakamura, Kyoko Motomochi (1986) 'The significance of Amaterasu in Japanese Religious History', in Carl Olson (ed.) *The Book of the Goddess, Past and Present: An Introduction to her Religion*, New York, Crossroad Publishing Company.
5. See Carmen Blacker's (1975) *The Catalpa Bow*, London, George Allen & Unwin, for a description of Amaterasu in this role. The *Nihonshoki* however, attributes the first recorded shamanic dance to the deities who tried to convince Amaterasu to leave the cave in which she had hidden after a quarrel with her brother.
6. Hori, Ichiro (1975) 'Shamanism in Japan', *Japanese Journal of Religious Studies*, 2 (4): 231–87.
7. Blacker, *The Catalpa Bow*.
8. Hori, 'Shamanism in Japan', p. 234.
9. The 1930s Japanese feminists used the motto: 'In the beginning was the sun, and she was woman'.
10. See, for example, Joy Paulson's (1976) 'Evolution of the feminine ideal',

in Joyce Lebra, Joy Paulson and Elizabeth Powers (eds) *Women in Changing Japan*, Stanford, Stanford University Press.

11. Joyce Ackroyd (1957) 'Women in Feudal Japan', *The Transactions of the Asiatic Society of Japan* (third series), 7: 31–68.

12. For the argument that women's menstrual blood was considered powerful rather than polluting in pre-Buddhist Shinto belief, see Smyers, Karen A. (1983) 'Women and Shinto: the relations between purity and pollution', *Japanese Religions*, 12 (4): 7–18.

13. See Chapter 1 for a broader treatment of women in Buddhism

14. Ellwood, Robert S. (1967) 'The *saigū*: princess and priestess', *History of Religions*, 7: 35–60.

15. Nakamura, Kyoko Motomochi (1981) 'Revelatory experience in the female life cycle: a biographical study of women religionists in modern Japan', *Japanese Journal of Religious Studies*, 8 (3–4): 187–205.

16. Uchino, Kumiko (1983) 'The status elevation process of *sōtō* sect nuns in modern Japan', *Japanese Journal of Religious Studies*, 10 (2–3): 177–94.

17. Kaneko, Sachiko and Morrell, Robert E. (1983) 'Sanctuary: Kamakura's Tōkei-ji convent', *Japanese Journal of Religious Studies*, 10 (2–3): 195–227.

18. See, for example, Ihara Saikaku's (1963) *The Life of an Amorous Woman* (ed. and trans Ivan Morris), New York, A New Directions Book.

19. Uchino, 'The status elevation process of sōtō sect nuns in modern Japan'.

20. It is only in Japan that this *bodhisattva* is associated with children. Originally known as *Kṣitigarba* or 'earth womb', he is the *bodhisattva* who, in central Asia and China, delivers souls from hell and helps people in their last moments before death. In modern Japan, there seems to be growing up a strong iconographical relationship between images of *Jizo-sama* and the Catholic Virgin Mary.

21. Nakamura, 'Revelatory experience in the female life cycle'.

22. Strict Buddhist sects such as Tendai and Shingon taught that women had to be reborn as men before they could achieve salvation (Paulson, 1976 'Evolution of the feminine ideal'). See also the summing up of Mahāyāna Buddhism's compromise on the question of women, rebirth and salvation in Thelle, Notto R. (1983) 'Women in society and religion', *Japanese Religions*, 12 (4): 38–55.

23. See, for example, Ian Buruma's (1985) *A Japanese Mirror: Heroes and Villains of Japanese Culture*, Harmondsworth, Penguin.

24. Yoshida, Teigo and Ueda, H. (1968) 'Spirit possession and social structure in southwestern Japan', *Proceedings of the VIIIth International Congress of Anthropological and Ethnological Sciences*, 2: 377–80.

25. The Japanese festival of the dead which now occurs throughout Japan on varying dates depending on whether the lunar or solar calendar is followed: on the solar calendar *O-bon* falls in July; in the more traditional lunar calendar it falls in mid-August. I have also attended *O-bon* celebrations as late as September.
26. Sugiyama-Lebra, Takie (1984) *Japanese Women, Constraint and Fulfillment*, Honolulu, University of Hawaii Press.

FURTHER READING

Aston, W.G. (1896/1956) *Nihongi: Chronicles of Japan from Earliest Times to A.D. 697*, London, George Allen & Unwin.

Davis, Winston (1980) *Dojo, Magic and Exorcism in Modern Japan*, Stanford, Stanford University Press.

Hardacre, Helen (1984) *Lay Buddhism in Contemporary Japan, Reiyukai Kaidan*, Princeton, Princeton University Press.

—— (1986) *Kurozumikyô and the New Religions of Japan*, Princeton, Princeton University Press.

Hori, Ichiro (1968) *Folk Religion in Japan, Continuity and Change*, Chicago, University of Chicago Press.

Japanese Journal of Religious Studies (1983) *Special Issue on Women and Religion in Japan*, 10 (2–3).

Philippi, Donald L. (1968) *Kojiki*, Princeton, Princeton University Press.

Murasaki Shikibu (1981) *The Tale of Gengi* (trans Edward G. Seidensticker), New York, Alfred A. Knopf.

Reader, Ian (1991) *Religion in Contemporary Japan*, Basingstoke, Macmillan.

Saikaku, Ihara (1980) *Five Women Who Loved Love* (trans Wm. Theodore de Bary), Vermont, Japan, Charles E. Tuttle.

Yoshida, Teigo (1990) 'The feminine in Japanese folk religion: polluted or divine?' in Eyal Ben-Ari, Brian Moeran and James Valentine (eds) *Unwrapping Japan*, Manchester, Manchester University Press.

Index